Progressive Rock, Religion, and Theology

Theology, Religion, and Pop Culture
Series Editor: Matthew Brake

The *Theology, Religion, and Pop Culture* series examines the intersection of theology, religion, and popular culture, including, but not limited to television, movies, sequential art, and genre fiction. In a world plagued by rampant polarization of every kind and the decline of religious literacy in the public square, *Theology, Religion, and Pop Culture* is uniquely poised to educate and entertain a diverse audience utilizing one of the few things society at large still holds in common: love for popular culture.

Select Titles in the Series
Progressive Rock, Religion, and Theology, by Frank Felice and James F. McGrath
The Spirit and the Song: Pneumatological Reflections on Popular Music, edited by Chris E. W. Green and Steven Félix-Jäger
Post-Christian Religion in Popular Culture: Theology through Exegesis, by Andrew D. Thrasher
Nazi Occultism, Jewish Mysticism, and Christian Theology in the Video Game Series Wolfenstein, by Frank G. Bosman
The Last of Us and Theology: Violence, Ethics, Redemption?, edited by Peter Admirand
Fantasy, Theology, and the Imagination, edited by Andrew D. Thrasher and Austin M. Freeman, with Fotini Toso
Theology and Wes Craven, edited by David K. Goodin
Theology and the DC Universe, edited by Gabriel Mckee and Roshan Abraham
Theology and Star Trek, edited by Shaun C. Brown and Amanda MacInnis Hackney
The Spirit and the Screen: Pneumatological Reflections on Contemporary Cinema, edited by Chris E.W. Green and Steven Félix-Jäger
Theology and the Avett Brothers, edited by Alex Sosler

Progressive Rock, Religion, and Theology

Frank Felice
James F. McGrath

LEXINGTON BOOKS/FORTRESS ACADEMIC
Lanham • Boulder • New York • London

Published by Lexington Books/Fortress Academic
Lexington Books is an imprint of The Rowman & Littlefield Publishing Group, Inc.
4501 Forbes Boulevard, Suite 200, Lanham, Maryland 20706
www.rowman.com

86-90 Paul Street, London EC2A 4NE, United Kingdom

Copyright © 2025 by The Rowman & Littlefield Publishing Group, Inc.

All rights reserved. No part of this book may be reproduced in any form or by any electronic or mechanical means, including information storage and retrieval systems, without written permission from the publisher, except by a reviewer who may quote passages in a review.

British Library Cataloguing in Publication Information Available

Library of Congress Cataloging-in-Publication Data

Names: Felice, Frank, author. | McGrath, James F. (James Frank), 1972– author.
Title: Progressive rock, religion, and theology / Frank Felice, James F. McGrath.
Description: Lanham : Lexington Books/Fortress Academic, 2024. | Series: Theology, religion, and pop culture | Includes bibliographical references and index. | Summary: "Co-written by a musician and a professor of religion, this book studies progressive rock music's profound engagement with religious themes. It looks closely not only at lyrics but at the music itself, which spans an array of artists and songs from its early days to the present"—Provided by publisher.
Identifiers: LCCN 2024032025 (print) | LCCN 2024032026 (ebook) | ISBN 9781978709515 (cloth) | ISBN 9781978709522 (epub)
Subjects: LCSH: Progressive rock music—Religious aspects.
Classification: LCC ML3921.8.R63 F54 2024 (print) | LCC ML3921.8.R63 (ebook) | DDC 782.42166—dc23/eng/20240710
LC record available at https://lccn.loc.gov/2024032025
LC ebook record available at https://lccn.loc.gov/2024032026

∞™ The paper used in this publication meets the minimum requirements of American National Standard for Information Sciences—Permanence of Paper for Printed Library Materials, ANSI/NISO Z39.48-1992.

*To Barbara and Laurie Wasserberg
for introducing James to classic Genesis
and to Ray and Mary Lodien
for introducing Frank to Neal Morse and Spock's Beard*

Contents

Introduction		1
1	ELP's "Tarkus": Religion and Politics in a Post-Apocalyptic Landscape	15
2	Yes: Prophets of a Spiritual and Musical New Age	31
3	Genesis's "Supper's Ready": Messiahs and Metamorphoses	63
4	Jethro Tull's Songs about God: A Prog-phetic Condemnation of Idolatry	83
5	Kerry Livgren's Kansas: From Syncretism to Monotheism and Complexity to Simplicity	95
6	Rush's "Freewill": Beyond Election to Choice as a Theological Anthem	115
7	Neal Morse's *Similitude of a Dream*: A Recasting of *Pilgrim's Progress*	131
Conclusion		157
Bibliography		163
Person/Band Index		171
Subject Index		175
Scripture Index		179
About the Authors		181

Introduction

Although this book's exploration of its topic will make clear how progressive rock highlights the inherent blurriness and permeability of genres, it is still possible to identify a few features that typify music labeled as "progressive rock," or "prog," a category with several synonyms or near synonyms, including "art rock." The distinctive elements that set prog apart from the rest of rock include the integration of elements from other varieties of art music (what the general public often labels "classical") and from folk, varying time signatures and whole songs in something other than common time, and lengthier compositions with changes of mood that one associates with symphonic music. Will Romano has noted the difficulty of tracing the origin of the designation "progressive rock," since *Billboard* was already using the term in 1967, before the emergence of most of what has been given the label.[1] Certainly, the arrival on the scene of the Beatles' album *Sgt. Pepper's Lonely Hearts Club Band* marked a key turning point. Many of the key directions that prog would explore in the years that followed can be found there, at least in nuce. The integration of rock (including psychedelic), classical, and folk elements on that album is noteworthy, of course, but at a more fundamental level, the defining feature is that it was experimental. Merely listing features such as the incorporation of sound effects or the fact that it was a concept album may be less indicative of what characterizes prog at its most basic level than the creative and innovative attempt to bring together musical genres and to do so in a manner not entirely like anything others have done before. Whether one categorizes *Sgt. Pepper* as a precursor to prog/proto-prog or as its beginning, it offers a useful watershed to which it is possible to point.

As a single book on a genre, there was no prospect of this book being comprehensive. It is nonetheless useful to draw attention to the difficulty of finding a clear beginning at the start of this book on theology and progressive rock, since the same type of issue emerges equally in the former as in the latter. Does Christianity begin with Paul or with Jesus, some have asked. How innovative was Jesus in relation to other individuals and groups that we know of, in particular John the Baptist, with whom he was closely associated? One may also ask very similar questions in relation to both music and theology as to whether this or that was "progressive" and what characteristics indicate that. Is sounding like 1970s prog music fifty years later still "progressive"?[2] If Paul's inclusion of Gentiles in the people of God was progressive in his time, is doing the same in the present enough to still be progressive, or is greater inclusivity now required for the label to be appropriate? If some aspire to the label, rightly or wrongly, others have resisted its application to themselves or denied it to others in ways that deserve to be questioned. Consider, for instance, Jerry Ewing's statement, "While no one would ever call Queen a prog band, early albums such as *Queen* (1973) and more specifically *Queen II* (1974) displayed a proggy art rock tendency."[3] For those who are fans of the genre, the irony is immediately apparent. Some most certainly *would* call Queen a prog band, and others would at least consider it an open question worth asking. Still, more would say that Queen overlaps several genres, something that in itself has been *a defining characteristic of prog*. To the extent that prog itself shifts over time from being a transgression of boundaries between genres to actually being a genre in its own right, inevitable questions arise, including where the genre could possibly go from there and whether a new difficulty doesn't arise of defining what is *not* prog. Derek Shulman of the band Gentle Giant said concerning Queen, "They were kind of prog, but they were also very pop . . . they crossed all sorts of borders . . . They combined rock, glam, pop, prog, everything into one package. In that respect, they were very original."[4] When Ian Mosley (Marillion's drummer) was asked if those in the progressive scene viewed Queen as prog at the time, he responded,

> No, that was left to the likes of Genesis, Crimson, Pink Floyd, and Yes, of course. I always thought of Queen as more of a rock band. I never really think of even progressive rock bands as progressive rock bands unless the lyrics are all about fairies and goblins.[5]

Defined that way, several prog bands are removed from the category, or at least most of their songs and many whole albums, including, of course, most of Marillion's output. Queen, on the other hand, once again seems to fit squarely in the category of prog due to songs such as "The Fairy Feller's Master-Stroke," which Dee Snider of Twisted Sister described as "prog-rock genius."[6] But does being the drummer for Marillion or the lead vocalist of Twisted Sister give you the expertise or authority to decide which bands do or do not fit in the genre of progressive rock? Another example that resides similarly close to the borderline is Led Zeppelin, which drew on J. R. R. Tolkien as well as Greek classical literature in its songs (See "Ramble On," "Misty Mountain Hop," and "Achilles' Last Stand").

We are not discussing this only because of the challenge of defining progressive rock. Scholars of religion and theology will tell you that the challenge of defining those areas and what fits into them can be just as difficult, and some would say impossible. Some things clearly fit the categories, however, they are defined, of course. The problem is with what is excluded and what fits awkwardly while still seeming to belong. Some simply opt to define smaller and smaller subgenres or to allow individual bands (or works of literature or whatever else) to stand alone. For example, Megadeth bassist Dave Ellefson says, "I think Queen is their own genre."[7] Rudolf Bultmann wrote that the Gospels are "a unique phenomenon in the history of literature."[8] Both claims are problematic and open to challenge, and yet both are appealing, if only as ways of acknowledging the problem of attempts to fit any distinctive work of music or literature into a category that seems to pigeonhole it.

The points of intersection between the two subject areas that form the title of this book are not only to be found in such analogies, nor only in engagement with religious themes in lyrics. Time and again, progressive rock artists cite not "classical" music in general but more specifically hymns as experienced, particularly in Anglican churches and school chapels in the United Kingdom where most of the major developments in proto-prog (the Beatles, the Moody Blues, Procol Harum), psychedelic (Pink Floyd, The Who), and then progressive rock in its own right (King Crimson, Yes, ELP, Jethro Tull, Genesis) all emerged. And, of course, Queen. The penchant for longer songs (sometimes but by no means always in the context of concept albums) meant that there was more room to explore fantastic narratives as well as serious subjects, and the lyrics were often more philosophical and/or mythological than was the norm in the rock songs on popular radio. Even on shorter songs, Queen veered in the direction of prog both musically (consider "Bijou" or the long instrumental ending on "A Beautiful Day (Reprise)") and lyrically (on their first album, "Jesus" not only connects with the theme of this book but also illustrates the storytelling capacity of rock when pushed beyond prevailing assumptions concerning what it ought to be about). The Queen song "Jesus" is also interesting because of how it says that "it all began with the three wise men." Freddie Mercury was, of course, born Farrokh Bulsara to Parsi (Zoroastrian) parents. Since the three wise men are regularly identified as Persian Zoroastrian magi, there is a fascinating connection between Mercury's religious heritage and this song about a figure who predominated in the context in which he found himself but who was not part of his own tradition.

Macan writes, "the counterculture was primarily a religious and humanistic, rather than a political or ideological, movement. . . it mirrored a generation's quest for some sort of metaphysical depth." He then set out to evaluate "to what degree (if any) rock can be seen to articulate a coherent theological viewpoint."[9] The present study of a sample of progressive rock will illustrate that Macan is right that there is a depth of metaphysical questing to be found in progressive rock across a wide array of different bands and different time periods. It also shows that individual questers did not pursue this spiritual search through music in the same way or with the same result. Neither their starting points nor where their journeys took them are identical or even particularly similar. What is similar, however, is the quest itself and the exploration of it through words and music combined in long-form expressions that allowed ample room to pursue this endeavor they share in common. John Corbett has provided an illustration of the way the experience and exploration of the Sixties influenced some, in the form of an anecdote about how an encounter with a hippie-witch influenced his parents. He writes,

> Mom and Dad interpreted it all as evidence of a spiritual dead end; these unfortunate young people, they reasoned, had tried it all—from sex, drugs, and rock 'n' roll to Zen, the Children of God, and crystals, and anything that seemed even slightly redemptive—and had come up empty. It scared my parents senseless. Generally open-minded, proffering a free-to-be-you-and-me attitude, they then and there decided that their children would grow up Episcopal, thinking that at least this would give us an anchor we could fasten ourselves to or discard.[10]

The decade of the 1970s both drew heavily on that which preceded it and reacted against it, and those two motions of ongoing questing and disillusionment with the period many considered its peak provide a crucial background to the spiritual and theological themes encountered in classic progressive rock.[11]

SOURCES AND THE DEFINITION OF THE GENRE

Genres are always subjects of debate, and progressive rock is no exception. Indeed, it presents us with a particularly clear example of the very reason why debates persist about genre, namely the fact that someone, somewhere, is always transgressing the boundaries of any categories that scholars, record stores, or anyone else might put in place. Some would go so far as to say that

> no exact definition of the form is possible. Progressive musicians borrowed and stole from every conceivable kind of music: rock, jazz, blues, classical music of every period, folk music from every country under the sun, electronic and

avant-garde experimentation, and more besides . . . Much of prog is indeed about the obliteration of categories.[12]

Many who are asked what typifies "progressive rock" would propose not merely the blurring of genre boundaries in general but the integration specifically of rock music and "classical" music. The latter term is actually quite complex and controversial for those who are avid fans or scholars of the genre. "Classical" strictly speaking refers to a period in the past, after the era of Renaissance or Baroque music but before the directions explored by composers from the nineteenth century onward in eras that have been labeled Romantic and then Modern. Yet contemporary composers are often labeled as "classical," even if those who work on music academically would undoubtedly prefer terms like "neo-Baroque," "neo-Classical," "minimalist," and the like. If we take a look at a range of "progressive" rock artists, even from the earliest period in the 1970s, we will see influences of contemporary composers and music from before the "Classical," era in the strictest sense of the word. Some were engaging with and drawing on the most avant-garde orchestral and chamber works and compositions, while others were squarely rooted in the Renaissance, well before what scholars of orchestral and chamber music call "classical" in the strictest sense. Terms like "modern" are notoriously problematic, as illustrated not only in the realm of music but also by their appearance in the titles of scholarly works on theology from a century ago that now seem rather dated and anything but modern in the sense of contemporary. Calling the most recent developments "postmodern" merely continues the process of painting (or composing or theologizing) into a corner, at least as far as the prospect for any new labels is concerned. To distinguish progressive rock from other kinds of pop music, one can make a contrast by comparing these elements: Lyrics were more poetic; technology was harnessed for new sounds; the music approached the condition of "art"; some harmonic language was imported from jazz and nineteenth-century classical music; the album format overtook singles; and the studio, rather than the stage, became the focus of musical activity, which often involved creating music for listening, not dancing.[13] Progressive rock has always been a genre that borrowed and incorporated from others around it, oftentimes giving rise to various subgenres such as Folk-prog, progressive hard rock, math rock and others.

As was mentioned briefly before, early in the phenomenon known as progressive rock, we see one particular strand of music tradition play a noticeably important role: the music of the tradition of Anglican chant and hymnody. For a few, modern and even avant-garde musical trends were significant influences.[14] While those with a superficial acquaintance with music connect progressive rock with "classical" music and by that I mean anything from Baroque to Early Romantic music by famous composers from Bach to Beethoven, the influence of Anglican hymns connected the genre more directly with late nineteenth- to early twentieth-century English composers such as Howells, Stanford, Parry, Elgar, Holst, and Vaughan Williams, while Keith Emerson and Emerson, Lake, and Palmer (ELP) also listened to and either covered or borrowed from music not only by Holst and Vaughan Williams but also Mussorgsky, Bartók, Ginastera, and Copland.[15] The phrase "classically-trained musicians" is sometimes used to indicate both this influence and the training in playing it, but like the term "classical" more generally, this is unhelpful as a perspective on the genre.[16] On the one hand, sometimes all this meant is that the individuals took music lessons as children, while on the other hand, those who have taken such lessons have played and continue to play all varieties of rock. Indeed, listening to and borrowing from composers of the same era is not limited to bands labeled progressive. For instance, when Sting used a melody from Prokofiev's Lt. Kije Suite in "Russians," it wasn't categorized as "prog." Yet the use of a melody from Vaughan Williams' "Fantasia on Greensleeves" by ELP in "Touch and Go" would be for the simple reason that they are already categorized as a prog band. Yet if that song had been by some other band, it might well not be categorized as prog at all. The fact that Sting also integrated and fused rock and jazz in his solo music also seems as though it might deserve the label "progressive," yet jazz rock and jazz fusion have rarely been placed in the same category. As we shall see, these are not the only labels and boundaries that are blurry, and if this makes a book like ours more challenging to write in some ways, the very fact that similar issues arise in music and in theology is itself instructive.

THEOLOGY OR THEOLOGIES? BANDS AND BLURRY BOUNDARIES

Was Paul a Christian or a Jew, or both, or neither?[17] People move between identities over the course of their lives and sometimes occupy multiple identities simultaneously. Thinking about bands and their members can provide a useful way for us to think about this subject. Many bands are like the proverbial ship of Theseus. If no members are the same today as when the band was founded, is it the same band? (The same thought experiment might also help us think about personhood and continuity across an individual's life as their cells die and new cells come into being, as matter is lost and absorbed, but that might be a bit much to try to tackle in the introduction to a book about theology and pop culture.) There are people who say that Phil Collins' influence killed the progressive character of Genesis. Indeed, there are some who will say this even though Peter Gabriel's solo offerings incorporate as much pop as anything done by Genesis or any of its other members, while *Invisible Touch* is full of songs which, while not precisely like what one heard on *Trespass*, are not at all standard pop fare. That, of course, relates to that other key question of whether making the same kind of music that was prog in the 70s counts as prog today, or whether, by definition, to be progressive involves continually experimenting, pushing beyond boundaries, and borrowing from across genre divides. But it relates directly to our present context, too. Was Genesis already Genesis even when it was The Anon and The Garden Wall? Was Paul a Christian even though he never uses the term, and was he still Jewish even while working to graft Gentiles into the people of God? Are Tony Banks and Mike Rutherford still Genesis today even if not working together as a band, given that there is always the possibility of a reunion?

Definitions, boundaries, and categorizations are messy, complicated, and controversial. When academics study religious phenomena and propose or apply categories, we aren't ending discussions and debates but contributing to them. Yet in our efforts to define some categories more clearly while problematizing others, we are prone to forget that labels can never be pinned down or have their boundaries marked with both clarity and precision in perpetuity. Engaging with a very different area, such as the history of progressive rock, can do more than merely illustrate this point. It can foster appreciation for this inherent blurriness at a deeper and more visceral level, just as music itself is prone to accomplish in relation to emotion. Returning to the question of whether a genre of music can have a "theology," the answer is, of course, not. Yet it may have related theologies and philosophies, which can be grouped together or at least meaningfully compared and contrasted within the framework of the shared genre, much as one might do with a philosophical trend unaccompanied by music. Returning to Edward Macan once again, he suggests that "progressive rock's philosophical 'message' . . . is a loosely linked network of attitudes, ideas, and issues, and not a coherent philosophical system per se."[18] Engaging with this evaluation from the perspective of musicology, not only within that framework but also from the perspective of religious studies, is not merely appropriate but necessary. That is our aim in the present volume. To prepare the ground for the specific artists and songs that will be the focus of the book's chapters, we have sought here to show the usefulness of this exploration on a variety of grounds.

If terms such as "progressive" are potentially vague and the focus of significant debate in the realm of music, that is all the *more true* in areas such as biblical studies. Was Paul progressive in his views on subjects such as slavery and women? If he was progressive within the context of his own era but his words are no longer progressive within the framework of ours, do we deny him the label, and if so, why would we not also revoke it from bands whose sound was fresh in 1974 but seemed downright old-fashioned by 2024?[19]

Comparison of the very notion and category of progressiveness in diverse realms such as ethics and music has the potential to afford insights and yet has not, to our knowledge, been undertaken. There is also another question that has been raised in relation to both music and religion, namely whether it *should* be progressive. While some found the musical exploration of prog rock exciting and innovative, others complained that it was not what rock was supposed to be. When the early Christian apologists engaged with philosophers and philosophical systems of their time, were they doing something indicative of their religion's vibrant living character or merely transgressing its boundaries in ways that inevitably led to "heresy"? Is there such a thing as the theology of a band or a genre any more than of a religion or a denomination? Are there rather only theological views of individuals, themselves inevitably bound to change and evolve over time, which may share family resemblances and yet whose uniqueness should not be subsumed under broader umbrellas when the effect is to cast a shadow on their distinctiveness? It may be helpful—but can at the very least be a fun thought exercise—to ask whether James and Paul were in the same band. The tensions between them do not answer that question, since bands without internal tensions caused by different visions are the exception rather than the rule. In the realm of music, as in religion, groups are regularly torn apart by the same tensions that are so generative of creativity when the tensions are maintained.[20] Was Barnabas akin to the drummer for both Peter and Paul, a figure who contributed to the music that each made separately, where we may never know how much he himself contributed to their songs? Could one write a history of Paul's band involvement from *The Pharisees* to *Jesus and the Christians*, akin to a musician's biography, if only we had sufficient source material to work with? We do not always have detailed records about band members' thoughts and motives, despite them being so much closer to us in time compared to early Christianity. If there are unique challenges to ancient history, many of the issues that arise are the same in the realm of the history of thought, regardless of where and when, and regardless of whether the worldview finds musical expression. Bill Martin suggests that cultural transitions are more decisive when it comes to the changes bands undergo than are changes in the lineup of musicians.[21] For those who work hard to situate writers like Paul in their cultural and historical context, the aim is never to simply explain their views away as a product of their time. All thought and all music is a product of its time and a product of its human creator. There is value to asking every sort of question possible, about the theology of early Christianity as well as of Paul and also of his individual letters, and about the theology of progressive rock and of Jethro Tull and of Ian Anderson. There is benefit to a literary/musical approach focused on the text as well as a historical one that asks questions about what is behind it.

Bridges and Boundaries in Music and Theology

In concluding this introduction, we acknowledge that another problematic commonality between the study of the history of Christian or other religious thought and the study of the history of prog or any other rock is the fact that there are famous stars in both categories. Historically, men have predominated, and thus matters of gender and representation arise. The kind of borrowing from Indian music that invigorated the music of the Beatles would today be labeled by some as a form of cultural appropriation.[22] Yet looking at music and theology together provides an opportunity not only for critique of historic patriarchy but also for problematization of categories, some of which are taken for granted in the criticisms as well as in those that are identified as problematic. If the majority of the early prog rock pioneers were white, is that surprising or problematic given that the genre emerged in a European (and more specifically, primarily a British) context? Rock music, to at least some extent, emerged through embrace of and creative engagement and fusion between music of European and African traditions. Here too, the categories are problematic, since the division among the continents of Europe, Asia, and Africa is a matter of human labeling. To be sure, there is a helpful convenience to being able to refer to parts of the world, just as is true of musical genres and theological traditions. Yet the boundaries are blurry and, to some extent, arbitrary. Applying yet another label ("the Middle East") to the region where land masses are joined only introduces another problematic term with boundaries that are just as blurry. Neither theology nor music has ever been hermetically sealed off from cultural exchange across boundaries, and if it is important to critique ways that this is done that are hegemonic and imperialistic, reifying a category such as "black music" or "white music" is not only problematic but reinforces a problematic racist framework even if it is done (as has sometimes been the case) in the interest of safeguarding a tradition of the oppressed from obliteration through processes of colonization and absorption. Ultimately, it must be acknowledged that *all* music is born from borrowing and appropriation, whether recognized or not by its creators. Progressive rock exists because its creators borrowed and blended from whatever previous music suited their aesthetic requirements. While especially characteristic of this genre, this is a historic characteristic of music itself as a global phenomenon.

It is common to point out that the Christians of its early centuries were influenced by Platonism and Stoicism as well as Judaism, and yet such ways of putting things are themselves problematic, since there was no sharp divide between these (as Philo of Alexandria perhaps illustrates better than anyone), even though it would equally misrepresent things to suggest that there were no characteristics that typically distinguished Jewish and Greco-Roman thinkers. Nor is Judaism merely an "influence" on Christianity. Before it ever bore that label, what we now call Christianity was a form of Judaism. How much interaction there was with various strands of non-Jewish thought at its earliest stage of development is difficult, if not impossible, to answer since the exchange of cultural ideas and language has never not been a characteristic feature of human societies, and the first-century Levant was no exception. Prog rock emerged at the intersection of rock music with European art music traditions, and rock itself was born out of a fusion between European folk traditions and the blues, which emerged in the context of African enslavement in the Americas. There is no way to tell the story of this music in a way that compartmentalizes music into neat categories of genre or region. If the aim is to accurately describe history while also taking a stand against discrimination and oppression, then that story can be traced in terms of the victory of African music in conquering Western European music, beginning with pioneers like Sister Rosetta Tharpe and continuing all the way to the influence of blues and jazz on composers as diverse as Maurice Ravel and George Gershwin. While the Hungarian musicologist-composers Bartók and Kodály studied folk traditions within a framework that was in the service of nationalism to at least some extent, their recordings and studies of that music spread its influence across boundaries of nation, language, and culture. Eventually, Bartók's own music would be co-opted (initially without credit) by Emerson, Lake, and Palmer. Any attempt to tell this story shows our categories of musical genre, national culture, linguistic difference, or religious and theological distinctiveness to be inherently problematic, all with the same blurry edges. Some have sought to label certain theologies as "syncretistic," as though theirs were immune from the influences of time, place, and cultural exchange. This has never been and could never be the case. Hopefully, this study will helpfully highlight this important fact, as well as illustrate a way of investigating the history of musical and theological exploration that takes this aspect fully seriously.

Audrey Lorde famously said that "the master's tools will never dismantle the master's house."[23] It is certainly true that there are systems such as capitalism that have inequity inherent within them, so that attempts to harness and use them to achieve greater equity prove self-defeating. In the case of music, on the other hand, we have a reminder that some tools are so ancient and so widespread that we cannot fully trace their heritage. Recognizing that the European piano had precursors in the African mbira and other instruments does more than simply illustrate this point. Tools and instruments, genres, and systems deserve to be carefully evaluated and critiqued. There is also often the potential within them to transcend boundaries that divide. The role of music in general and rock music in particular in transgressing not only musical divisions but racial-ethnic ones is important. Music in the service of an ideology can be a powerful tool, whether the aim is to foster nationalistic fervor or to challenge it. No musical instrument or genre is the exclusive property of the oppressors. The same may also be true of theology, albeit to a lesser extent. There too the capacity of biblical texts to both defend and challenge slavery also comes to mind. The range of different theological views and types of individual personalities involved in the creation and performance of the music that we subject to close analysis in this book is extremely varied. This book offers a study of a few important moments in the history of musical engagement with profound questions about religion and spirituality. It is precisely because of the paradoxical and tension-laden phenomenon of rock music being "counter-cultural"[24] while also being inherently wedded to the record industry that it seems so important to highlight these broader questions about method and ideology in the introduction. As authors with personal and/or professional connections to music and theology, we make no claim to impartiality. We do, however, strive to accurately describe, study, and reflect upon this small sample of musical-theological explorations in the interest not only of greater appreciation and enjoyment thereof but also consideration of the wider societal ramifications of musical and theological trends. In an era in which nationalism is on the rise and historic divisions are being broken down in some quarters while reinforced in others, studying the tools that have historically served both aims is important. Both theology and rock music have been popular and unpopular at the same time, depending on whom one asked. The power of the two combined is significant and deserves the kind of careful study we seek to offer in the pages that follow.[25]

The remainder of the book will offer chapter-length studies of key progressive rock artists, with a primary, but not exclusive, focus on a particular work or two. Each chapter explores matters of theological and religious interest in relation to the band, the specific work that is the chapter's focus, and then connections between that work and other works by the same artists, concluding by tracing the connections of theme and influence that run inward or outward between the work in question and other musical creations. In several instances, the works in question are themselves as long as the side of an album or even span multiple LPs. First, we will turn to Emerson, Lake, and Palmer with a focus on the song "Tarkus." Next is Yes and two of their longest works, *Close to the Edge* and *Tales from Topographic Oceans*. In the chapter on Genesis, the focus is on "Supper's Ready," and in the chapter on Jethro Tull, we focus on one classic and one very recent work, "My God" and "Mine is the Mountain." In the chapter on Kansas, we make something of a departure from this usual structure because Kerry Livgren's own religious journey is so directly reflected in the band's songs over an extended period. The chapter on Rush returns to the usual format with a focus on "Freewill," and the final major chapter focuses on the Neal

Morse Band's concept album *The Similitude of a Dream*. A brief conclusion rounds off the book, but even prior to that the individual chapters highlight along the way the connections between many of these bands at the level of membership as well as influence and inspiration. Each chapter could have been expanded to cover still other works and more of each artist's story to become a book in its own right. Since the topic has been relatively neglected, it seemed better to offer a study that provided a wider array of representative cases and that highlights the connections, similarities, and contrasts. It is the hope of the authors that others will build on the foundation we offer here and will dig deeper still into this richly rewarding musical genre.

NOTES

1. Will Romano, *Close to the Edge: How Yes's Masterpiece Defined Prog Rock*. Milwaukee, WI: Backbeat, 2017, p. 14.

2. Indeed, much of what was labeled as "neo-prog" was trying to recast musical elements from the early 1970s into the 1990s. On the question of whether 1970s-style prog rock is still "progressive," see Igor Khoroshev's thoughts in Chris Welch, *Close to the Edge: The Story of Yes*. London: Omnibus, 2008, p. 250.

> I always played progressive rock and then I found out that what I thought was progressive in the Seventies had become kind of regressive! Now I try to write music that nobody has done before. It's not commercial but it's unique. It's nothing like Yes might write. I am more into Prodigy and The Chemical Brothers. That's what I think is progressive music today.

See also Tim Morse, *Yesstories: Yes in Their Own Words*. New York: St. Martin's, 1996, p. 77 for thoughts from Rick Wakeman on Yes evolving and Marillion coming in to do what Yes used to.

3. Jerry Ewing, *Wonderous Stories: A Journey Through the Landscape of Progressive Rock*. London: Flood Gallery Publishing, 2018, p. 122.

4. Speaking with Martin Popoff, who published the quote in *Queen: Album by Album*. Beverly, MA: Voyageur, pp. 13, 20. Shulman also says that Brian May's guitar style was "progressive because it wasn't the norm" (p. 16).

5. Popoff, *Queen: Album by Album*, p. 153.

6. Popoff, *Queen: Album by Album*, p. 32.

7. Popoff, *Queen: Album by Album*, p. 67.

8. Rudolph Bultmann, "Evangelien." In *Religion in Geschichte und Gegenwart*, 2nd ed. (Tübingen: Mohr Siebeck, 1928), vol. 2, 419, trans. JZ Smith in "On Comparison," 39 and quoted in Jennifer Eyl, *Signs, Wonders, and Gifts: Divination in the Letters of Paul,* edited by Hermann Gunkel and Leopold Zscharnack, Oxford: Oxford University Press, 2019, p. 22. On this point, see now Helen Bond, *The First Biography of Jesus*. Grand Rapids, MI: Eerdmans, 2020, p. 1.

9. Edward Macan, *Rocking the Classics: English Progressive Rock and the Counterculture*. Oxford: Oxford University Press, 1997, p. 6 (concurring with an earlier study of his).

10. John Corbett, *Pick Up the Pieces: Excursions in Seventies Music*. Chicago, IL: The University of Chicago Press, 2019, p. 3.

11. It's interesting to compare the progressive rock that has emerged in the 1990s and continues up to the present—aside from a number of Christian-based prog groups such as the Neal Morse Band, some of their work recasts myths into modern contexts (cf. Dream Theater's *Change of Seasons* or *Metropolis, Scenes from a Memory*), or reflects a paradoxical unease/embrace of secular humanism.

12. George Forrester, Martyn Hanson, and Frank Askwe, *Emerson, Lake, and Palmer: The Show That Never Ends. A Musical Biography*. London: Helter Skelter, 2001.

13. Allan F. Moore, *Song Means: Analysing and Interpreting Recorded Popular Song*. London: Routledge, 2016. Archived from the original on 7 November 2021. Retrieved 12 October 2016.

14. Pink Floyd was "a unique mix of John Cage meets Karlheinz Stockhausen meets Bo Diddley" (Mark Blake, Joe Boyd, Victoria Broackes, Anna Landreth Strong, Howard Goodall, Jon Savage, and Rob Young, *Pink Floyd: Their Mortal Remains*. London: Victoria and Albert Museum, 2017, p. 8).

15. Alberto Ginastera endorsed Emerson's version, saying (as recorded in the liner notes of the album *Brain Salad Surgery*), "Keith Emerson has beautifully caught the mood of my piece."

16. The inappropriateness of the phrase, and what it connotes for fans, is summed up well by John Corbett in *Pick Up the Pieces,* p. 118. In essence, it denotes virtuosity that went beyond the level of average fans' own musical abilities. In some instances, it fits, for example, Tony Kaye and Patrick Moraz, and in others, such as Tony Banks and Keith Emerson, we have specific evidence that they learned pieces of what may be broadly called "classical music" (often more precisely music from the Romantic to modern eras). See also Welch, *Close to the Edge*, pp. 95,112,152,187, and 249–250; Morse, *Yesstories*, pp. 4–6 on various members of Yes. The blurriness of genres not only between varieties of rock but also rock and classical is further illustrated by Yngve Malmsteen's Guitar Concerto and Deep Purple's Concerto for Group and Orchestra. Are these prog, hard rock, heavy metal, or all of the above?

17. On this, see for instance, Pamela Eisenbaum, *Paul Was Not a Christian: The Original Message of a Misunderstood Apostle*. New York: HarperCollins, 2009 as well as the extensive literature categorized under the heading "Paul within Judaism."

18. Edward Macan, *Endless Enigma: A Musical Biography of Emerson, Lake, and Palmer*. Chicago, IL: Open Court, 2006, p. 251.

19. In music, progressive has become a mere label, the same way that Baroque, Classical, Bop, and Gamelan have all done so; in defining the style and applying its label, the central tenet of what is progressing beyond the current time, method, order, etc. has become moot.

20. In this book, we will see instances of this in Yes and ELP in particular; in one case, the result being a changing lineup, while in the other, there was more continuity

despite the tensions. Other bands, such as Styx, are also worth exploring through this same lens.

21. Bill Martin, *Music of Yes: Structure and Vision in Progressive Rock*. Chicago, IL: Open Court, 1996, pp. 208, 219.

22. To challenge the broad application of this phrase to all forms of cultural borrowing is not in any way to suggest that there is not an appropriate critique to be offered of specific forms of disrespectful emulation, as in the classic example of the use of some traditional cultural attire as a Halloween costume. The concern here is to show that there are boundaries (blurry, as always) beyond which the critique becomes inappropriate and even risks reinforcing racism and segregation. No one that we know of would suggest that medicines or computers developed in Europe or the United States cannot be produced and distributed elsewhere. Why should the same not be true of musical instruments, which are also a form of technology?

23. This phrase formed the title of a 1979 address, which has been published multiple times and is widely cited. See, for instance, Audre Lorde, *Sister Outsider: Essays and Speeches*. New York: Penguin Books, 2020, 100–103.

24. There is a bit of irony involved that many of the subjects and lyrical topics in much of progressive rock music can be viewed as *counter*-counter-cultural: not so much about sex, drugs, and rock and roll, but, as was mentioned above, about spirituality, religion, and "fairies and goblins."

25. The introduction was written by McGrath with input from Felice, as were chapters 2–5, while chapters 6–8 were authored by Felice with input from McGrath. Allowing the perspective of a specialist in music and a religious studies specialist to each be heard in their authentic voice, while also reflecting the input of both throughout, seemed to offer the best and strongest exploration of this book's subject matter. The authors recognize that neither of them writes about the other's area of expertise in a manner normally characteristic thereof, and this needs to be embraced in interdisciplinary collaborations such as this.

Chapter 1

ELP's "Tarkus"

Religion and Politics in a Post-Apocalyptic Landscape

THE BAND

The extent to which progressive rock bands have overlapping members means that tracing the story of any one of them brings others into the picture. If this poses the challenge of being unable to easily separate and disentangle them, it also has a positive advantage in relation to the approach we have adopted in this book. As we focus in on a handful of famous songs and bands, we actually tell the story of many more. Arguably this is nowhere more true than in the case of Emerson, Lake, and Palmer (ELP). Indeed, one of the challenges they faced was that they were hyped up as a prog rock supergroup even before they had released any album.[1] This was due to the fact that each of its members had already made a significant impact on the music world before coming together to form ELP. Greg Lake was in King Crimson and Keith Emerson in The Nice prior to the formation of ELP, while Carl Palmer went on to form Asia after ELP broke up (but returned to each thereafter as the bands reunited or reshuffled). Asia also included Steve Howe and Geoff Downes from Yes, and Greg Lake even did a brief stint on vocals at one point to fill in for John Wetton.[2] Wetton in turn was in King Crimson for a time, simultaneously with Bill Bruford who was in Yes and later toured with Genesis.

Emerson's band, The Nice began as a backing band for vocalist P. P. Arnold. The band got its name when Arnold, learning that they did not have one, suggested "the Naz," meaning Jesus, short for "the Nazarene." The British band members misheard Arnold's suggestion as "The Nice" and used that.[3] In developing their own music, The Nice were at the forefront of integrating classical and jazz elements into rock and of the creation of rock arrangements of classical pieces. This would continue in ELP, reflecting the fact that Emerson enjoyed and played music by composers such as Prokofiev,

Bartók, Ginastera, and Vaughan Williams. Already in The Nice, Emerson was telling stories through music, with liner notes about his "Five Bridges" suite interpreting the work as inspired by trains in Newcastle-upon-Tyne and symbolizing the danger of technology run amok. That theme, of course, is central to ELP's "Tarkus" and "Karn Evil 9."

Prior to ELP, Lake was involved in a number of bands, including one called The Gods, which has resulted in statements by him such as "the Gods never did anything."[4] That could sound very theologically interesting to someone who did not know a band was the reference! Lake was later recruited to join Giles, Giles, and Fripp, which rebranded itself with the name King Crimson. You will find it repeated widely that the band took its name, King Crimson, from the demon Beelzebub.[5] Peter Sinfield denies that, arguing that it is simply adapted from "In the Court of the Crimson King," which was written before the band had a new name.[6] They knew they needed a name, something catchy and powerful. But who is the crimson king in those lyrics? A King Crimson fan website maintained by Jon Green suggests the album and its lyrics are an evocative exploration of the story of the Holy Roman Emperor Frederick the Great, a major patron of philosophy and music renowned for fostering the freedom of thought that characterized the Enlightenment.[7] The critique of religious dogma and elevation of secular over ecclesiastical power that characterized the Enlightenment in general and Frederick in particular certainly resonate with many of Sinfield's lyrics. Sinfield served as a lyricist not only for King Crimson but also for a number of ELP songs, and his influence is detectable at times in lyrics Lake penned.[8] Robert Fripp, on the other hand, has specifically identified the crimson king as Beelzebub.[9] In widely-quoted liner notes, he claims, "The name King Crimson is a synonym for Beelzebub, which is an anglicized form of the Arabic phrase B'il Sabab. This means literally the man with an aim and is the recognizable quality of King Crimson."[10] Without clarification from Fripp himself, it is impossible to know how he came up with the curious notion that this ancient name of a demon derives from Arabic and that this was its meaning. That the crimson king was the devil or a similar figure appears to be the most widely-held view among band members and interpreters alike. Ian McDonald says that the song "In The Court of the Crimson King" poses the question of whether we are "the devil's playthings." He then emphasizes that it isn't *promoting* something demonic but posing a question about control.[11] This case serves as another excellent example of the fact that the meaning of lyrics (as in the meaning of a great deal of poetry more generally) can be neither monolithic nor static even from the perspective of their author. The process of creating lyrics reaches into the depths of the human mind and what emerges often surprises even the one whose mind it is.

As both Emerson and Lake found themselves looking for new musical challenges, Emerson proposed to Lake the possibility of a collaboration. The result was a band that stood out as distinctive in a number of key respects even in the highly creative world of progressive rock. Among the early and most influential bands, none other consisted of members who had previously been in bands that had been influential and garnered a significant reputation. In these early years of progressive rock, there was little opportunity for that, to be sure, since psychedelic and prog had not been around that long. Nevertheless, when ELP formed in 1970, there was relatively little prior history to prog, the initial spark usually being traced to the Beatles' 1967 album *Sgt. Pepper's Lonely Hearts Club Band*. During that brief time, both The Nice and King Crimson had been at the forefront of what came to be known as progressive rock. The makeup of the ensemble was also distinctive in not having a separate lead guitarist in the manner that other bands did. The fact that Lake provided vocals, guitar, and bass meant that the focus in any given song tends to be on Emerson's keyboard playing and the lyrics. The former ranges across an array of styles but is centered in the realm where rock and twentieth-century "classical" music most naturally converge. The latter brings the dark poetic strain characteristic of King Crimson lyrics, which evocatively engage with subjects like war, politics, the future, and the meaning of existence. While cynicism about church emerges more explicitly in King Crimson's songs after Lake's departure (e.g., in "The Great Deceiver"), it is clearly present in the lyrics of the first two King Crimson albums, with which Lake was associated. While The Nice was arguably the band most associated with rock arrangements of art music, King Crimson also did this in their use of Holst's "Mars, Bringer of War" from the *Planets* in the instrumental piece "The Devil's Triangle." ELP would later include an arrangement of "Mars" on their one album as Emerson, Lake, and Powell.

The first ELP album includes a great deal of instrumental content. In the lyrics of "Knife Edge," there is reference to kneeling and praying for guidance and to people waiting patiently for their turn to be hanged, who "sing the praises of the hallowed." The overarching theme is madness and maintaining one's reason, and within this context, the religious imagery highlights how, on the one hand, people seek divine assistance in maintaining sanity, while on the other, religion can make the collective insanity of a society seem sane. The climactic moment in the lyrics asks about self-actualization and identity, things that people acquire in large measure from their social context and which are threatened when one dares to question what is accepted. The balance between being in society and daring to be different enough to question and change it represents one possible interpretation of the knife edge mentioned in the song's title and the final line of its lyrics. The one who is seeking to maintain their balance is said to be weighed down by their talents, an interesting image given that the talented (in the modern sense of the word) are often the most torn between creative innovation and societal expectations, while the word has its roots in the Greek word *talanton*, which means a measure of weight rather than abilities. The interpretation of the parable of the talents in the Gospel of Matthew (25:14-30) as about using one's abilities undoubtedly influenced the shift in meaning. The song thus highlights that abilities (especially artistic ones) can be both burdensome and liberating at the same time. This first foray into dark evocative poetry would not, however, have prepared listeners for the much more direct criticism of religion that would follow on ELP's second album, *Tarkus*.[12] The mention of machines, on the other hand, does indeed hint at what would be a recurring theme running through some of ELP's most influential and memorable music.[13]

THE SONG

We emphasize throughout this book that it is important to consider both music and lyrics when discussing the theology of a particular song, album, or band. Yet as happens in composition in all genres, sometimes the words come first, sometimes the music, and at still other times the two come together more or less simultaneously. In the case of "Tarkus," Emerson and Palmer developed the main part of the music before bringing it to Lake for lyrics. Lake, in turn, was not immediately enthusiastic about what they had come up with but created lyrics that only found a unifying thread of meaning when William Neal created the cover art for the album.[14] "Tarkus" thus represents an example of music inspiring lyrics, which in turn inspire visual artwork that casts the music and lyrics in a new light. Lyrics by their very nature tend to predominate when there is a question about the meaning of a song. In the case of Tarkus, I think it is safe to say that no one would envisage, on the basis of the song lyrics alone, the battle among powerful creatures depicted and narrated in the album liner notes. Neal had this to say about the name Tarkus: "The name Tarkus has puzzled many, and been open to all manner of misrepresentations, it is however an amalgamation of two elements. The first is found in the Bible at the second letter of Peter chapter 2 verse 4. A condition of deep spiritual debasement is mentioned called 'Tartarus'. The other is the term 'Carcass' hence the name was painted in bones . . . Thus Tarkus essentially stood for the futility of war, a man-made mess with symbols of mutated destruction."[15]

On the artwork on the album sleeve, Tarkus emerges from an egg alongside a volcano. A mixture of tank and armadillo, Tarkus battles with and defeats other hybrid creatures that merge animal features with weaponry. Eventually, the Manticore fights Tarkus. The Manticore is not quite "man to the core" but has a body like a lion, a scorpion's tail, and a human face. The Manticore is the only one that manages to defeat Tarkus, and it is surely symbolic that the Manticore is the only creature that lacks artificial weaponry, as well as being the only one to incorporate human features. Unless the scenario depicted is either pure fantasy or reflects an admittedly widely-held misconception about evolution, then machine-creatures like Tarkus must be or have developed from war machines created by human beings. The egg from which Tarkus is born might suggest otherwise, or may merely indicate that these creatures are the result not merely of human machine engineering but human experimentation with animals. We should also pick up on the clue from Neal and posit that this is a world in the aftermath of nuclear war, which has caused significant mutations to what living things remain. Ultimately, the imagery is symbolic and does not strive for realism.[16] Symbolically, the message is about the potential for human beings to create machines that kill so effectively that they may wipe us out entirely, and yet ironically go on fighting with one another. The Manticore offers hope for organic life to persist and even emerge victorious, yet from our perspective, the Manticore is still grotesque. If there is hope in the message of "Tarkus," it nevertheless chastens us, warning that the path that leads to the world depicted is not one that would see humanity ultimately survive in its present form. We may perhaps be the ancestors of the Manticore. Even if it did not evolve from us, as organic beings, we may still take some comfort in its victory. We should still avoid heading in that direction at all costs and seek to chart a path to a different sort of future altogether, before it is too late for us to do so.

Edward Macan argues that Tarkus represents the Establishment while the Manticore represents the counterculture. While culture, art, and religion prove powerless to stop Tarkus, the counterculture had the potential to do so, although as the song conveys through the final reprise of music from the first movement, the Establishment has not truly been defeated or at least has the potential to reemerge as a force at any time.[17] This reading is not at all implausible, yet if we take seriously all the information we have—the lyrics, the album art, and the commentary by musicians and artists involved—we get the sense that the song is at its core about war and religion at a much more literal level. The song can be subdivided into three songs with instrumental segments before and after each. If we simply begin at the beginning, we may be liable to allow the lyrics which are the most obscure to shape our understanding of parts that are clearer and more thematically cohesive. Lake's penchant for playful rhyming is well known, as is the fact that at times he allowed assonance to take priority over meaning and thematic coherence. The song's meaning arguably becomes increasingly clear as it proceeds, but in the present context, it may make sense to turn first to the central section, titled "Mass," which focuses on religious hypocrisy and complicity in war and other societal and cultural evils. This upbeat central movement features a series of characters: preacher, minister, pilgrim, cardinal, messenger, bishop, and choir. Nearly all of them are explicitly religious. All of them are, as the refrain puts it, "the weaver in the web that he made." As a culture, a society, a religion, or a church (and sometimes all of the above simultaneously), we create webs of meaning and symbolism which do not merely interpret the world we find around us but shape, direct, motivate, and inspire us to make the world a particular way. There have been countless instances in which someone felt they had no choice but to act a certain way not because of any physical constraints or compulsions but because of an inability to perceive options beyond those dictated by one's culture and its norms. The values we define, the definitions we produce, can entangle us so that we are not merely unable to see beyond them, but are influenced and perhaps even controlled by them so that they prompt us to do what we otherwise would not. The examples in the lyrics are ones we likely would have called to mind in a discussion of this topic even if the song's words had not demanded that we do so. We have a preacher and a cardinal, both of whom are depicted as offering prayers to protect people, presumably soldiers. The high priest, meanwhile, "blesses" those who pray and obey with a blade. The prevailing emphasis is on religion as a supporter of militarism, both by encouraging those who give their lives to consider them as heroic, "for God and country," while at the same time offering false hope of protection to the loved ones of soldiers who hope they will return safely from the battlefield. The wedding of religion and war, church and army, is recognized as being profoundly ironic, much like the bishop's bell that rings "without a sound" and the "silent choir."

The pilgrim, the one who makes a journey motivated by religion, may seem the least implicated, the ordinary religious person as opposed to the authority in a church-state hierarchy supporting the current war effort. Yet here too there is a self-made entanglement, one that seems to echo directly with ideas expressed by the apostle Paul, most explicitly in the seventh chapter of his letter to the Romans. Defining something as sin fails to help us avoid it. Indeed, it makes whatever it is all the more enticing. Hence the irony that the pilgrim wanders in committing sin, and it is "so good." The naughtiness of prohibited actions may make them seem all the more enjoyable within a certain framework, but at the very least all the more attractive. This is the point at which it makes sense to make connections with the first vocal segment of Tarkus, "Stone of Years." It consists of a series of questions, each a puzzle, but one of which suggests that the person being addressed will realize their sin. If sin can be viewed in the "rock and roll" framework as "so good," it is also recognized here as something that corrupts and undermines one's wellbeing. The puzzles posed may be mysterious but the overall message is to ask how much we understand about wisdom and perception. The ambiguous questions set the stage for the clearer rhetoric addressing religious hypocrisy in the central lyrical section. In turn, this leads us into the third vocal segment, which focuses on war but is intimately linked to what preceded it. We weave webs of war seeking victory and find ourselves entangled in a process that leads to our own annihilation as a species.[18] We weave theologies that then serve to obligate us to self-sacrifice for church and/or nation.

Let us now return to the least specific lyrics of the song in the first vocal section, "Stones of Years," even the title of which is allusive and elusive. The words are typically understood as being addressed to Tarkus.[19] The first enemy that Tarkus faces (reading the scenes from left to right and top to bottom, as is clearly intended) is different from all the others in ways that have not been discussed by those who have proposed interpretations of the song. The others are hybrids of animals and weapons, except for the Manticore, who stands out as a purely organic, if hybrid organism. Tarkus' first opponent, however, does not resemble any known creature on Earth, nor is it one that appears to be mobile, whereas others can fly, jump on grasshopper-like legs, or walk. The opponent resembles a building, and so we might surmise that this is the last refuge of human beings. There are eyes on stalks, and so the building itself is a kind of hybrid entity. Humanity has made killing machines so lethal that they have completely taken over the world, where they fight against one another so lethally that it is not even safe for humans to go outside. To protect ourselves from our creations, we made a sealed fortress from which we can peer out by means of telescoping eyestalks that may or may not incorporate an organic or quasi-organic element. It may have tentacles and be capable of some sort of limited mobility, but the things that look like that may also be armored tunnels in which surviving humans live and move. We have created hybrid organic-mechanical autonomous weapons, and they are now the only things that can live on the surface of our world—at least until the Manticore emerges to change that. No other living things are visible in the panels, nor can human beings be seen since we are completely sealed off. These killing machines must be highly intelligent in some form, even if not self-aware or capable of reasoning in ways that correspond to what a human mind would do. It is thus possible to understand "Stones of Years" as being addressed to the remnants of humanity, perhaps by none other than Tarkus, but perhaps by some alien onlooker witnessing these events as they observe from space. It makes more sense for holed-up humanity to be confronted with the question of whether the dawn has ever seen our eyes, whether we have any remnant of understanding of how organic life once reproduced on our planet, and whether our feet have walked on the ancient stones of our world. It likewise makes more sense for us to be asked about our lack of wisdom and challenged to realize our sin. The questions return in the final section, and we may interpret them as being posed to humankind as well. There is a victory, and perhaps somehow humankind managed to produce the Manticore to serve as its champion. But the earth has been scorched by our warfare, and the mention of *leaves* of sorrow hints at the obliteration of plant life as a casualty.

The song as a whole is very critical of institutional or organized religion at the very least, and perhaps of religion in general. The opening section of the song has at least slight wisps of connection with biblical wisdom literature, in particular the questions God poses to Job in the final section of the book. That biblical text challenges the traditional theology of its time, and thus there is no contradiction between a song that is critical of religious hypocrisy and falsehood drawing on such a source. If theodicy, the problem of undeserved and unjust suffering, remains a thorn in the flesh (or a stinger in the eye, if you prefer) for many theologies, some came to view the development of doctrines about afterlife and resurrection as resolving the problem. It is thus intriguing, to say the least, that Tarkus ends with words that echo Rev. 21:4 and its promise that in the new Jerusalem there will be no more sorrow or pain.[20] Of course, pain can end through death as well as through healing, and we are thus led to ask whether the ending is a hopeful one beyond our self-inflicted cataclysm or one that lacks the presence of human beings, whether viewed hopefully or despairingly from some broader perspective of either the divine or of organic life.

Turning once again to the song as a whole, we should ask who tells the story of the Manticore. This battle is remembered and sung. Who does so? Paul Heggarty and Martin Halliwell view the scene as akin to that envisaged in the Genesis song "Watcher of the Skies," that is, one in which an alien has come to Earth and is surveying what humanity has left behind.[21] In that song, it seems that humanity has transcended its earthly cradle, while Tarkus seems more pessimistically to view our planet as our tomb, a place where aliens might one day find evidence of our penchant for self-destruction rather than our ability to transcend our planet of origin. Perhaps the answer provided by the album is that the story of humanity's self-destruction is remembered by the Manticore and its descendants. It is an appropriately chastening rebuke of humanity that we think our battles with one another (whether over dogmas, tracts of land, or anything else) are sufficiently important to merit the creation of weapons capable of destroying *all of humankind*, including those who foolishly try to wield them; and that we are concerned only with *our* survival as a species (or in many cases as a subset of humanity). The Manticore may be a better form of life than we have shown ourselves to be, and from a broader perspective, its victory may be a happy ending, perhaps an even happier one than if humanity persisted to continue our self-destructive way of life. The fact that the Manticore incorporates animal characteristics mentioned in the Book of Revelation may be significant. In Rev. 9:7-10 locusts are sent upon the Earth as punishment for humanity's sin. The locusts have faces like human beings, teeth like lions, and stings in their tails like scorpions. The Manticore has a lion-like body rather than either a body like that of a locust or teeth like a lion. (Locust-like legs are found on one of the other creature-machines in the album cover art). Read with an awareness of these intertextual echoes, the song may be understood as having a similar aim of warning about humanity's sinful imperial militarism and the religion that supports it. Whereas in Revelation, God is said to very directly send the plagues that punish, Tarkus has the plagues be the direct product of our own sinfulness. It is a common theme in secular apocalyptic literature and film that it is we who inflict judgment on ourselves as our own actions and way of life bear their bad fruit.

If Tarkus is not only secular sci-fi apocalypse but prog rock wisdom literature, the voice of God from the whirlwind in Job is replaced by an anonymous one. Here too, the gulf is not as great as it might seem. Ancient theological literature is human literature. The fact that God appears only to ask Job about the weather and wild animals indicates that the book's human author was being ironic. People claim to receive profound revelations yet they do not tell us things we could not have deduced from observing the world around us. Human wisdom is limited as our perspective is limited. We are not gods, much less God. Theological hubris that claimed to understand the moral workings of the universe inflicted suffering on Job. Technological and political hubris that claims to be able to safely wield doomsday machines and to have the right to do so inflicts physical suffering. Tarkus warns us that when human religious and military power join hands in an unholy alliance, the result may indeed deserve to be classified as apocalyptic, as eschatological, as having to do with the end of the world or at least of human history. Such warnings are not intended to depress us about the inevitability of what is foretold but begs us to wise up and change our ways before it is too late—to disentangle ourselves from the web that we made.

BEYOND THE SONG

While "Tarkus" dared to poke fun at and challenge religion, even more shocking criticism of religion was to find expression elsewhere on the album. Not only listeners, but Emerson and Palmer were shocked when they heard the lyrics Lake had come up with, which ask "Can you believe, God makes you breathe? Why did he lose six million Jews?"[22] Macan describes the song in question, "The Only Way," as "a hymn to an agnostic, humanist, seemingly materialist worldview . . . Lake's treatment of Christian beliefs is shadowed by an underlying sense of anger."[23] Macan goes on to observe that the song "Tarkus" had already undermined for listeners the call that Lake would issue that faith be placed in the human race. He argues that humanity's track record makes it unrealistic to think that humans will themselves provide the redemption that is no longer sought from a spiritual divine entity, and he considers this a shortcoming not only of *Tarkus* but also Jethro Tull's *Aqualung* inasmuch as they offer a philosophy or metaphysics.[24] Be that as it may, the song is certainly striking for the way it offers a song that musically has definite hymn-like characteristics, complete with pipe organ prelude, and yet calls on people to not simply obey the Word but to believe instead that "man is man-made."

"Karn Evil 9" from the album *Brain Salad Surgery* has direct connections with Tarkus.[25] If one judged based on song titles, I doubt anyone would guess that one of the most popular and widely known bits of prog rock music would be something with the title "Karn Evil 9 First Impression Part 2." This turns out to be another point of intersection with classical music. Who, based on the title, would guess that something called Symphony No.9 "From the New World, 2nd movement: Largo" would be incredibly popular and immediately recognizable? In both prog rock and symphonic music, composers create large-scale works from which tiny fragments may become popular, divorced from the meaning provided by their original context. Anyone who listens to classic rock radio knows "welcome back my friends." Few of them are aware of the post-apocalyptic story told by the song in context. With lyrics by Peter Sinfield, whom Lake knew from their time together in King Crimson, it mentions pulling Jesus from a hat and thus adopts the same critical-satirical stance toward religion. Its connections are much deeper, however, at the level of concept and narrative. It is only toward the end of the song that we discover that the remnants of humanity, in this barren landscape in which a single blade of grass is a rare novelty item, face yet another threat in the form of machine intelligence that we have created. If dystopian post-apocalyptic stories are by definition pessimistic, what are we to say of one that envisages things getting even worse? The threat posed by this machine, coupled with the nearly lifeless landscape, suggests that this song or suite could be understood as a prequel to Tarkus. If so, then perhaps we should optimistically take "The Score" from the album *Emerson, Lake, & Powell* to be the sequel to Tarkus.[26] Not only does it return to the "show that never ends," but it has musical elements that also hark back to "Karn Evil 9," if updated for the 1980s. The more positive feel of its synth fanfare might even suggest a happy ending to the tale. The lyrics are vague, but if there is a connection to a larger musical narrative, then the singer's lack of regrets about the journey that led to this point converges with the upbeat musical language in a major key to suggest that the struggle was worth it. Perhaps it is inevitable that AI technology, like the exploitation of fossil fuels, will lead to harm, but it may also be the case that it is better to develop these technologies and address the negative consequences than to never do so and forego all the benefits they bestow on humanity. Faced with the choice, few actually prefer the simplicity of life in a garden like Eden (or Socrates's idyllic vision for human life depicted in Book II of *The Republic*) to one with struggle and challenges that make existence seem worthwhile and to have a trajectory rather than being static.

While not part of the same story per se, Jerusalem's mention of "satanic mills" serves to nicely frame and introduce the technologically-accomplished post-apocalyptic dystopia of "Karn Evil 9." Where Genesis merely alludes to that classic English hymn in "Supper's Ready" (more by way of introduction than direct echoing or quotation), ELP performs the complete hymn in their own arrangement. The lyrics are from a poem by William Blake that appears in the preface of his *Milton a Poem*, and Blake also authored an epic poem with the title "Jerusalem." Since there is no reason to think that ELP were aware of or interested in the original context of the hymn's words, we may forego exploring them here. It is worth noting, however, that Blake's *Milton* as a whole offers many more references to Satan's "mills," which recommend a different interpretation than those which assume the reference to be to the impact of industry and technology. The members of ELP most likely took for granted the popular understanding of the lyrics (reflected also in Sting's reference to satanic mills in his song about coal mining, "We Work the Black Seam").

Other songs reflect ELP's critical and far from serious take on religion. In "Benny the Bouncer," the central character dies in a fight and in the hereafter becomes a bouncer working for Jesus at St. Peter's gate. That is another song in which Sinfield was involved in the lyrics, as he also was in the song "Hallowed Be Thy Name" from the album *Works Vol.1*. In that collaboration between Lake and Sinfield, we encounter a madman whose "wisdom" incorporates (and in one case inverts) lines from the Lord's Prayer. The band's solo efforts also engaged with religion in interesting ways in conjunction with Christmas. Greg Lake's "I Believe in Father Christmas" (ELP later recorded a version on *Return of the Manticore*) places in parallel the experience of realizing that Santa Claus is not real and identifying the religious beliefs that one was taught as fairy stories. More cheerful is Keith Emerson's "Captain Starship Christmas," which appears to take up the idea that had been expressed in song some years earlier by Chris De Burgh in his "A Spaceman Came Traveling."[27] There is obviously also a connection here with the sci-fi story or stories in Tarkus and Karn Evil 9.

BEYOND THE BAND

Having already begun to see connections with songs by other artists, this is a natural point at which to bring that to the center of our focus. There is plenty of room for comparison between how bands like Yes and ELP tackle subjects like war and environmentalism, given their rather different spiritualities. Neither is a fan of the traditional church in their native England, but neither ELP's music nor interviews with its members indicate any interest in the alternative spiritualities that many gravitated to in the 1960s and 1970s, including Yes' Jon Anderson. Both Yes and ELP converge in exploring science fiction themes (see Yes' "Arriving UFO," "Starship Trooper," and perhaps most directly connected with this chapter, "Machine Messiah"), as do other bands like Genesis ("Watcher of the Skies"), Styx ("Come Sail Away" and "Mr. Roboto"), and Rush ("The Body Electric" in which an android "prays to the mother of all machines").[28] The intersection of prog rock and sci-fi could be the subject of a book in its own right.[29] While Rush is the subject of its own chapter, it is still appropriate here to note connections with the ELP songs that have been the focus here. The songs "Distant Early Warning" and "The Body Electric" (when considered together, as is natural to do as both appear on the album *Grace Under Pressure*) explore human inhumanity to other humans and presumably our enslavement of the intelligent machines we created. The latter leads to apocalypse in countless science fiction franchises, including The Matrix films, the backstory of which is explored in one of the animated shorts in *The Animatrix*. The same may be true as backstory to Tarkus and/ or "Karn Evil 9." Also to be mentioned because of its exploration of religion and a post-apocalyptic future is Rush's concept album *2112*.

CONCLUSION

Returning our attention to ELP's Tarkus now that we have traced a number of threads far and wide, it becomes clearer still that the meaning of Tarkus is far more vague than the songs we have just been mentioning. The lyrics of "Tarkus," taken on their own, convey nothing of the sci-fi and post-apocalyptic meaning that emerges when the album artwork is considered as a pointer to the song's meaning. Progressive rock artists like ELP, Yes, and Genesis regularly offer abstract lyrics that may be interpreted in more than one way. The case of Tarkus offers an opportunity to ask whether the album art, which entered the picture (pun intended) late in the process, should be allowed to not merely influence but constrain our interpretation. Taken on their own, the song's lyrics are far more concretely about religion and war. Unanswered prayer, hypocrisy, and human sacrifice are among the clearer religious images that precede the depiction of the battle. Fighting for freedom, the earth has been scorched and children are starving. The futility of war, its self-defeating nature, makes the fact that religion is so often harnessed to support it all the more disturbing. There are multiple points of contact with the surreal apocalyptic vision of "Supper's Ready" by Genesis. Both take a close look at this subject, albeit in very different ways, and each offers its own critique of religious leaders who offer a call to arms. Both end with language from the Book of Revelation. Neither seems to have been copying the other in doing so, and thus taken together, these songs suggest that, just as there seems to be a natural if unholy alliance between religion and war, there is a natural pairing of song and the Christian Bible's apocalyptic finale in offering a call to humankind to avoid an apocalypse of our own making.

NOTES

1. Will Romano, *Mountains Come Out of the Sky*. Milwaukee, WI: Backbeat Books, 2012, p. 47.
2. Lake tells the story of how this happened in his interview with Anil Prasad, "Greg Lake: New Perspectives," *Innerviews,* 2011. https://www.innerviews.org/inner/lake.html.
3. Macan, *Endless Enigma*, p. 14.
4. Interview with Nick Logan in *New Musical Express* quoted in Macan, *Endless Enigma*, p. 57.
5. See for example, Macan, *Endless Enigma*, p. 63.
6. Recorded interview in the Japanese music documentary "Song to Soul." https://www.youtube.com/watch?v=-JcisCoqUK4.
7. On Frederick's outlook and influence, see in particular Immanuel Kant's 1784 essay *An Answer to the Question: What is Enlightenment?* King Crimson itself exemplifies the changing lineups of progressive rock bands. Peter Sinfield's website quotes Robert Fripp as saying, "King Crimson lives in different bodies at different times, and the particular form which the group takes changes. When music appears which only King Crimson can play then, sooner or later, "King Crimson Appears to Play the Music." https://www.songsouponsea.com/Promenade/CourtH1.html.
8. Macan writes, "Peter Sinfield's lyrical imagery, with its highly characteristic mixture of sci-fi apocalypse and mystical medievalism, made a huge impact on later progressive rock" (Macan, *Endless Enigma*, p. 68). To provide one example here, in reference to "In the Wake of Poseidon," Macan writes,

> Sinfield's lyrics, which engage the twelve archetypes of De Jongh's cover art, move into a deeper symbolic realm than anything from their debut album, with some of the references to the Magi and Jesus Christ, in particular, luminescent with multiple shades of meaning. (Macan, *Endless Enigma*, p. 81)

The progression from music to cover art to lyrics mirrors the process in the case of "Tarkus" we explore later in this chapter.

9. See also https://www.songsouponsea.com/Promenade/ChapterOneA.html.
10. The source given for the statement is liner notes from *The Essential King Crimson: Frame by Frame.* http://www.progarchives.com/forum/forum_posts.asp?TID=43262. On Fripp's interest in Wicca, see Romano, *Close to the Edge*, p. 172.

11. Romano, *Mountains Come Out of the Sky,* p. 37.

12. Greg Lake has said, "When I started serious writing, which I suppose was in the days of King Crimson, my lyrics were very brutal. We were busily observing all the things wrong in the world and the Church was one." (quoted in "Greg Lake – God versus Rock and Roll," *Sounds Magazine,* May 25 1974. https://geirmykl.wordpress.com/2018/12/24/article-about-greg-lake-elp-from-sounds-may-25-1974/.

13. Macan, *Endless Enigma*, p. 123 detects Orwellian/Huxleyan aspects to the song and indeed sees the album as a whole as unified by a dystopian vision of the future in which ensouled machines emerge that no longer need humans, their creators (pp. 127–128).

14. Lake shared a little about the process on his website http://www.greglake.com/one2one.php?page=11. On Lake's reaction see http://albumlinernotes.com/Emerson__Lake___Palmer.html.

15. Information from William Neal's website. https://web.archive.org/web/20130301165104/http://www.williamneal.co.uk/index.php?option=com_igallery&view=gallery&id=2&Itemid=18.

16. Macan, *Endless Enigma*, p. 148 emphasizes that a crassly literal interpretation of the story told through the artwork, and the assumption that it provides the literal meaning of the song, would reduce the symbolic depth and significance of the song. He also notes (p. 146, also in *Rocking the Classics*, pp. 87–88) that a singular dogmatic interpretation would not be in keeping with the "hermetic ethos of the psychedelic era," which expected songs' meanings to be hidden and require searching out. Stephen Lambe, on the other hand, describes Neal's liner art as a "surreally literal" interpretation of Lake's "abstract lyrics about war and organized religion" (Stephen Lambe, *Citizens of Hope and Glory: The Story of Progressive Rock*. Gloucestershire: Amberley Publishing, 2011).

17. Macan, *Endless Enigma*, p. 149.

18. Fans of science fiction may think of the episode from the original series of Star Trek, "The Doomsday Machine," which depicts a killing machine that continues to wreak devastation long after its creators and their enemies are no more; or the original Battlestar Galactica, in which the Cylons were a reptilian race that no longer existed but whose robot soldiers continued to fight on their behalf.

19. Peter T. Ford, "Compositional Style of Keith Emerson in Tarkus (1971) for the Rock Music Trio Emerson, Lake and Palmer." Master's Thesis, Indiana State University, 1994, p. 52. http://hdl.handle.net/10484/3914

20. The song lyrics are "there will be no sorrow, be no pain" while the verse in Revelation reads "there shall be no more death, neither sorrow, nor crying, neither shall there be any more pain."

21. Paul Heggarty and Martin Halliwell, *Beyond and Before: Progressive Rock across Time and Genre* (Updated and Expanded Edition). London: Bloomsbury, 2021, pp. 86–87.

22. Emerson described his reaction to Lake's lyrics in an interview with Joe Bosso. https://www.musicradar.com/news/guitars/interview-keith-emerson-talks-elps-tarkus-track-by-track-565038.

23. Macan, *Endless Enigma*, p. 159.

24. Macan, *Endless Enigma*, p. 160. Macan also offers two concluding observations about "The Only Way" (p. 161): "First, one wonders if ELP intended a bit of unspoken irony by accompanying this hymn to agnostic humanism with music that makes numerous references to that paragon of Protestant piety, J. S. Bach. Second, one wonders if Emerson and Lake noticed how prominently their solemn D minor melody featured the tritone C# - G —the *diabolus en musica*—in a hymn devoted to an agnostic worldview. More unspoken irony?" Macan feels that "Infinite Space" moved toward "a more mystic/Gnostic outlook" (*Endless Enigma*, p. 162), but the entire sequence seems to have a unified and coherent humanist message. See pp. 162–3 for more on Eastern mysticism, this song and Lake's vocals on it, and Jon Anderson. See p. 240 for the religious/spiritual roots of the counterculture of that era.

25. The title (according to Jerry McCulley's liner notes for the Brain Salad Surgery DVD) comes from a combination of the song's carnivalesque aspects and Keith Emerson's idea for a sci-fi story featuring a planet called Ganton 9. The liner notes can be found transcribed at http://www.ladiesofthelake.com/cabinet/bssliner.html.

26. Macan, *Endless Enigma*, p. 490 notes the possibility of hearing echoes of "Karn Evil 9, 3rd Impression" in the mood and major key fanfares in "The Score."

27. De Burgh credits the idea for the song to, among other things, reading Erich von Däniken's *Chariots of the Gods*. De Burgh explains this in an interview with Liam Allen, "The Stories of the Christmas Hits," *BBC News,* December 26, 2010. https://www.bbc.com/news/entertainment-arts-12049738.

28. The title The Body Electric stems ultimately from a poem by Walt Whitman, but also connects with Ray Bradbury's short story collection *I Sing the Body Electric*, the song featured in the motion picture *Fame*, and several other literary and musical references. For other examples of the intersection of rock with at least somewhat progressive tendencies, spirituality or religion, and aliens, see Larry Norman, "UFO"; and "Angels and Aliens" by Pinnick Gales Pridgen, which reflects Dug Pinnick's experience of an angelic presence, which he later came to interpret as an experience of an extraterrestrial.

29. Author Michael Moorcock collaborated with Hawkwind, first providing lyrics and then a musician himself, contributing musically. On this, see Michael Toland, "Q&A: Michael Moorcock Plays Hawkwind Sci-fi Author Joins Two-Day Tribute to Space Rocker," *Austin Chronicle,* March 28, 2019. https://www.austinchronicle.com/daily/music/2019-03-28/qa-michael-moorcock-plays-hawkwind/. Interestingly in the context of the present chapter, Moorcock also wrote fantasy about a king with crimson eyes, Elric of Melniboné. On the intersection of science fiction and rock in general, see Robert McParland, *Science Fiction in Classic Rock Musical Explorations of Space, Technology and the Imagination, 1967–1982*. Jefferson, NC: McFarland, 2017.

Chapter 2

Yes

Prophets of a Spiritual and Musical New Age

Among the early pioneers of the genre of progressive rock, there is no other band more worthy of inclusion in a book on this topic than Yes. If "The Revealing Science of God" does not correspond in some way to "theology," then surely nothing in the music of this era and genre does. Yet the precise meaning of this phrase (which serves as the title of the first part of the double LP concept album *Tales from Topographical Oceans*) is not self-evident nor easy to pin down. The same can be and indeed has been said about Yes lyrics in general. Yet as with theological discourse in general, failure to find meaning in Yes lyrics often reflects either a lack of careful close attention, or the incomprehension of the outsider with respect to an esotericism into which it is possible to be initiated. If Yes represents the most overtly spiritual progressive rock band from those early years of the genre, and at the same time has lyrics that convey little clear or overt theological meaning, that fact is both theologically and musically interesting in and of itself. As some find meaning in the songs while others find them incomprehensible (both musically and lyrically), it forces us to reflect on whether the theology of Yes, of Jon Anderson, and/or of specific songs are things that are to be found in them, that we construct in our engagement with them, or perhaps both.[1]

THE BAND

It is difficult to generalize about the band Yes since there has been so much change in the lineup over the years. There are nonetheless overall continuities in the involvement of Chris Squire and Jon Anderson, the founding members who continued to appear on most albums. Just as we also see in the case of Genesis, the original lineup is not the "classic" configuration responsible for the best-known work of the band. The founding members, however, often have a formative influence regardless of how long they continued to participate directly in its ongoing history.

Unlike in the case of the band Genesis, whose original members all met at the same single middle-class public school in England, the backgrounds of the members of Yes have been more diverse from the outset, ranging from working class to middle class and from extensive formal musical training to none whatsoever, and this has continued to be true right up to the present. While not to be related in any kind of simplistic causal way to the meaning and significance of their musical output, neither is the upbringing and background of key members irrelevant. While Jon Anderson says that all of them sang in school choirs, Chris Squire had significant training specifically in the context of church choirs.[2] Jon Anderson has said that his upbringing involved parents from different church backgrounds (Catholic and Church of England) while he attended a Methodist school. This may well have fostered spiritual curiosity and a recognition of the appropriateness, if not indeed the necessity, of seeking and exploring, of experimenting and testing rather than simply taking the familiar for granted.[3]

Once again, we must acknowledge that, as much as we may wish to approach the music of a band holistically, the lyrics sung play a dominant role in any discussion of the music's or the band's theology. This, in turn means that the lyricists have a disproportionate influence on our impression of their theological perspective.[4] In the case of Yes, Jon Anderson by no means wrote all the lyrics, but even when he did not, he had a penchant for placing his distinctive stamp on them. Anderson's interest in spirituality is impossible to miss, as it is not merely a matter of his background but of fervent convictions about which he has spoken regularly in concerts and interviews. Chris Welch writes,

> Jon has long aspired to different religions and varieties of mysticism, and he was a natural convert to the hippie idealism of the Sixties which sought to unify all religious beliefs into a kind of single Earth spirit . . . There is no doubt that his beliefs run deep. The quest for wider arcane knowledge is as important to him as the creation of good music.[5]

In the band Kansas, the conversion of Kerry Livgren to evangelical Christianity led directly to Steve Walsh's departure, as the latter was not comfortable singing the former's lyrics. While Yes' history is marked by frequent departures and returns of individual members, there is no clear indication that Anderson's (or anyone else's) religious views or lyrics were the reason. Most, if not all of the band members appear to have had conventional British backgrounds which usually included some intersection with church and

Christianity. In some instances, this influence persisted or was revived in adulthood, while in others, this was not the case, and more often than not, we do not know. Steve Howe, for instance, seems to fit the label "spiritual but not religious."[6] In the case of Rick Wakeman, we are not reliant only on his solo albums (with titles that include *The Gospels, Prayers*, and *A Suite of Gods*) to infer his stance. Wakeman appeared on the 700 Club and talked about his upbringing in the church and returning to Christianity with renewed personal interest in the 1980s.[7] From the perspective of Pat Robertson's variety of American evangelicalism, Wakeman might appear to best be categorized as "religious but not spiritual." Yet, in British Christianity, Wakeman's infamously coarse sense of humor, swearing, and beer drinking may be felt perfectly compatible not only with a nominal Christian affiliation but a personal connection of the sort that would account for his focus in several of his solo albums. Geoff Downes, who would later join the band, was the son of a church organist, but by the time he became part of Yes, its penchant for exploring spiritual themes and for incorporating church organ was already well established. However, Downes has opined that his story is by no means unique, suggesting in an interview that "A lot of prog rockers got their introduction to music through churches."[8] In some cases, an affiliation with Christianity remained or was revisited; in others, it diminished or was abandoned. However, it is, as a rule at least part of the background and cultural context of British musicians in this era. In the case of Yes, it is coupled with the kinds of hippie and New Age forms of spirituality that draw eclectically on Indian, Native American, and other religious traditions. These were part of the culture of the era that gave rise to prog rock, but not all bands embraced that cultural trend and gave it expression in their music. Even those that did, such as the Beatles, did not do so in the same way that Yes did, nor to the same extent, in wedding an eclectic approach to both spiritual and musical sources.

If in some ways the overt spirituality of many song lyrics and Anderson's public statements about them offer an overabundance of resources for the purpose of a book like this, in other respects they pose a dilemma, both with regard to how to narrow our focus sufficiently to fit within the confines of a chapter, and with regard to how to evaluate the interpretations Anderson himself offers. The lyrics themselves are often difficult to interpret in their own right, adding another layer of complexity. John Corbett writes:

> Yes is what happens to psychedelia when it hits the seventies. It goes corporate—not prog rock strictly speaking, with its analytic and experimental embrace of avant-gardism, but a kind of uplifting prog pop. This music is free of hippiedom's lifestyle implications. It's meant for solitary epiphany rather than communal enlightenment, emphasizing synergetics rather than group gropage, deploying ambiguous themes that are overwhelmingly positive—hey,

man, they are called Yes after all—and *Dianetics*-like in their mix of light-of-the-world quasi-biblical message and schnazzy new-tech gleam. *Achieve it all with music that came quickly from afar* goes the first verse of the title cut [of *Close to the Edge*], suggesting something mystical or technological, a psychic or radiophonic transmission from another plane. Anderson has explained that the lyrics to *Close to the Edge* were inspired by Hermann Hesse's *Siddhartha*, and they have an oblique poetics that was, to us, impossible to understand with any specificity but suggested something profound: the abstruse universal.[9]

Anderson has said that his poetic lyrics are more about conveying impressions through their sound than literal meaning that can be captured by parsing the prose.[10] As Thomas Mosbø helpfully puts it, they *suggest* rather than *convey* meaning.[11] This may hinder interpreters from engaging in the kind of close reading with attention to grammatical, syntactical, and lexical details and relationships that is the go-to method of academics discussing texts. He has also said that the meaning he perceived in them was often something he found in them *after* composing them, rather than something he set out to convey through them.[12] A good example of this is "Long Distance Runaround." In 1989, he said that for him the song had come to be about

> how religion had seemed to confuse me totally. It was such a game that seemed to be played and I was going around in circles looking for the sound of reality, the sound of God. That was my interpretation of the song, that I was always confused. I could never understand the things that religion stood for. And that through the years has always popped its head up in the songs I've been working with.[13]

Elsewhere he says the song

> was all about the craziness of religion. You're taught that Christianity is the only way. All those people in China are going to the devil, stupid doctrine, you know. And when you're a kid, you're 9 years old, you don't know any better. You were taught at school that everything started in Greece. Sorry. Not true.[14]

In a similar vein, he says of "Your Move,"

> There are so many different ways to look at it. Every time I would think "Cause his time is time in time with your time" I was trying to say that I will do anything that is required of me to reach God. And I think that whoever is listening to it should feel the same thing, that they are in tune and in time with God.[15]

I suspect that few who look closely and honestly at the lyrics of these two songs in the absence of Anderson's commentary will detect the meaning Anderson articulates as inherent in them. On the contrary, this seems the sort of interpretation that would be judged to be reading meaning *into* words rather than out of them, if it were offered by anyone other than their author.[16] Nonetheless, as we also see in the chapter on "Supper's Ready" by Genesis, the explanation offered by a lyricist is not always a trustworthy guide to what we might term intended or original meaning. Sometimes the reason is wit, playfulness, and/or a desire not to have great weight placed by others on words that are deeply meaningful to oneself in a personal way. In other instances, the reverse may be true, and the interpretation may reflect a desire to take what was initially mundane and elevate it to loftier heights.

Anderson has said that he offered "meaningful lyrics." He has also indicated that it is fine with him and to be expected that different people will interpret a song like "Close to the Edge" differently, and yet in the very process, he suggests there is a "full meaning" for the audience to get or not get.[17] At other times, he suggests a different process, one of finding meaning rather than conveying it intentionally:

> After we've put the song together and recorded it, I start to look at the thing as a whole and decide there is a meaning to it—if I can find a meaning. And possibly those who listen to it will find different meanings.[18]

Chris Squire responded to the suggestion that Yes lyrics are "philosophical" by proposing *vague* as a more appropriate description.[19] Can all of these seemingly contradictory affirmations about the meaning of Yes lyrics be true? Or perhaps more to the point, is the meaningfulness inherently multifaceted and multiple, as much in the mind of the beholder as anywhere else? Even for those who create words and music, the meaning thereof is not static. Those who seek to find meaning in music or scripture inevitably confront the question of the relationship between the author's intention and the reader as interpreter. Even for an author, what a song means is a complicated matter and liable to change as a result of its reception and the experiences and evolution of the author in the time after composition. What, then, is the status of the divergent interpretations of a text? Yes songs do not solve this challenging hermeneutical conundrum, but they do help us to bring it sharply into focus and understand it better as a result.

It must also be said that Yes lyrics are often singled out for criticism with respect to their obscurity and the difficulty in pinning down their meaning. It is not clear, however, that they stand out among other progressive rock lyrics or indeed among rock lyrics as a whole.[20] If we think of songs like "Whiter Shade of Pale" by Procol Harum, "Stairway to Heaven" by Led Zeppelin, or "Hotel California" by the Eagles, the lyrics feature many details that seem mundane, couched in clear prose, and yet the *meaning* of the song is much debated. Other examples such as the Beatles' "Lucy in the Sky with

Diamonds" could also be mentioned. Yes lyrics also become clearer when one reads them on a page and realizes that the sense units, the phrases, often do not align with the natural versification of the song. Yet listeners ought to be clued in to expect this, given the penchant of Yes to do things such as add an additional word that completes a sentence after a pause that misled us at first to think that the phrase was finished.[21]

Will Romano interviewed Jon Anderson in the early 1970s, when Anderson appeared to be "working through some form of spiritual transformation," prompted perhaps by the convergence of his fame alienating him from his working-class roots, and the urgency created by the decline of the psychedelic era of the 1960s and profound questions the entire society faced about what came next.[22] The exploration was a deeply personal and fundamentally musical one. In the interview, Anderson spoke of the influence of reading Herman Hesse and wanting to express his feelings about it in lyrical form, precisely because he didn't have some of the more common experiences songwriters draw upon. "I don't have the blues, so what do I write about?"[23]

As we reflect on the meaning conveyed through lyrics, we should consider that Anderson has even invented his own language for the track "Can I" as also for use in the song "Sound Out the Galleon" on his first solo album *Olias of Sunhillow*.[24] "Khatru" may also be an invented word.[25] The creation of words and use of sounds for purposes other than conveying meaning verbally is widespread in religious contexts. Om, the primordial sound according to the Hindu tradition, features prominently in Hesse's novel *Siddhartha*. In examples ranging from texts found at Nag Hammadi to contemporary Pentecostalism's practice of speaking in tongues, the use of language-like speech not connected to lexical meaning and its cognitive counterparts can serve to facilitate and/or give expression to altered states of consciousness, allowing the brain to "switch gears" as it were.[26] Will Romano notes the influence of chant and related musical forms on Yes's music and the chant-like elements that are incorporated[27]. All of this is at least in principle capable of fostering a meditative or other altered state of consciousness. Romano also notes how the combination of incense, multicolored light through stained glass windows, and the reverberating music of a pipe organ within the context of a church service "can be devastatingly effective and psychically transformative. The ceremony itself becomes a psychedelic and mystical experience . . . "[28]

It may be that the song "The Prophet" provides a key to making sense of what we see in Jon Anderson's lyrics and his diverse statements about them.[29] Perhaps he seeks to allow that his inner voice is a source of divine wisdom that his conscious mind may be less aware of. He allows words to gush forth in rhythmic rhymes rather like an ancient oracle, and he then seeks to parse in them a deeper meaning than he was cognizant of at the moment of their composition.[30] If so, then not only do we need to consider the theological views expressed by the band through their music, but also the theology of inspiration, of prophecy, that is at work and underpins it. It is easy to connect music and prophecy on a general level. On the one hand, singers of protest songs were at the forefront of challenging the status quo in the 1960s in a manner akin to what we see in some ancient prophetic figures, especially but not exclusively in the biblical tradition. On the other hand, music as a means to prophetic (and, more broadly, mystical) experience is mentioned in the Bible as well as by members of the band Yes (1 Sam. 10:5; 2 Kgs 3:15-16; 1 Chron. 25:1; Ezek. 33:32). Jon Anderson has said, "During the show, you're in tune with the forces that surround, which is God." In a similar vein, Trevor Rabin said, "I'm in another world onstage, it's like a religious experience to me."[31] Here they are referring, of course, to performance, but losing oneself in music is also something that can happen during the composition process. In turn, individual Yes songs have characteristics in their instrumentation, harmony, and alteration of tempo and mood that can facilitate an altered state of consciousness for listeners.[32]

Anderson has said, "There is a messenger within you . . . There's that point within you that knows you: we call it God, right?"[33] He further describes the process of creating lyrics in these terms:

> I just let the spirit flow and write down what comes. I never felt so much that I was a poet but a writer of ideas. Then sometimes I look at it and realize that it is poetry. It does have a balance and a literary point of view. It had substance. I never tried to create that, it just happened. So I realized I was being well used and I was a good vehicle for words and expression. It just seemed to happen naturally.[34]

This is a common experience of those creating music or crafting words, and it is a reason why there is a long-standing tradition of referring to this as "inspiration."[35] Whether one considers Yes lyrics "inspired" in a religious or even a more general sense, one thing should be undeniable: they represent the creative artistic product of the human minds of the band members, and are laced with religious and spiritual overtones, and thus deserve to be taken seriously and given the attention they are due in connection with a study of the theological significance of the band's musical output.[36]

THE SONGS

In the case of some bands, there may be only one song or a small handful that engage directly with theology, religion, and/or spirituality. In the case of Yes, it is the songs that do not do this that are the exception. On the other hand, the ambiguous and allusive character of Yes lyrics makes it difficult and perhaps impossible to choose one song and have it provide a sufficient focus for exploring the band's theological engagement and significance on its own. By considering two of Yes's longest musical creations, there is, of course, the risk that we may fail to do justice to the details. On the other hand, bringing more than one point of reference into the discussion promises to help clarify things that might remain obscure if the songs were considered in isolation. Both of the works that are the focus of this chapter would have been included, the only question being where. The present arrangement, which keeps them together, thus seems best.

Steve Howe indicated at one point how he understood the character of the songs the band was working on at the time, saying that he and Jon had been working on songs that might have a "religious feel." Interestingly, Tim Morse understood the reference to be to *Close to the Edge*, while Chris Welch took it to be to *Tales*.[37] The latter appears to have heard this directly from the source and thus is probably correct, but Howe may have made more than one statement to this effect. It may also be the case that music began to take shape at that point that ended up on or influenced the character of both albums. Either way, the suitability of the description as applied to both pieces of music is instructive and points to the shared aspects that make it appropriate to consider these two works in tandem.[38] Moreover, both are related to the religious thought of India. Both are long-form prog rock compositions (while *Tales from Topographic Oceans* has four tracks, each the length of an LP side, they are conceived as four movements in a thematically linked whole). They were created in close succession, and both highlight water imagery (river and oceans). Anderson seems to connect the two water images in the liner notes to the 2013 reissue of *Close to the Edge*: "The river leads you to the ocean, all the paths lead you to the divine."[39] Both early on feature chant-like singing with numerous repetitions of the same note. [40]The manner in which *Tales* begins with nature sounds also suggests a relationship if not indeed a continuation of the earlier work's exploration in the latter. The final movement of *Tales* includes a bridge section that quotes themes not only from other movements of *Tales* but also "Close to the Edge."[41] Anderson has spoken of the large-scale works from "Close to the Edge" through "Awaken" as reflecting his own *ideology*.[42]

Jon Anderson's website says,

> The lyrics are frequently inspired by various books Anderson has enjoyed, from Tolstoy's "War and Peace" to Hermann Hesse's "Siddhartha". A footnote in Paramahansa Yogananda's "Autobiography of a Yogi" inspired an entire double album "Tales From Topographic Oceans" (1973). Recurring themes include environmentalism, pacifism and sun-worship.[43]

That last point is intriguing for our purposes, as well as more generally, as it is an aspect of Anderson's outlook that has not been given the attention it is due and which is not always noticed by listeners. There is a need for a more detailed study of the role the sun plays in Jon Anderson's spirituality and in Yes lyrics than we can provide here. See, for instance, the song "Heart of the Sunrise," the "Music of the Sun," and other references in "Close to the Edge," the names of the sun in many languages in *Tales*, the reference to the sun leading us on in "The Gates of Delirium," the wish (echoing the Book of Joshua) for the sun to stand still in "Awaken," the reference to the "order of the sun" in "Shock to the System," and the list could go on and on.[44] Nevertheless, either this is a viewpoint Anderson has moved away from, or it is but a way of labeling his viewpoint that seemed preferable to him than labels such as "hippie spirituality" or "Neo-Pagan" which, for some, have negative connotations. It seems unlikely that Anderson, if an ardent sun-worshiper, would speak as he does of believing in the God within us rather than a God *in the sky*.[45]

Determining as much as we can about what Anderson believed and practiced, and what he read, may be helpful and yet at the same time should not constrain our interpretation in any rigid fashion. The meaning of these musical works is not found in purported source material such as the books Anderson was reading at the time. The songs rather provide a glimpse of Anderson's reception of and reactions to those literary works. The most useful parallel to highlight is Hesse's *Siddhartha*, which takes inspiration from the life of Siddhartha Gautama according to Buddhist tradition and literature, incorporating some historical and legendary details, and yet also changes the story dramatically in numerous respects, in particular by making Siddhartha and the Buddha separate characters. Awareness of source material can help us parse meaning, but not only through continuity. Sometimes the significance of the relationship is in enabling us to see what the later author chose to change and rework. Just as Hesse was not bound to the sources he used, neither was Anderson. As Thomas Mosbø writes, "It is important . . . for us to draw a sharp distinction between the *inspiration* for a particular song and the *content* of that song."[46]

Taking this point to heart will also allow us to see where source material may have been misunderstood or interpreted in a very different manner than the meaning of the source when treated on its own terms. That Anderson departed from his source of inspiration is nothing out of the ordinary. Nonetheless, Anderson has acknowledged that however much the ideas he encountered in that footnote may have inspired him, he did not understand them. Rick Wakeman was especially critical, pointing out that Anderson had taken a footnote about Shastic Scriptures that it would take eighty years to read and proceeded on that basis as though he truly grasped their content and meaning.[47] The fourfold structure of *Tales from Topographic Oceans* is not related substantively to the four categories of text mentioned in the footnote that sparked the idea. Indeed, Jennifer Rycenga has remarked, "it is embarrassing how little Anderson knows about Hinduism," not even managing to spell correctly either the first or last name of the author of the book whose footnote he cites as the inspiration of the work.[48] He also misspells the second division of the shastras, smritis, as suritis. Rycenga points out Anderson's ignorance not as an overall negative judgment, but to direct attention away from its loose and superficial connection with Hinduism so that we seek to understand it on its own terms.[49] Progressive rock (and music in general) is full of instances in which reading a text inspired a work, but that work should not be understood as a retelling of the same story. Anderson himself said in 1994, "I spent a year of my life going crazy, creating a piece of music that even I didn't know what it was all about."[50]

Sometimes a source of inspiration may relate to the subsequent work antithetically. The much later song from the *Union* album, "Dangerous (Look in the Light of What You're Searching For)," is very reminiscent of material toward the end of Hermann Hesse's novel *Siddhartha*, which Anderson has said inspired the song "Close to the Edge." However, in the novel, the character Siddhartha offers a warning that seeking can prevent us from noticing things we should learn because we seek with a particular goal in mind which narrows are perception. The song seems to advocate what Siddhartha cautions against.[51] Another possible relationship between source and song is that found in Jewish Midrash and the Qur'an when it takes biblical stories and elaborates on them, fills in gaps, alludes to them in poetry, and in other ways explores around the edges of those stories rather than retelling them in anything like a straightforward fashion. The attentive listener might find that "Close to the Edge" seems to have little direct connection to Hermann Hesse's *Siddhartha*, or might experience it in a manner akin to a programmatic tone poem, in which the composer's prompting that the instrumental work is based on and explores a particular story leads the listener to seek connections between the emotions and moods conveyed through the music and key moments in the narrative. In the realm of symphonic music from the Romantic era, we know that sometimes composers began with the story and deliberately sought to convey its plot through their music, while others found that a work they composed reminded them of the contours of a story and added the connection as an afterthought. The connection to a text may also intervene at any point between initial conceptualization and post-completion labeling.[52] There is no reason to expect rock to be any different.

"CLOSE TO THE EDGE"

Having made these points, we are now free to note points of contact with sources of inspiration and yet ask about their meaning within the context of the songs. Lyrics do not always take shape in the order in which they will be sung. Nevertheless, the beginning words of a song are important regardless of when they took shape in the compositional process. Beginning at the beginning brings the challenge of interpreting the lyrics into very sharp focus. Why begin with a witch at all, and what does it mean to describe her as "seasoned"? Why is the liver important? Would it be disappointing if the solution to this riddle turned out to be that Anderson once ordered a chopped liver sandwich and, when the person taking the order called it out to the kitchen staff, it was abbreviated to "a seasoned 'witch," and that he (as songwriters are often prone to do when they hear a striking phrase) thought, "that should be in a song"?[53] Even if the lyrics had a humorous mundane spark that prompted them, that would not render the end result frivolous. Indeed, it is relevant to note how frequently the prophets of ancient Israel saw mundane objects and saw deeper significance in them. Within the context of the lyrics, the listener is the one who may have (and thus is implicitly invited to have) the experience described. It is emphatically about what could be, even if drawing on what the singer or someone else has presumably experienced. An encounter with an expert in esoteric knowledge leads to inner transformation (the liver and mental states being connected in ancient thought about human anatomy in ways few today would).[54] This may have happened to the singer previously, but now Anderson himself may be the one who passes on the invitation to enter into new mysteries. For both, this experience involves music. It would, on the other hand, be easy to seek a connection with Hesse's novel and identify the seasoned witch with Kamala in the novel, who initiates Siddhartha into the sexual arts, an important aspect of his overall journey on the path to Enlightenment, even if one that he eventually forsakes like so many others, as offering insight and yet merely a stepping stone toward the recognition that the pleasures or pursuits in question are transitory and do not ultimately satisfy.

The refrain in "Close to the Edge" connects with the thematic use of rivers in Hesse's novel. Siddhartha considers suicide by throwing himself in the river at one point. His crossings of the river are each significant both to his character and to the narrative. The river makes him aware of the transitory nature of reality since a river is a constant flow that gives us the illusion that it is an object. Finally, in the end, Siddhartha becomes a ferryman and takes the river as his teacher. The ebb and flow of life and its cyclicality represent another prominent theme in the song that is also found in Hesse's novel. Seasons and change go hand in hand with the ups and downs that bring one back to a point where one was before, yet hopefully, like the river, not in fact the same even if externally this might appear to be the case. If we see only the "cycles of the past" we may still fail to grasp this crucial insight. We are prone to be deceived into seeing only what is constant or what is transitory when reality encompasses both, even in the very same thing. In the most radical of chemical transformations, matter is nonetheless conserved—the total mass (or more correctly the totality of matter and/or energy, the two being interchangeable) is retained. The interjection of "not right away" into the refrain the first time it occurs nicely conveys the postponement of enlightenment as a phase in Siddhartha's journey.

Anderson says that the block chords toward the end of the song symbolize that "religion as it stands is subsequently destroyed and there is hope for real understanding."[55] Anderson further explains, "We destroy the church organ through the Moog. This leads to another organ solo rejoicing in the fact that you can turn your back on churches and find it within yourself to be your own church."[56] This interpretation seems to be another example of one that is offered after the fact, as the proposed meaning is not conveyed by the broader musical context in which this segment is found. The overshadowing of the church organ with the sound of the modern synthesizer does not convey that they are in conflict, nor does the appearance of the Moog lead to harmony. Rather, it is immediately followed by a more dissonant rendition of one of the song's earliest melodic themes. Any suggestion that here at last the cycle is broken and Enlightenment achieved by moving beyond traditional religion is thus undermined by what the music conveys. There is an interesting intersection between life, history, and music at this point. Historically, Buddhism arrived on the scene as a teaching that called for major revisions to the way human life and its eternal trajectory were understood in India at that time. In actual fact, however, while Buddhism did emerge and flourish as a religion of its own, Hinduism was able to embrace aspects of Buddhist thought and practice within its own pluralistic framework. It has done the same with Jesus, and Anderson is but one example of a European who has felt able to follow the same logic in the other direction, embracing religious ideas from Buddhism, Hinduism, and elsewhere without jettisoning Jesus and everything that is part of his Christian heritage (not that a complete break with the past is ever possible). His lyrical trajectory will likewise move from a Buddhist story adapted by a European novelist, to Hindu scripture as described in a footnote in a book aimed at Western audiences, and later still in "Awaken" he would find inspiration in a retelling of the story of Jesus, Calvin Miller's *The Singer*. He may leave certain aspects of theology behind along with his worries, but his lyrics recognize that the changes are in fact left "far from far behind." Even when you are said to be whole, the reality of ongoing change persists. Enlightenment may have been attained, but nirvana has yet to be reached. Tension is relieved, and yet the revelation of the master's name seems to be set against that as something that brings tension.

There seems to be no way to determine whether the master whose identity is revealed here is the Sun, the self, Siddhartha (as a figure suddenly revealed in the novel to be distinct from the Buddha and yet able to be a guide toward Enlightenment nonetheless), or someone else.[57] Within the framework of eclectic New Age spirituality, there may be no need to choose one possible referent to the exclusion of others. Such spirituality has room for many masters, and usually, the ultimate arbiter and revelator is the self, while not excluding learning from others. There are plenty of ways that the story of Jesus can be glimpsed as in the background, and some have attempted to make that the key to the song's meaning.[58] The crucifixion of the singer's hate is an image that would fit just fine in Paul's theology. The woman who takes the blame for the crucifixion of her own domain fits less obviously well within the framework of Christian tradition, even if no modern European making reference to crucifixion could fail to have Jesus in mind.[59] One could readily find in this a parallel between God the Father sending his son whom humans crucify, the humans that God made; and Mother Earth who is crucified by the humans that sprang from her womb.[60]

The reference to manna from above echoes both the wandering of Israel in the wilderness and the adaptation of that imagery by Christians in connection with the Eucharist. Heavenly food often serves as a means of initiation and transformation.[61] Having noted intertextual echoes with literary sources external to the band's output, we should not neglect relevant echoes to earlier Yes songs (just as we may detect echoes of "Close to the Edge" in later songs). The reference to "your disgrace" calls to mind the one who is reassured with the message "Yours Is No Disgrace" in the song of that title. In that song, the one sung to is a soldier, returning with feelings of shame and guilt from a war they did not start but nonetheless fought in.[62] The references to sad courage claiming victims and armored movers suggest a military reference is possible in "Close to the Edge" as well. It is unclear whether the same individual is addressed, on this occasion not being reassured but invited to allow their feeling of disgrace to prompt them to seek deeper enlightenment, or if someone else is in view who should in fact feel disgrace. If the former, then the music that calls to them from afar could in fact be that earlier Yes song. There are too many possible meanings for us to explore them all here, never mind hope to decide between them.

The one who has outstretched arm offers a revelation and could easily be the Buddha or even the crucified Jesus. The singer's smile in response suggests that he feels he already knows the things this other claims to reveal. This meshes with Anderson's stated conviction that God is, in fact, one's higher self, to be found within, and thus one does not ultimately require another teacher besides oneself. How this relates to the original invitation to an esoteric transformation with which the song began is unclear. If the singer can smirk at an invitation to learn in this way, what is to prevent hearers of the song from responding likewise to the song's own invitation?[63]

The song's musical interlude section is reminiscent of what we today know as New Age music. The genre existed when "Close to the Edge" was created and was likely an influence. Indeed, many of Rick Wakeman's solo instrumental albums are placed in that category. Toward the climax of the song, the melody to which the lyrics "I get down" are sung moves in an upward direction, creating a contrast between the words about descent and the ascending melody soaring up to a high note. Then the church organ enters for the first time. This vocal idea is repeated, making sure we don't miss the point. Then the synthesizer enters, leading to a more dissonant revisiting of an earlier theme before the music takes us first instrumentally and then also vocally back to the early chant-like section but now with a far more forceful feel, before the lyrics revisit "I get up, I get down," and then the song ends with a return to the sounds of nature where it all began. In an era when people seek to escape from life by getting high or "getting down," the song encourages an embrace of the more mundane ebb and flow of life with its typically more subtle ups and downs.[64]

TALES FROM TOPOGRAPHIC OCEANS

Thomas Mosbø suggests that *Tales from Topographic Oceans* represents the first rock symphony, a categorization that seems extremely apt in numerous ways.[65] First, when compared with all the shorter works from the brief prelude or song to the extended suite or tone poem, all of those hold the listener's attention in specific ways for a short duration that contrasts with what a symphony demands of listeners. Symphonies regularly have melodic moments and themes that listeners love, but the overall context of them, the process of developing them and exploring them at length, often leaves not only listeners but critics cold. In the realm of rock, extended works are all in essence individual songs of the kind that listeners are used to (at least as far as their length is concerned) joined together. They may have linkages among and between them, and reprises. But these are akin to the suites, tone poems, and operas of art music. A rock opera like *Tommy* or *Jesus Christ Superstar*, and whatever one judges the best category for a concept album like *The Wall* or *Thick as a Brick*, they are all works that are comprised of smaller segments in a way that *Tales from Topographic Oceans* is not. This is crucially important both to make sense of the album and to evaluate the frequent negative assessments of the album by those who, even if they were already fans of progressive rock, were not primed or prepared for the kind of attentive listening that a symphony—whether "classical" or "rock"—demands. Second, if we think of a symphony that incorporates vocal elements, such as Beethoven's 9th or Mahler's 2nd, 3rd, or 8th, the "meaning" of the work is not discerned by focusing exclusively or even primarily on the lyrics. The words are important, but just as one part of a larger musical whole, in a way that is not true of an opera or oratorio.

The music on *Tales from Topographic Oceans* incorporates elements that may be described as avant-garde. The move to this and then to a more folk-influenced feel in the "Ritual: Nous Sommes Du Soleil" section is emotionally powerful. That the title for this section is *ritual* should lead us to reflect on the way that the interplay of fast and slow music, of dissonance and harmony, creates emotional effect (for example, in settings such as that of modern evangelical Christian worship). Many evangelical Protestants believe themselves to be at the other end of the spectrum entirely from liturgy and ritual, when in fact they use many of the same elements found in traditional liturgy and ritual, just in different ways and with different labels.[66]

Bill Martin writes on the subject of the religious outlook of *Tales*,

> this religious vision is representative of a complete philosophy; it is not "religious" in the contemporary secular sense of a set of beliefs that can be compartmentalized in the form of a metaphysical creed. The vision of *Tales* concerns difficult questions of society, gender, ecology, and the possibility of being at home in the cosmos. Its sense of making progress with these issues is neither purely meditative nor otherworldly. Its notion of transcendence is not presented in a mode of denial; the vision here is one of *working through*, not a contemplative leap beyond. As with "Close to the Edge," there is a complex intertwining in *Tales* of "Christian" and "pagan" themes.[67]

Martin's key insight here is also expressed slightly earlier in the book when he characterizes Yes as having a *hermetic* rather than *gnostic* outlook.[68] The difference is that the former label does not entail otherworldliness of a sort that ignores or rejects life in this material world. The label *pagan* is also apt inasmuch as the religious outlook reveres the Earth and nature. This refusal to dichotomize flesh and spirit, body and soul, sacred and secular finds expression in the fact that Yes's songs (and Jon Anderson's commentary in concerts) do not leave religion as a private matter as most secular bands with religious members do, nor do they compartmentalize their sacred and secular output. Life in this world and its metaphysical underpinnings and context are viewed as a whole. In the same way, the members of the band are by no means on the same page religiously, and yet any dichotomy to ultimate separation is resisted (with the exception of the album *Fragile*). The whole of Yes is greater than the sum of its parts without invalidating those parts (even if the album-making process did sometimes result in individual members' musical contributions to songs being obscured either in the mixing or the assigning of credit).

Considering this helps us to make sense of the otherwise ambiguous and indeed paradoxical title of the album. The oceanic and the topographic normally represent polar opposites. That which is solid has topography, while liquid is in flux. Yet a major theme in Siddhartha is that a river appears to our eyes to be an object with a location, yet in fact is constantly changing. *Tales* promises to narrate stories to us that give us glimpses of the world viewed holistically. Progressive rock obviously provides an ideal musical language for expressing this vision, with its fusion of diverse styles and traditions, old and modern, harmonious and dissonant, fast and slow not just across the songs of an album but within a single piece. Nor should we miss that Yes did not merely happen across this genre and find it provided a suitable medium. Yes played a pioneering role in creating the genre, and their unique sound reflects the spiritual vision described here in a way that other bands of their time did not.

Not that the union is always a harmonious one (any more than Yes's *Union* was a result of happy, harmonious collaboration). Whether one affirms an underlying monism of all reality or views unity as a future goal to emerge from a genuine plurality of the present day, tensions are real and unavoidable.[69] After the open-ended sense of questing with which side 2 ended, on side 3 of *Tales* the soundscape seems to depict a back and forth between rhythm and melody, between primal beat and church hymnody. From this emerges a melody that is at once lilting and not quite conventional in its tonality. Raucous electric guitar plays a role as part of a more elaborate and tumultuous section, then gives way to acoustic solo guitar with hints of a Spanish feel. When the whole band reunites, the lyrics ask questions even as the music contrasts this with a cheerfulness that must be viewed as ironic. The solo guitar then returns, followed by a return of rhythmic interjections reminiscent of the earlier part of the side, before the whole fades mystically away.

It is surely significant to the meaning of side 4 that themes from side 1 and other segments are repeated there, woven into a new context. There is also an echo of "Close to the Edge," as well as a moment when the words sung are repeated in a manner that "Awaken" would later echo.[70] Even as audaciously large as *Tales* is, it can be viewed as part of a still greater whole. The lyrics may seem to take a surprisingly mundane turn, but no more so than in the love between two individuals that features in Genesis's surreal "Supper's Ready." In the hands of Yes, the seeming resolution of this spiritual quest in human love is followed by frenetic percussion and building chords on the keyboard, to which dissonant and surprising sounds are added into the mix. We have not arrived to a point of rest and stability. Nonetheless, the guitar manages to interject and bring back the melodies we had previously heard, after which gentle piano and voice join in, and then at last we truly feel that home has been found. Even so, the band enters in full force one last time to remind us of the struggle that it has taken to reach this point, before the album fades out to ambiguous chords that rob the listener of any sense of finality. Present happiness without genuine recognition of the struggles it takes to get there would be trite, and failure to acknowledge the uncertainty of the future would be an unrealistic delusion. The conclusion to the album conveys this dramatically and poignantly.

If we return now to the question posed early on side 1, we may detect a certain irony in the question "what happened to this song that we knew so well?" Occasionally in this rock symphony, small sections emerge from amid the grandiose, experimental, and unconventional. Several sections have melodic and structural characteristics that would not be out of place on pop radio, although they are not crafted and shaped in such a way as to actually allow this to be done. The interspersing within longer avant-garde works of sections that are accessible to a wider listenership is a common recurring feature across Yes's opus. The lyrics on one level seem to voice the question some critics would ask, those who did not embrace the format nor the specific characteristics of a long-form rock composition such as this double LP concept album represented. Yet what many critics panned was a natural expression of the band's drive to explore and experiment. Even as the lyrics refer to a moment for which they have waited their whole lives, it comes after a pause, and multiple voices sing "moment" entering in an unsynchronized manner.[71] Spiritual and musical seeking and experimentation make for a natural pairing. Once again, there is a convergence of medium and message.

The most disturbing line on the album is "let them rape the forest," a surprising perspective when the value of the natural world and humanity's interconnectedness with the wider cosmos are themes articulated so frequently in Yes songs.[72] Other words, such as a more accusatory "you/they will rape the forest," would have fit equally well. It is the "let them" that disturbs. This surprising line may prove especially helpful in making sense of this album's meaning and its theology. One peril of monism is, of course, that nothing can ultimately be judged good or evil since all is divine. Rycenga's characterization of Yes's outlook as panentheist rather than pantheist, together with Anderson's apparent adherence to sun-worship, serve to bring clarity to the perspective offered here.[73] Fighting violently to stop the destruction of Earth's natural resources leads down a path that turns the defender of the Earth into its future exploiter, the oppressed into a future oppressor. Yet mere passivity seems inadequate, especially in relation to the many nature-oriented spiritualities that tend to emphasize the uniqueness of Earth, that harming it will destroy ourselves as well as much else that is valuable. From a truly cosmic perspective, the Earth is just a small part of the whole, and humanity a small part of Earth's story. If one regards the sun rather than the Earth as central to the story, as ultimately what gives life to Earth and thereby to humans and forests alike, then from that perspective the Earth may be valuable but it is not ultimate. Humans are prone to exploit the forest, turning that land into cities we can call home, turning the wood from trees into lumber to build houses we call home, as the lyrics hint. From a wider perspective, it is still tragically short-sighted, but nonetheless possible to get over the loss of the overhanging trees. We make ourselves feel more secure through these efforts to turn the natural world that is our natural home into something we build and pave. In the very process, we find ourselves alienated from the Earth and Nature as mother. The perspective of the Sun may be what is offered here, offering as long-term comfort the fact that humanity may harm the forests and the environment, but Sun and Earth will outlive them. Yet even viewed in this light, there remains a striking difference between the message in the words "let them rape the forest" compared to, say, "don't kill the whale." If it is surprising that those who are "of the sun" would be willing to resign themselves to the exploitation of the Earth, it is still nowhere near as egregious as the positive justification of doing whatever one wishes with natural resources because "this world is not our home" and there will be a "new heavens and a new earth."

It is tempting to connect this vision with that of the sad woman in "Close to the Edge." If the lamenting woman there is Mother Earth, the reference to the crucifixion of her domain is poignant. The Sun calls humankind to recognize something greater than its limited horizon. The Earth gives itself endlessly. In the interplay between the divine Earth and the divine Sun, the transcendence and immanence of the divine are both affirmed. The Earth will become a scapegoat that we crucify for our own ends unless we crucify our own hate and selfishness. Even while speaking in terms of a nature-oriented spirituality, the ongoing influence of Christian terminology and concepts remains. Yet this language is not used uncritically, and the fact is not ignored that warring factions on this planet have been motivated by "one cross" even while the world and humanity were crucified in the name of the Crucified. From the perspective of the Sun, Earth may lose the battle, just as evil regularly appears to triumph in monotheistic religions in which this creates an especially difficult theological conundrum. The Sun and the rest of the cosmos will continue, and so will life itself. This broader perspective ironically allows for an appeal to be made to self-interest and a narrower human-centered perspective. If the forest is plundered and the planet is ravaged, we do harm other living things, but the greatest harm is to ourselves, both our moral character and our long-term prospects for survival.

BEYOND THE SONGS

Spiritual themes and imagery pervade Yes's entire opus and there will thus there can be no attempt to fully list and catalog them here. Indeed, having made more than one extended musical work the focus in the previous section, we may be excused for keeping our broader survey brief. Songs from the early years of Yes indicate both that impenetrable lyrics were not always the norm (although there were hints of where things might be headed) and that the interest in religion and spiritual matters was there all along. One song that we have already mentioned, "The Prophet" from the album *Time and a Word*, illustrates this particularly well. That song sums up the approach to spirituality of the 1960s, one that has persisted and remained influential down to our time. Anderson says the song is about a man that everyone follows, yet who "tells them they should find and believe in themselves and be their own prophets and not just follow like sheep."[74] It is, of course, profoundly ironic that this self-defined spirituality was not made up of wholly unique individual approaches but constituted a movement of like-minded individuals who followed a very small number of individuals, most of whom depended heavily on still others before them, often drawing (however imperfectly or imprecisely) on traditions that are among the oldest known. Those who pride themselves in not following the crowd like sheep are typically just part of a smaller crowd, something which is not inherently praiseworthy. The majority may be misguided, but rejecting the path followed by the many does not always make one right. It should also be noted that, especially in the Abrahamic faiths, true prophets were above all else those who challenged people, calling them away from a focus on self and going their own way.[75] The song's central character might be perceived as a true prophet calling people away from mindless adherence to tradition and things they have been told, or a false prophet leading people to focus on themselves. Perhaps the prophet of the song is a bit of both. At the very least, one may concur with Bill Martin's assessment that the lyrics are

> a bit hokey and immature . . . Certainly an aspect of redemption is breaking out of mental cages, seeing the world in a new light. But breaking out of cages, including mental cages, requires struggle, and there is no sense of this in the song.

By way of contrast, the song "And You and I" is judged to be more mature "in conveying that redemption, the path to utopia, is struggle and work and not simply solitary enlightenment on the model that many Westerners want to read into Eastern philosophies."[76]

A few other songs may be mentioned briefly. "Mind Drive" from *Keys to Ascension* shows that there is a consistency of outlook throughout the history of Yes as far as Jon Anderson's lyrical output is concerned. "Circus of Heaven" provides a very unusual depiction of a carnival of supernatural and mythical beings arriving in a Midwestern town.[77] The song "Endless Dream" on the album *Talk* critiques modern televangelist religion, mentioning in conjunction with "tin Jesus on the radio" pledging in exchange for a spot in eternal life, and the extent of payment determining the degree of ferventness of prayers that will be offered. "Where Will You Be" alludes to ideas such as the immortality of the soul. Many solo and side projects could also be mentioned.[78] Jon Anderson's solo output, in particular, includes a great deal that is relevant to this, more than can be discussed in this chapter in a way that would do justice to it. Very recently, Anderson has uploaded songs to YouTube and elsewhere online that are not found on albums (at least not yet). These include "Music is the God of Love" and "Surfing With God."[79] From his earlier solo works, particular mention needs to be made of lyrics such as "Talking to their God, Talking to their child, Talking to their understanding truth" from "Understanding Truth." See also the thanks offered to Buddha, Jesus, Mohammad, and Krishna in "Big Buddha Song." The song also mentions "Divine mother." The song "We Are Truth" says, "We are truth made in heaven we are glorious." "Ave Verum" speaks of the majesty of God, pure light, and the "God of love, of light." "Leap into the Inconceivable" mentions "safe religion" declining, asserting that "All is One." There are references to "soul" incredibly frequently in Anderson's lyrics. Some of this is clearer than others. What should we make, for instance, of the words "Magical Trinity" in the lyrics to "All God's Children"? Jon and Vangelis' "He is Sailing" talks of religions and of the savior and the kingdom coming, but what savior or kingdom is unclear. All of these connect in some way with the themes that predominate in "Close to the Edge" and *Tales*. It is not clear that they add anything substantial to our understanding of them.

BEYOND THE BAND

As a pioneer in the realm of progressive rock, Yes's influence is all-pervasive. On the one hand, there is a distinctiveness and an inimitability about Yes, from their lyrics to their style and even the timbre of Squire's bass. Yet at the same time, we can see their impact on how other bands explored the potential of the prog rock genre, perhaps in particular in how progressive metal took certain seeds from Yes (and others such as Van Der Graaf Generator) and created a subgenre of their own. If *Sgt. Pepper* opened the door for rock to move in a progressive direction, *Close to the Edge* was received as illustrating what precisely that could look like in practice, the potential for long songs with varied rhythms and elaborate structures to explore new musical and lyrical possibilities.[80] *Tales*, in turn, represented an exploration of the potential of the concept album to tell a story with at least some unified elements.[81] Examples include Pink Floyd's *The Wall*, Andrew Lloyd Webber's *Jesus Christ Superstar* (a rock opera), Genesis's *The Lamb Lies Down on Broadway,* Rush's *2112*, and Neal

Morse's *Sola Scriptura* and *Jesus Christ, Exorcist*. All of those have religious aspects to the story they explore.[82] Several of them are at least indirectly in conversation with one another. All of them require audiences with a different approach to and expectations from rock music than had been the norm prior to Yes or indeed can be considered the norm today. The development of rock opera and the embrace of elements of musical theater (e.g., by The Who and Styx), and Peter Gabriel's exploration of costumes, recognized this to an extent that Yes live performances did not to the same degree. Perhaps this is indicative of a sense that, for Yes, in a way that was not as true of other bands in the same genre, concerts were conceived as transformative spiritual experiences in which the audience shared, rather than "performances" as traditionally understood.[83] Although often viewed as representative of high culture now, opera has always been primarily about entertainment and engaged audiences differently than symphonies have. Yes's music has inspired many songs and albums much as developments in the realm of the symphonic have influenced opera in the same and later times.[84]

As influential as Yes has been musically, they have been far less so lyrically, with little imitation of their attempt to weave overt New Age spirituality into mysterious poetic lyrics that mystify, playing fast and loose with the rules of grammar in doing so. One exception is Magma, which features an invented language as part of its interplanetary storytelling. For that band too, comprehension while listening was not the point of the experience. The music of this era is characterized by the inclusion of Hindu, Buddhist, and other non-Abrahamic religious sources, combined with an interest in UFOs and science fiction, as well as a heightened awareness of the fragility of Earth's ecosystem. When Yes shares such elements in common with other bands, there is no way to determine whether there was a direct line of interest as opposed to a shared participation in the culture and interests of their era. It is not clear, nor to be expected, that any other band that explores such realms does so by directly drawing on Yes's approach. Yes, however, certainly played a role in legitimizing such exploration through rock music, offering an invitation to others to do likewise even if in different ways. Because context and meaning are inseparable, our awareness of that broader context and the many other ways it found expression in music provides important and at times crucial evidence that helps us make sense of Yes and the theology of their musical creations.

CONCLUSION

The theology of Yes's music is, to a large extent, simply the theology of the 1960s hippie movement as it has persisted and developed in the New Age movement and other trajectories. This entire phenomenon is, on the whole, a nebulous array of loosely related spiritualities, all of which claim to offer substance and depth, yet regularly show themselves to be superficial on closer inspection.[85] Lest this judgment sound smug, it must be said that this is true of a great deal of theology. Indeed, it might be fair to say that most theology seems superficial or devoid of substance when viewed from outside the worldview that gives it meaning. Theological language is inherently symbolic (even slogans like "taking the Bible literally" do not correspond literally to reality). Yes engages with this directly, and thus offers something more substantive and rewarding than most. Their music pushes listeners to reflect on the nature and limits of language when expressing spiritual mysteries and convictions. Moreover, in the realm of rock music in which songs about lust and cars and other superficial concerns abound, it would be ironic to criticize a band whose lyrics have a spiritual focus as being in any sense "superficial."[86]

The songs and lyrics of Yes, considered in conjunction with the band's history, should lead us to reflect on the fact that theology and lived practice are inseparable. Tensions between what people claim to believe and how they actually live are not to be ignored. Does a failure to exemplify love, peace, and harmony undercut or undermine the message of the lyrics? Geoff Downes has said, "For a band with a positive, affirmative name like Yes it does seem strange there is a lot of backbiting and squabbling."[87] For those seeking to critically engage and evaluate the theology of Yes, what we know of the band members' lives and relationships raises questions about the notion that all paths lead equally and inevitably to God, to harmony, and to love. Subscribing to this view clearly does not lead inevitably to harmonious collaboration and coexistence with others! The practicalities of the music business, of art and the effort to achieve excellence, naturally lead to a competitiveness that can, if left unchecked, produce the very inequalities and conflicts that are criticized in Yes's song lyrics. Nevertheless, this discrepancy between ideal and practice should not lead to a smug dismissal of the message, unless one is going to equally take similar divergences in one's own tradition (e.g., Christians' failure to love their enemies) as discrediting it in similar fashion. Yes embodies the tension that characterizes human existence. Those who make art struggle with how to be true to their vision while satisfying audiences and earning income. Those who follow Jesus struggle with the tension between the demands of his teaching and the practicalities of life in human society. When one aims for a lofty goal, one will often fall short, and such failures to attain a high standard do not mean the standard or the effort is misguided. Aspiration may be inherently worthwhile.

The religious traditions of India that inspired many musicians in the English-speaking world during the 1960s and 1970s likewise provide evidence that tensions and seeming contradictions such as these are ancient and not the exclusive purview of any one religion. Some have embraced an ethos of non-violence based on the idea that all things are ultimately divine expressions of one Brahman. Others (as famously articulated by Krishna in the Bhagavad Gita) have taken the same premise to mean that, since no one truly dies, there is no reason to hesitate from killing and engaging in battle.[88] The view that the Ganges is divine has led some to be confident that it needs no human assistance and others to champion an environmental ethos that seeks to defend and protect it from human harm. Neither is the sole obvious corollary of the theological premise in question. Wrestling with the songs of Yes can help bring this aspect of the relationship between theological theory and practice into sharper focus. It also helps us to assess the role of religions (in particular Christianity) that were familiar and traditional in Europe and the Americas prior to the surge of interest in "Eastern" spirituality in the era that gave rise to progressive rock, and more recently, to the "nones" who consider themselves "spiritual but not religious." Just as this music was a wedding of different musical traditions to produce something new, the arrival of Hinduism and Buddhism as contenders for adherents in the English-speaking world did not represent a replacement but a fusion.[89] Even the most radical of revolutions is shaped by what was already there, not only as a force that is countered in a reactionary way but also as an ongoing influence even when it is not acknowledged. The infusion of other ancient traditions from around the globe, in the context of modern individualistic societies, will continue to transform all these converging trajectories. Whether anything genuinely new, stable, and long-lasting will emerge as a result remains to be seen.

That which classical music and jazz offered to rock was not forms of music that were new in and of themselves. They may have seemed new to those who had, up until that point, worked within the framework of genres and styles such as 4-bar blues. Adding more complex time signatures, changes of pace and mood, and new lyrical directions was exciting in that context. The punk backlash would soon illustrate that not everyone appreciated the move in those directions the way their adherents and fans did. The same is true in the realm of theology. Exploration of neglected and alternative possibilities that are a focus in another tradition can invigorate one's own theology with fresh ideas and avenues. The new is not always bad, nor is it always better. It is clear, however, that some of the most interesting theological creativity (as well as some of the most disappointing reactionary polemic) has been produced when representatives of one tradition have engaged and interacted with another.[90] The 1960s and 1970s witnessed all of the above and more. Some thought of themselves as embracing another religion entirely, when in fact their religion was not (as they alleged) the traditional spirituality of peoples more in tune with nature, but an "alternative" that was in fact a creation of British and American young people with only the most superficial understanding of the beliefs and practices they claimed as influences. The creation of these was a response to and reaction against a Christianity that had not only become too familiar and comfortable, but had failed to adequately critique and respond to the trappings of materialism and capitalism. Far from consistently offering alternatives, this movement produced new products and commodities that were just as deeply rooted in "Western" individualism.

Yes has been many different bands over the decades. No band, and no religion, remains static.[91] The question is always how much of the past is carried forward in each new composition or album. When Steve Howe or Rick Wakeman joined Yes, there is an analogy that can be made to religious conversion in connection with our discussion above. They brought things with them that they could contribute, even as they embraced being part of something that already existed.[92] Some became disillusioned and left, only to return again. That too often happens with religions. One reason why "Eastern" spirituality has been and remains attractive to people who are unsatisfied with something else they were brought up with, such as Christianity, is that its newness (to them) promises answers to questions their own tradition has failed to address to their satisfaction. What people regularly discover on their spiritual and ideological pilgrimages is that all human constructs—all theologies, cultures, and worldviews—have strengths and weaknesses. None of them answers every possible question and responds to every objection in a manner that is satisfying to everyone. Some meander from tradition to tradition, questing for a better understanding. Some chart their own course, drawing eclectically from here and there. And some cycle back sooner or later to their own heritage with a new appreciation of it, with its strengths and weaknesses, as a beautiful but imperfect expression of human existence. That can be true of a religion, and it is inevitably true of bands and musicians. To be a true fan of Yes doesn't mean rejecting anything other than the original lineup. Nor does it mean liking *Tormato, Drama*, and/or *Big Generator* equally with one another, or ranking them a particular way in relation to the other albums that are usually considered to represent Yes's greatest musical achievements. Being a fan of a band, or an adherent of a particular theology, should mean recognizing the value of what it has to offer without pretending there is nothing more to learn from elsewhere, that our favorite has no shortcomings.

If there is a theological lesson that can be learned from Yes, perhaps it is the fact that the band's defining characteristic over the years has been a shared pursuit of musical excellence combined with an ability to not take themselves too seriously. The members of Yes are the first to acknowledge that their output has not been even, even as they disagree about which songs and albums they think are truly excellent. For all the adamance, intransigence, and dogmatism that various members have exhibited, they all also engage in humble self-deprecation. Offering a vision of shared human identity, a connection with something greater than ourselves, a striving for excellence coupled with humility and awareness of our own shortcomings in relation to those values and vision—isn't that what theology, and music, are ultimately all about? The appropriate answer, in the context of this chapter, is "YES."

NOTES

1. On Jon Anderson's lyrics and his spiritual vision see further Randall Holm, "Pulling Back the Darkness: Starbound with Jon Anderson," in Michael J. Gilmour (ed.), *Call me the Seeker: Listening to Religion in Popular Music*. New York: Continuum, 2005, pp. 158–171 (here pp. 160–163).

2. Jon Anderson's statement is recorded in Morse, *Yesstories*, p. 100. On Downes see Welch, *Close to the Edge*, p. 187. On Chris Squire's choral training see Morse, *Yesstories*, pp. 1–2; Welch, *Close to the Edge*, pp. 24–27; also Romano, *Close to the Edge*, p. 26. Bill Bruford (Morse, *Yesstories*, p. 128) has compared Chris Squire's bass lines to church music. While members of Genesis Tony Banks and Peter Gabriel mention the influence of singing hymns in school (as also at football matches) the role of hymns and church music in Chris Squire's formative years goes beyond that significantly. Martin, *Music of Yes*, pp. 198–199 notes that Squire included Barry Rose playing pipe organ on his solo album *Fish Out of Water*. Rose was, the choirmaster at a church where Squire had been a chorister, St. Andrew's in Kingsbury. On this see also Sid Smith, "The Making of Chris Squire's Fish Out of Water," *Louder*. https://www.loudersound.com/amp/features/the-making-of-chris-squires-fish-out-of-water.

3. Malcom Dome, "Touching the Face of God: Jon Anderson on Religion," *Louder*, October 25, 2016. https://www.loudersound.com/features/religion-jon-anderson.

4. Thomas J. Mosbø, *Yes – But What Does It Mean?* Milton: Wyndstar, 1994, p. 25 emphasizes that for Yes more than perhaps any other band, meaning is conveyed through the music as well as—and at times more than or rather than—through the lyrics.

5. Welch, *Close to the Edge*, pp. 10,15. On Jon Anderson's spirituality and beliefs see also Anil Prasad, "Jon Anderson: Harmonic Engagement." *Innerviews*, 2005. https://www.innerviews.org/inner/jon-anderson.html.

6. Howe's autobiography *All My Yesterdays* mentions helping a small local church in Devon as well as connecting with his spiritual side through music, but little else and nothing that could be considered religious in a traditional sense. See also http://yesworld.com/2013/06/ask-yes-friday-21st-june-2013-steve-howe/.

7. Jerry Lucky, *Progressive Rock*. Burlington, VT: Collector's Guide Publishing, 2015, pp. 144–145. See also the article published in the *Harvard Courant* on October 17, 1997, "Yes Is Ready to Jam at Meadows Music Theater." https://www.courant.com/1997/10/17/yes-is-ready-to-jam-at-meadows-music-theatre/.

8. Ewing, *Wonderous Stories,* p. 16. David Gallant, *Asia: Heat of the Moment.* New York: Asia Music Limited, 2007, p. 14 writes, "The youngest of the original Asia family, Geoff Downes also received his passion for music through a family connection; his father had been organist and choirmaster at a church in Stockport." Romano, *Close to the Edge,* p. 20, notes that the same was true of Doug Ingle who wrote Iron Butterfly's "In-a-Gadda-Da-Vida."

9. Corbett, *Pick Up the Pieces,* pp. 117–118.

10. Romano, *Close to the Edge,* pp. 143, 151; Morse, *Yesstories,* p. 124; Mosbø, *Yes,* p. 11. On the other hand, some lyrics are surprisingly literal, as for instance Roundabout which is based on a drive from Aberdeen in Scotland to London in England (Morse, *Yesstories,* p. 28; Mosbø, *Yes,* p. 95).

11. Mosbø, *Yes,* pp. 31–32.

12. See especially his interview with Carl Wiser of SongFacts: https://www.songfacts.com/blog/interviews/jon-anderson-of-yes.

13. Morse, *Yesstories,* p. 31.

14. Interview with Carl Wiser, SongFacts: https://www.songfacts.com/blog/interviews/jon-anderson-of-yes.

15. Jon Anderson, quoted in Morse, *Yesstories,* p. 24.

16. See Morse, *Yesstories,* p. 24 for another example.

17. Morse, *Yesstories,* p. 43.

18. Morse, *Yesstories,* p. 121.

19. Welch, *Close to the Edge,* p. 128. Martin, *Music of Yes,* pp. xxv and 57 discusses the characterization of prog lyrics in general and Yes lyrics in particular as "bad Romantic poetry."

20. This point is made very well and fairly by Jennifer Rycenga, "Tales from Change within the Sound: Form, Lyrics, and Philosophy in the Music of Yes," in Kevin Holm-Hudson (ed.), *Progressive Rock Reconsidered.* New York: Routledge, 2002, pp. 143–166 (here pp. 144–145).

21. Examples range from "I must have waited all my life for this…moment" in "The Revealing Science of God" on *Tales* to "the dreams we make…real" in "Leave It" on 90125.

22. Romano, *Close to the Edge,* p. 100.

23. Romano, *Close to the Edge,* p. 101. Anderson recounted having a religious experience of being visited by an angel while in a hotel in Las Vegas (p. 103). On the influence of reading *Siddhartha* see also Morse, *Yesstories,* pp. 33–34.

24. Mosbø, *Yes,* p. 10; Welch, *Close to the Edge,* p. 271. Cp. The new language Kobaïan which Christian Vander invented for use by his band Magma.

25. Note how Anderson offers contradictory meanings for khatru even within a single interview (Morse, *Yesstories,* p. 39). See also Romano, *Close to the Edge,* pp. 151–152.

26. On speaking in tongues and the altered states of consciousness experienced through music and flow (in the sense defined by Mihaly Csikszentmihaly) see Margaret M. Poloma, "Glossolalia, Liminality and Empowered Kingdom Building: A Social Perspective," in Mark J. Cartledge (ed.), *Speaking in Tongues: Multi-disciplinary Perspectives.* Bletchley: Paternoster, 2006, pp. 147–173 (here p. 153). See also Benedict

Carey, "A Neuroscientific Look at Speaking in Tongues." *New York Times,* November 7, 2006. https://www.nytimes.com/2006/11/07/health/07brain.html; also B. Grady and K. M. Loewenthal, "Features Associated with Speaking in Tongues (Glossolalia)," *The British Journal of Medical Psychology,* 70(2) (1997): 185–191. For a musical connection see Jonathan Rowlands, "John Coltrane's A Love Supreme as Prayed Glossolalia: A Suggestion," *Journal of Pentecostal Theology,* 28(1) (2019): 84–102.

27. *Close to the* Edge, pp. 127, 138–139, also 105–107; Mosbø, *Yes,* p. 235. Morse, *Yesstories,* p. 43 records Howe saying a doctor told him Close to the Edge benefited his patients.

28. Romano, *Close to the Edge,* p. 121. Watching Jon Anderson singing the first part of "Awaken" on stage with his eyes closed while playing the tambourine illustrates this powerfully, as does his tambourine-playing and hand-raising. The contrasting moods of the sections and the instrumentation are also relevant to the experience once again, including the use of a literal church organ at the end of the studio recording. On Yes lyrics fostering mystical experience see Rycenga, "Tales from Change," p. 145; Mosbø, *Yes,* p. 53. See also Romano, *Close to the* Edge, pp. 198–199 on possible influence of *2001: A Space Odyssey* and its important opening music, Richard Strauss' *Also Sprach Zarathustra,* which was sometimes used as a prelude to Yes concerts, as were other symphonic works.

29. Mosbø, *Yes,* pp. 42–43.

30. Mosbø, p. 217.

31. Morse, *Yesstories,* pp. 11–112.

32. "Heart of the Sunrise" provides a particularly good illustration. See once again Poloma, "Glossolalia."

33. Morse, *Yesstories,* p. 62; Mosbø, *Yes,* p. 41.

34. Morse, *Yesstories,* p. 124.

35. Martin, *Music of* Yes, pp. 62–66 offers a useful discussion of authorial intent as well as of the tendency of some who understand Anderson's lyrics to represent a "stream of consciousness" as an excuse for not engaging with their meaning. See also Morse, *Yesstories,* p. 62 on an automatic writing technique or something along those lines used by Jon Anderson.

36. See also Mosbø, *Yes,* p. 75 on Anderson as *artist* and "Messenger of Hope" rather than "messiah" or something else of that sort.

37. Morse, *Yesstories,* p. 97; Welch, *Close to the Edge,* pp. 109, 126.

38. Mosbø, *Yes,* p. 19 considers the two albums to represent music that people will still be listening to a century later (see also p. 273). These works represent the result of collaboration between Howe and Anderson, who together are most directly responsible for the songs that are most germane to this book's focus.

39. Quoted in Romano, *Close to the Edge,* p. 98, where an interview with Howe reveals that the original idea of "close to the edge, down by the river" was contributed by him, initially having a literal reference. The connection of river and corner juxtaposes a natural landscape and urban setting (Martin, *Music of Yes,* p. 140), although admittedly the two are located in close proximity in many cities in England and elsewhere. See also Romano, *Close to the* Edge, pp. 243–255 on the symbolism of water imagery, and p. 251 on the idea of all paths leading to the same divine

destination. Martin, *Music of Yes*, pp. 81–82, 196 and Mosbø, *Yes*, pp. 36, 67–68 note other examples of water and river imagery connected with spirituality in "A Venture," Wonderous Stories," and "Hearts" as well as on Jon Anderson's solo album *Olias of Sunhillow*.

40. Cf. Mosbø, *Yes*, p. 235.

41. As noted by Martin, *Music of Yes*, p. 154, and discussed in some detail in Mosbø, *Yes*, pp. 264–268. Note as well that the main guitar melody that features while Anderson sings "nous sommes du soleil" is very similar to a theme in the first movement, a theme which is itself echoed even more closely on the electric guitar in close proximity, as if intending the listener to notice this connection.

42. Martin, *Music of Yes*, p. 204. As mentioned earlier, "Awaken" was inspired by The Singer in which rivers also play an important role, although not in a central way.

43. See his website: http://www.jonanderson.com/about.html See also Mosbø, *Yes*, pp. 221–222.

44. See further Rycenga, "Tales from Change," p. 147; also Mosbø, *Yes*, p. 70 on the sun giving better reasons in "Birthright" on the ABWH album, pp. 195–196 on the sun and divinity on Anderson's solo album *Olias of Sunhillow*. and pp. 221–222 on this in *Tales from Topographic Oceans*.

45. See the quote with which we began this chapter: "I'm very open and very conscious of my love of life and love of Mother Earth and love of the god within rather than the god out there - the God in the sky. God is here around us. We are collectively this energy force field."

46. Mosbø, *Yes*, p. 37.

47. Welch, *Close to the Edge*, p. 142.

48. Rycenga, "Tales from Change," p. 148.

49. Rycenga, "Tales from Change," p. 150.

50. Morse, *Yesstories*, p. 44. On humility when speaking about religion see p. 47.

51. Also on the *Union* album is the song Angkor Wat, apparently inspired by watching a documentary about Cambodia which made reference to Cambodian beliefs about the afterlife, which are then specifically referred to in the lyrics. This information comes from the fanzine *Notes from the Edge* #16, June 28, 1991. https://web.archive.org/web/20080509191610/http://www.nfte.org/back-issues/0016.

52. On this genre see for instance Lawrence Gilman, *Stories of Symphonic Music A Guide to the Meaning of Important Symphonies, Overtures, and Tone-poems from Beethoven to the Present Day*. New York: Harper & Brothers, 1907, pp. 1–6.

53. The stories behind the Beatles' "Hard Day's Night" and Chicago's "25 or 6 to 4" provide examples.

54. See Michele Augusto Riva, Enrica Riva, Mauro Spicci, Mario Strazzabosco, Marcello Giovannini, and Giancarlo Cesana, "'The City of Hepar': Rituals, Gastronomy, and Politics at the Origins of the Modern Names for the Liver," *Journal of Hepatology*, 55(5) (2011): 1132–1136.

55. Quoted in David Weigel, *The Show That Never Ends: The Rise and Fall of Prog Rock*. New York: W. W. Norton, 2017, p. 72. On religion as opposed to rather

than fostering understanding of deeper spiritual truths for Anderson see Holm, "Pulling Back the Darkness," p. 168.

56. Morse *Yesstories* p. 36; also quoted in Weigel, *The Show That Never Ends*, p. 105; Dirk von der Horst, "Precarious Pleasures: Situating 'Close to the Edge' in Conflicting Male Desires," in Kevin Holm-Hudson (ed.), *Progressive Rock Reconsidered*. New York: Routledge, 2002, pp. 167 182, here p. 177. Anderson has also referred to "And You and I" as a "hymn" while at the same time distancing it from any connection with church (Morse, *Yesstories*, p. 37; Romano, *Close to the Edge*, pp. 149–150).

57. It should also be asked whether this is the same figure as the master(s) of images, soul, light, and time addressed in the song "Awaken."

58. See for one example Martin Jacobsen "Analyze it to Life: Yes – Close to the Edge." This online article from May 21, 2015 reads the story of Jesus into the lyrics. http://www.deathmetal.org/article/analyze-it-to-life-yes-close-to-the-edge/.

59. Being crucified is also mentioned in "Dear Father" about which Anderson told Will Romano, "I wanted to know what the truth of God is. Everything is within you. Each human has the same light, has the same collective knowledge within . . . it is not out there" (*Close to the Edge* p. 48).

60. As Jon Anderson said in an interview with Carl Wiser, SongFacts (https://www.songfacts.com/blog/interviews/jon-anderson-of-yes), "I'm very open and very conscious of my love of life and love of Mother Earth and love of the god within rather than the god out there - the God in the sky. God is here around us. We are collectively this energy force field. It's a wonderful experience to grow into that as you get older."

61. On this see Meredith Warren's work on theophagy, in particular *My Flesh Is Meat Indeed: A Nonsacramental Reading of John 6:51-58*. Minneapolis, MN: Fortress, 2015.

62. See, e.g., Mosbø, *Yes*, pp. 46–47.

63. Mosbø, *Yes*, p. 41 detects a humility in Anderson's spiritual message, which extends an invitation as a fellow-seeker, rather than claiming to know and dictate to others. This should be considered as tempering the extent to which the appropriate category for Anderson is "prophet," with "mystic" perhaps being a better description, although the two categories do overlap significantly.

64. Anderson has connected the song's final verse with a dream he had about dying that resulted in him no longer being afraid of death thereafter. See Mosbø, *Yes*, p. 48; Morse, *Yesstories*, p. 36.

65. Mosbø, *Yes*, pp. 213–214, 271–272.

66. On ritual as an aspect of both "Close to the Edge" and *Tales* see Mosbø, *Yes*, pp. 127–139.

67. Martin, *Music of Yes*, p. 147.

68. Martin, *Music of Yes*, p. 140.

69. Martin, *Music of Yes*, pp. 154–155 articulates it in terms of the dialectic between unity and struggle.

70. Mosbø discusses similarities between the two works in *Yes*, p. 252.

71. On this see further Rycenga, "Tales from Change," p. 151. This element is appreciated but not explained by Martin in *Music of Yes*, p. 149.

72. Rycenga, "Tales from Change," pp. 144, 158.

73. Rycenga, "Tales from Change," pp. 145–146.

74. Morse, *Yesstories*, p. 18.

75. On Yes songs as prophetic see Martin, *Music of Yes*, pp. 22–23, 30–31, 83–84.

76. Martin, *Music of Yes*, p. 30.

77. Cf. also Jon Anderson's solo song, "Heaven Knows."

78. On some of the religious elements in ABWH see Stuart Chambers, *Yes: An Endless Dream of '70s, '80s and '90s Rock Music: An Unauthorized Interpretative History in Three Phases*. Ottawa: General Store Publishing House, 2002.

79. "Music is the God of Love" was written by Alessandro De Rosa and is available on YouTube and SoundCloud. This song with a reggae feel asserts that religion is unnecessary and that music is the God of this world. https://www.youtube.com/watch?v=-fgXaS2PYsM; https://soundcloud.com/alessandroderosa-com/music-is-god-anderson-de-rosa?in=alessandroderosa-composer/sets/alessandroderosa-com-music. "Surfing with God" is likewise on YouTube: https://www.youtube.com/watch?v=2CdFQigZfNY.

80. On the impact of Yes and Close to the Edge see Romano, *Close to the Edge*, pp. 233–255.

81. In a 1978 interview with Ed Sciaky (available on YouTube at https://www.youtube.com/watch?v=yyl2Eqs3JgQ), Jon Anderson said that Topographic is "never far from our hearts" and they (or at least he) continued to think about performing the entire thing at least once more.

82. Dream Theater's "Twelve Step Suite" also deserves mention, although it is a sequence spread across multiple albums.

83. The disconnect between this vision for rock music and what some fans and musicians wanted from the genre sparked the punk movement. The theology of punk as it relates to prog as an impetus deserves to be explored in its own right. On rock concerts, ritual, and liminality see Danielle Anne Lynch, *God in Sound and Silence: Music as Theology*. Eugene, OR: Pickwick, 2018, pp. 92–93.

84. Rush took to opening concerts with Richard Strauss' *Also Sprach Zarathustra* during the *Counterparts* tour (mentioned by Martin Popoff in *Driven: Rush in the '90s and "In the End"*. Toronto: ECW Press, 2021). It seems unlikely that they were unaware of Yes doing so before them. The Nietzschean connections of that work are arguably closer to the outlook of Rush than Yes.

85. This is not merely an outsider's perspective. Trevor Rabin remarked when opining that the *Big Generator* track Holy Lamb was weak, "What's a harmonic convergence? I don't know. Ask Jon." Quoted in Welch, *Close to the Edge*, p. 223.

86. Mosbø, *Yes*, p. 73 emphasizes that Yes's music is anything but superficial, as that book as a whole hopefully demonstrates more than adequately.

87. Quoted in Welch, *Close to the Edge*, p. 255.

88. On Anderson's embrace of the idea that one's consciousness never dies, see Romano, *Close to the Edge*, p. 104.

89. See Martin, *Music of Yes*, pp. 17–20 on Jon Anderson's embrace of "Eastern" spirituality as a Western appropriation.

90. In our time, the word "apologist" has come to refer almost exclusively to superficial critiques of other viewpoints that will convince few who are not already persuaded. The figures known from church history as the apologists of the second century, by contrast, exemplify the kind of creative engagement that produces things that are genuinely new and interesting.

91. Romano, *Close to the Edge*, p. 230 writes, "No one can repeat what's past, and most are not foolish enough to attempt to do so."

92. It may be less helpful to think of the expulsions of some from the band as "excommunications."

Chapter 3

Genesis's "Supper's Ready"
Messiahs and Metamorphoses

THE BAND: GENESIS

It would be easy to be distracted by the name of the band *Genesis* when discussing them in a book on theology and progressive rock. Producer Jonathan King, who is responsible for the name and for giving them their start, called them that because he viewed the band as "the start of my serious production career."[1] This name was acceptable to the band, whereas an earlier suggestion, Gabriel's Angels, a pun on the lead singer's surname which also had biblical overtones, was adamantly rejected by all—except for Peter Gabriel. Their first album, From Genesis to Revelation, was conceived as a concept album based on Bible.[2] The band was nonetheless disappointed that their album, when it was to be found in record stores, was often mistakenly placed in the religious music section.[3] The band's outlook was not overtly religious either in the beginning (pun intended) or at any point subsequently. Their British context led to inevitable intersections with religion, but there is also evidence of genuine spiritual curiosity and interest from individual band members, resulting in more engagement with religious concepts and texts than was typical in progressive rock music (or any other form of rock music for that matter).

The music center at Charterhouse School, where the band's founding members met, was named after Ralph Vaughan Williams, one of the school's famous alums.[4] Interest in music in general was encouraged and fostered, but anything to do with rock music was prone to be discouraged, albeit not equally so by all the teaching staff. Chris Stewart, the original drummer, says they stole "occasional melodies [from] the hymn book."[5] Whether he meant that literally or metaphorically, it indicates what we might have surmised otherwise from what is generally known about British public schools, namely the presence of things like hymn singing and related musical influences associated with the Church of England. Durrell Bowman talks about the influence of church music at Charterhouse School, which the founding members attended, saying that on the album *Trespass*, "Most of the songs have a kind of searching quality, with some semi-religious, arguably post-Christian, lyrics."[6] Peter Gabriel has said, "Hymns played quite a large part. They were the closest I came to soul music before I discovered soul music. There are certain hymns that you can scream your lungs out on, and I used to love that. It was great when you used to get the old shivers down the back."[7] Gabriel has elaborated on this point, indicating that he loved hymns for the melodies, as one sings them at a football match as is the long-standing practice in the United Kingdom, and not for the religious aspects.[8] Founding member Anthony Phillips has also indicated a love for hymns, not due to being especially religious, but a love of melody.[9]

If we look at the broader musical culture in which students at such a school and their families were steeped, it would have included music by figures like Hubert Parry, who composed music for the church as well as pieces like "Blest Pair of Sirens" that drew on Greek and Roman mythology. This was the culture of the Anglican Church and of the British upper and middle classes, and thus also of the public schools that served them and educated their children. It is no coincidence that Genesis reflects this culture probably more than any of the very earliest progressive rock bands. We see elements of the Bible as well as classical myth woven into the fabric of their songwriting, not as an expression of personal piety but as simply the lyrical language that came naturally in the cultural atmosphere within which they lived.[10] As Sarah Hill writes, "Not all progressive rock albums were conceptual, though many betrayed a group's interest in some aspect of literary or spiritual life. Because the original members of Genesis shared a background in the British public school tradition, there is in their early recordings an unsurprising reflection of the Englishness and Anglicanism of their early education."[11] Guitarist Steve Hackett commented on the band's popularity in Italy, attributing it to "the theological nature of many of the songs" as well as their familiarity with some of the Greco-Roman source material: "Catholic countries throughout the world subscribed to early Genesis. They liked the stories. These were very religious countries and it struck a chord deep within them."[12]

In the early days, the band assembled things they came up with separately into songs, with the result that, as Mike Rutherford has said, "We wrote long songs because we weren't good enough to write short songs."[13] This "composition by committee" approach is mentioned by many members, and while it was sometimes frustrating when someone's contribution was nixed by the others, it also led to the musical results that fans of the band's classic material love best. Even on songs largely written by one member, the musical contribution by others added something substantial. That said, it was more often than not the case that the lyrics of a song, and sometimes of an entire album, would be written by vocalist Peter Gabriel. In the case of the song that is our focus in this chapter, "Supper's Ready," Gabriel's usual practice during this period of going into the studio after the musicians had all laid down their parts and recording the vocals on his own meant that he could sing in a section that keyboardist Tony Banks thought of as "his bit," although Banks later came around and appreciated the result.

Gabriel's family background and personal spiritual journey are relevant to the effort to interpret what he wrote. His father had a bookshelf full of volumes reflecting theosophical and Eastern religious perspectives.[14] His family was Church of England but not devout.[15] His ex-wife Jill would later say that "Peter believes in God, and he believes in Christ, but I don't think he believes in the church."[16] Gabriel himself attested around the same time that he was "not a practicing religious person, in the sense of belonging to a faith or church."[17] When we place Gabriel within the context of the formative influences of his family and his education, important tributaries that fed into his lyrics become visible, and attention to these can help us to understand some of the more allusive and poetic elements that often puzzle listeners.

THE SONG: "SUPPER'S READY"

The song "Supper's Ready" (especially when considered in the context of Peter Gabriel's live performances of it during his time with the band, complete with preceding storytelling and costume changes) falls squarely in the genre of surrealist British humor, which many even outside the United Kingdom will be familiar with through its most famous exemplar, the comedy group Monty Python. That troupe, and this song and many others like it from the band Genesis during this era, offer a lot that is philosophically profound under the guise of the comical and farcical, including quite a bit that has to do with religion. Whether considered comical or profoundly serious, however, the religious and theological aspects of "Supper's Ready" are impossible to miss and deserve to be explored in a substantive way.

About "Supper's Ready," Bowman writes:

> Given the origins of Genesis in a Church-of-England-affiliated school, it makes sense that Gabriel's lyrics were partly inspired by John Bunyan's 17th-century *The Pilgrim's Progress*, as well as aspects of 19th-century British fantasy literature by Lewis Carroll and the Bible's Old Testament Book of Ezekiel and New Testament Book of Revelation. The epic song takes an even stranger path than *The Pilgrim's Progress* to establish a kind of post-Christian religious allegory. Lewis Carroll's work includes such things as absurdist nonsense, inventive

word play, and fanciful creatures, and Gabriel also makes use of those ideas. The Bible's Books of Ezekiel and Revelation speak of a New or Heavenly Jerusalem, and that idea is transformed at the end of "Supper's Ready."[18]

The musical feel of the opening section creates tension, and the disjuncture between that and the mundaneness of the initial lyrics creates an eerie effect. The multiple twelve-string guitars (including one played by Tony Banks who was normally on keyboards) often have a quasi-renaissance feel, hinting at music of a bygone era. This effect was often used in conjunction with stories that were mythical in character. In the opening section of "Supper's Ready," called Lover's Leap, there is musical tension created through the choice of chords, which provide no sense that there is a tonic (it begins with an Am6 chord which is an inversion of an F#ø). In other words, there is no sense of having a secure musical home, making for a striking contrast with the song's ending as we will see later. This effect is also accomplished through the fact that the lyrics offered against this musical backdrop initially depict the most mundane of settings: a sitting room (in American English "living room") with a television and the sound of cars audible from outside.[19] Yet as the two individuals look at each other, one perceives some kind of change in the other's appearance. Peter Gabriel has recounted that this is based on a real experience that he and his wife Jill had, in which she seemed to have been possessed.[20]

As the scene the song opens with progresses, but before a long instrumental section takes them away on the first leg of their surreal journey, we increasingly get a sense that all is not right. The narrator has been far away, which could quite easily reflect the real experiences of a musician spending time touring away from home, a frequent subject of songwriters.[21] It is not always clear who is speaking, whether we hear from only one or from both members of the couple. One or both of them is trying to reassure the other, and/or themselves, that the love they share is true. On the mundane level, the change in the other's appearance reflects the experience of reunion after lengthy separation. Both the fact that aging continues during such periods, and the fact that one does not see the other as frequently in person, make the renewed sight of them uncanny and potentially unsettling, however welcome it may be. The lyrics take this as a jumping-off point (a "Lover's Leap") for a deeper exploration of the instability even of the most familiar. The route traveled may be characterized as supernatural or spiritual, or in that era perhaps psychedelic might be the best term. There is no need to choose from among these categories as they can and often do overlap. A moment of recognition that things, like the appearance of a loved one, cannot be taken for granted can lead to a revelation that perceived reality as a whole may not be all there is, or at the very least is not as stable as one might presume. The instability of the scene grows further as ghostly figures are spotted outside. This trajectory will continue throughout the song as deception and harm connected with religion, war, politics, and economics all receive attention. Along the way, listeners are treated to regular references to figures from classical mythology and (especially toward the song's climax) the Book of Revelation, as well as famous examples of English hymnody.

The story is allusive and at times surreal, but beginning with the sense that one's home and true love are not as stable as a trite love song might suggest, the song proceeds to pull back the mask on other aspects of life, including religious teachers offering assurance about the afterlife, the celebration of war as a supposed means to peace, patriotism, and gender identities. Once one has perceived this as the song's unifying thread, the whole hangs together in a cohesive manner even as it takes delight in disconcerting us by pulling things apart that we take for granted. One of the particularly effective ways it accomplishes this is through a contrast and regular inversion between the unsettling elements being conveyed through the music or the lyrics. After the mundane initial scene of two people at home, television, and supper, set to music that lacks a sense of home, the lyrics move to two more seemingly mundane individuals, a farmer and a fireman. Yet by saying that the farmer looks after the farm and the fireman looks after the fire, the song shows the unpredictability and at times absurdity of language. These two job titles refer to farm and fire and yet the roles so designated do not normally relate to them in comparable ways. The song is full of puns and wordplays that could easily be viewed as mere linguistic fun, and on one level they are. Yet, as one would expect from surrealist art, Genesis songs characterized by these traits also poke at assumptions about reality and say something profound in the process.[22] Whether visual or verbal, surrealism shows the fluidity and instability of the things that we see and say, making a point in both cases about the things we think we *know*. This is not a departure from the starting point, which could in theory have continued as a simple love song just as it began. How does one know someone else's love is true? The uncertainties inherent in language have real practical relevance to everyday matters, including but not limited to romantic relationships. The varied punctuation in the titling of the first section makes ambiguous (perhaps intentionally) whether the reference is to a location where one or more lovers leap, or to one or more of them leaping. The ambiguity highlights that this is a starting point where romance and/or tragedy might ensue, depending on what happens next.

From there, we are introduced to the Guaranteed Eternal Sanctuary Man, whose religious deception is set to music that is majestic and hymn-like. Even as the song warns that those addressed have been fooled, the music intones the claims of this false prophet in a manner that conveys how what is offered could be compelling. The invitation to look into his mouth and walk inside highlights, through its surreal image, the role of speech in deception.

The ending of the section features a chorus of children singing a version of the "Rocking Carol," with a little snake taking the place Jesus occupies in the original.[23] The image conjured up thereby (even if one misses the reference to the carol and the significance of its words as background) indicates that the "children lost down many paths" are deceived into taking a literal or metaphorical devil into their midst, and having done so, they nurture it and adore it.

Next on the journey is a battle scene that is vibrant and celebratory. The introduction ties it explicitly to the overall theme of communication and the potential for tension or even contradictions between what is beneath the surface and what is visible: "Wearing feelings on our faces while our faces took a rest." The reference to a "prayer capsule" together with the mention of a "wonderful potion" conveys how religion, patriotism, and chemical narcotics may each have a similar effect of dulling or heightening senses, facilitating situations in which people engage in actions and have experiences that they otherwise would not. This is likely the same substance proffered as a "spoonful of miracle" by the Guaranteed Eternal Sanctuary Man, thus showing that we are still tracing the same story in this section. The lyrical and musical moods finally coalesce in the brief fourth section, which surveys the aftermath of the battle as a gruesome scene of carnage, while also paying a visit to the mythical figure of Narcissus whose story is echoed in the section's title, "How Dare I Be So Beautiful?"[24] The phrase was more directly borrowed from their producer Jonathan King who gave them their start in music, but brings to mind the classical myth nonetheless. The narcissism that leads to the celebration of war is highlighted before the song transitions abruptly into its fifth section, "Willow Farm," which was originally planned as a separate song but was incorporated here in the process of writing "Supper's Ready."[25] That section stands out musically and in many respects represents the pinnacle of the suite's deconstruction of stable categories and binaries.[26] We are told that everyone lies, that birds not only were previously eggs but also other animals (perhaps an allusion, even if a biologically inaccurate one, to evolution as an example of continuous flux that underlies and creates each epoch's seemingly stable array of flora and fauna). One can feel one's body melt, going from mum (in American English "mom") to dad and back, and between the roles traditionally assigned to men and women in society.[27] This theme of gender fluidity appears regularly in Genesis songs, as we will discuss later in this chapter. Winston Churchill appears in women's clothing, having previously been a British flag and a plastic bag, the ultimate in cherished national symbols and disposable everyday items juxtaposed. Brought together in this way, they challenge the listener not to take for granted any of the many items listed in what might seem to be a mere collection of rhymes. On closer inspection there is a deeper insight, the lyrics forcing into our conscious awareness that those things we assume to be deep and solid (mother and father, or a revered national leader) may be shallow and unstable, and indeed something else entirely than they appear. If they meet our expectations now, they may not always do so, because things change.

The next section's title ("Apocalypse in 9/8") brings the Bible directly into focus, as well as the unusual time signature in this part of the song. The subtitle says that it costars the "Delicious Talents of Gabble Ratchet." The phrase Gabble Ratchet was apparently originally "Gabriel Ratchet," which, of course, echoes the lead singer's name as well as the biblical angel, both of which are relevant to this section. The expression "gabble ratchet" denotes a flock of wild geese, which was sometimes treated as an omen. At times, they were identified with the "hounds of hell" because the unseen birds' yelping cries from the sky sounded like hounds, and in the dark, it would be impossible to perceive precisely where the sound originated.[28] The presence of hunters (also doubling as the horsemen of the apocalypse) on the album cover and the sound of wild geese on the album, if you listen closely, seems to clinch this as the reference. This detail in the title of the penultimate section thus brings to the fore the theme we have detected thus far of the potential for the mundane to serve either as a window to or a veil obscuring the spiritual or paranormal depth that lies there if one only perceives what is beneath the surface of visible reality.

This is followed by a final section which combines a British expression "sure as eggs is eggs" which denotes something that one can be absolutely confident about, and an allusion (highlighted in the liner notes on the album) to the hymn "Jerusalem."[29] Peter Gabriel often introduced the song with a story about worms in which he whistled this hymn tune. "Eggs is eggs" is a tautology, and not even a grammatical one, and so there is irony woven into the very fabric of it. Moreover, the inclusion of the egg as one of many stages in the change undergone in the "Willow Farm" section undermines any possibility of treating eggs as more stable or certain than anything else we might imagine. The song as a whole highlights the possibility that a deeper spiritual reality may lie beneath the surface of mundane reality, but also that the "spiritual" is not necessarily good. The spirits of religious deceit, narcissism, nationalism, and war can all be spotted behind the curtain, as well as angels of God. The egg reference thus likely reflects the quest for certainty and the feeling of certainty, but at the same time it exposes its inherent limitations.

That the trumpeting angels who appear just prior to the final section play "sweet rock and roll" is not just a nod to the genre of music being performed. In an era when rock was still countercultural and considered to be a destabilizing influence, as part of the lyrics of a song by musicians who met at a school where they were warned against such music, it is clear that their vision of a new Jerusalem is not that of the hymn, nor even in a straightforward way that of the Book of Revelation. Rather, the hope expressed for something better looks to a future that will emerge from (rather than in spite of) the enormous changes taking place in society in the 1960s and 1970s. The song highlights the irony: a school that educated the children of the British middle class who historically took up roles that safeguarded the status quo kept new music at bay thinking it would thereby maintain stability.[30] Yet the school had them reading Ovid and probably also viewing modern art, both of which are influences that can be detected in the song and in the band's other works.[31] From such sources, classical and modern, one learns that what seems solid is, in fact, fluid and what seems eternal is, in fact, ephemeral, which scarcely supports the upholding of the status quo or unquestioned allegiance to tradition. One might also learn through the stories the Greeks and Romans told about their gods and heroes alongside those in the Bible that theology, symbolism, and transcendence are not the exclusive domain or possession of any one religion. The reference to the pied piper leading the children underground, away from the battle might be a reference to the underground music scene, or at least the often hidden engagement of the younger generation with the new music that was leading them away from their parents' and culture's traditional values. Yet, as in the song lyrics, those undergoing these shifts are rooted in the soil of the earth and of their culture, the English landscape of the hymn that frames the song. The imagery calls for a willingness not only to challenge the traditional and ancient but also the innovative and modern.

The lovers' journey ends with a recap of the melody from the first section, with which the story began, and then shifts to the same music that was used for the Guaranteed Eternal Sanctuary Man. Now, however, the story is about the lovers: their souls are ignited and they find themselves free to get back home. Whether that is the home they share in which we find them at the beginning, returned to in a new light, or the celestial home of the new Jerusalem, or the one as a symbol of the other, is difficult to say, and it may not be necessary to choose between these options.[32] One possibility is that those who have been freed to get home to eternal rest are the two figures who supposedly, in one interpretation offered of the eerie experience alluded to in the song's opening, met on that occasion through Peter Gabriel and his wife Jill, whether possessing them or as past lives of theirs.[33] Pythagoras subscribed to a doctrine of metempsychosis or reincarnation, and this is associated with him by Ovid. Thus, while the liner notes characterize Pythagoras as merely a "Greek extra," the very act of singling him out and explaining his presence shines a spotlight on him that suggests his presence is far more significant. That Pythagoras' "brand new tune" is the last thing mentioned before the vocal melody returns us to the opening section's refrain likewise suggests that the mention of this philosopher is extremely important. Pythagoras has supposedly written a brand new tune, and yet what we hear next is a reprise of the song's beginning. The mention of blood and a looking glass echoes the passage in Ovid in which the philosopher advocates vegetarianism on the basis that the soul, life itself, migrates between different bodies.[34] The earlier reference to having been stamped "human bacon" also resonates with that section of Ovid's *Metamorphoses*, as does the use of religion to justify social practice and to mislead, since Pythagoras is depicted as blaming humans for invoking the gods' alleged desire for blood sacrifice to legitimize our practice. It is difficult to know whether Pythagoras writing his new song "in blood" affirms the view articulated in that classical source or inverts it by suggesting that Pythagoras has "changed his tune." What seems clear, however, is that the Book of Revelation is here being joined with Pythagoras' song of revelation, the seer John and the Delphic oracle joining forces to offer a vision of the world in which all things change, and yet there can also be a hope of ultimate fulfillment and final rest that is often lacking in religious systems that subscribe to metempsychosis.[35]

The musical language returns to the beginning with transformed meaning even as the place of peace (which the liner notes highlight as the meaning of the name Jerusalem) may now be the home where they were at the beginning, which they dwell in having managed to connect emotionally and spiritually in a way that they did not feel connected at the song's start, despite the emphasis there on their close physical proximity. Like the other concepts and categories problematized over the course of the song, home can be a place of conflict, one of verbalizations of love masking underlying discord, or a place of peace where communication occurs that manages to transcend the capacities of words. The musical language provides a sense of connectedness throughout this journey so that the story of the lover and the beloved receives a sense of resolution, while the mythic story also reaches closure as the appearance of an angel from the Book of Revelation announces that "supper's ready."[36]

Although it may be missed by many listeners, there is a repeated motif of the same four notes that occurs throughout the very last segment. Together with the section heading that "eggs is eggs," we are primed to hear in this an exploration of the quest for stability, for what is certain and trustworthy, in our world of false prophets, melting bodies, and ever-changing colors. The music, including that note of stability, fades out into eternity.

Some may find the notion of an absurdist or surrealist theology difficult to entertain. It should not be. In Buddhism, a key teaching tool is the koan, a puzzle or paradox the point of which is not to solve it through logic but to be prompted to transcend mundane thinking by contemplating it. Perhaps one reason that so many seem to find "Supper's Ready's" meaning impenetrable is that it has been treated as a riddle to be solved rather than something more akin to a koan or a surrealist painting.[37] If we look at some of the key thinkers in the realm of Christian theology and philosophy in the era in which Genesis created this prog rock masterpiece, we find a great many resonances. The song ends with a return home to live within the world of uncertainty, and yet at the same time hints that there might be an ultimate resolution to the frustrations caused by present uncertainty and the absurd. John Hick proposed the idea of "eschatological verification," the notion that one could affirm things one cannot prove in hope of their confirmation in the end.[38] In the same era, Paul Tillich emphasized that, while words could not do justice to the subject matter of a transcendent God, language could be used symbolically in a manner that was not literally true yet still meaningful.[39] The existentialism that underpins much of Tillich's thought is closely related to the many tributaries that influenced surrealism.[40]

The Book of Revelation could itself easily be categorized as surreal. A lion is announced, only for a lamb to appear (not on Broadway in this instance). The lamb has seven horns and seven eyes. Robes are washed white in the lamb's (red) blood. Such images would not be out of place on a Genesis album cover, nor in Genesis lyrics, from the Peter Gabriel era. Gabriel has said (in connection with the influence of the Book of Revelation on him as he was writing the song) that for the first time "I was really singing from my soul—almost like singing for my life."[41] This is an important clue that there is much more significance and depth to the song than the farcical explanation of its meaning in the album liner notes would indicate.[42] The comical commentary or introductions need not be viewed as at odds with that deeper significance, but they do have the potential to obscure it from view.[43] The use of cockney rhyming slang can also seem to detract from any sense of seriousness. Yet by saying "aching men's feet" in one expression he can talk of "making ends meet" through word play and yet also allude, as the liner notes do in a mere tantalizing hint, to the hymn "Jerusalem." The Britishness of the phrases and imagery makes the song even more impenetrable to listeners from elsewhere. They are also an important clue to the meaning of the song's theological and social vision. We have already mentioned the way it is framed by the hymn "Jerusalem," which begins with the possibility that Jesus might have visited Britain as a child, and ends with a patriotic determination to build Jerusalem there. "Supper's Ready" challenges that vision as it begins with the most humdrum aspects of life, takes a journey that exposes the way a society that thinks of itself so highly and narcissistically as the pinnacle of all things is built on mountains of bodies sacrificed in war, and the survivor is still grist for the nation's satanic mills even as he imagines he dwells in peace: "He is you." The children, on the other hand, are determined to pursue a different vision.[44] The new Jerusalem will indeed arrive, but will not be what the nationalistic poem by Blake, set to music by Parry to become the influential national hymn, had in mind.[45] Indeed, its use of a religious story that is almost certainly completely fictitious to instill patriotic fervor that will go to war for the nation encapsulates in one place everything that "Supper's Ready" critiques.[46] The supper of Revelation 19–20 is in fact an invitation to the birds of the air to dine on the flesh of kings and all humankind who have destroyed themselves in the climactic battle against God. Being part of a generation that emerged after the carnage of the two world wars, the members of Genesis, like others of their time, hoped that something new was waiting to be born.

BEYOND THE SONG

In principle, it might be possible to find out the curricula in Classics, theology, and philosophy at the Charterhouse School, where the founding members of the band met, including Gabriel who is responsible for the lyrics of "Supper's Ready."[47] However, the question of what may or may not have been assigned reading is less important than what kinds of things were likely to have been read by teachers and those who preached in chapel and on the shelves in the library, all available as potential influences on thoughtful and reflective students, both directly and indirectly. Even on the basis of the songs themselves, aided by things that band members have said by way of commentary, we can discern that Ovid's *Metamorphoses*, the Bible, and the various ways that religion pervaded British life have had an impact on the band's music that ranges far beyond the boundaries of "Supper's Ready" or any other specific song or album.

Genesis is, to my knowledge, the only band that has had not just one, but *two* of their songs compared to a modern-day Pilgrim's Progress. "Supper's Ready" is something of that sort set in the English countryside, while *The Lamb Lies Down on Broadway* is that as well, this time set in New York City.[48] Gabriel himself made the comparison in the case of *Lamb*, saying it was supposed to be "an adventure through which one gets a better understanding of self—the transformation theme."[49] That theme persists throughout much of Genesis's music as well as Gabriel's solo work. It is there in the death, rebirth, and rapid aging in The Musical Box, whose only real religious reference is the vague one early on, in which the nurse tells children lies about "a kingdom beyond the skies." How does that kingdom relate to the one that seems real enough at the end of "Supper's Ready"? It is of course possible to lie about a real kingdom, whether an earthly or a heavenly one. Tony Banks has said that "Supper's Ready" was intended to be a follow-up to "The Musical Box," and "the musical box" is mentioned in the lyrics of the "Willow Farm" section of "Supper's Ready." Hermaphroditus and Tiresias are interesting as figures who embody the transcending of gender boundaries and distinctions.[50] In Donald Podulska's survey of myth in the arts, Genesis provides the only entry for Hermaphroditus, and yet the band is surprisingly not referenced in conjunction with Tiresias, who is mentioned by name in the chorus of "The Cinema Show," even if the story of Tiresias is only alluded to rather than actually retold in the song.[51] Tiresias was changed into a woman and then back again and was asked to share his insight on the experience of male and female from that unique perspective. Narcissus, who appears briefly in "Supper's Ready," is the focus of a tale in Ovid's *Metamorphoses* which is introduced by Tiresias, and the story of Hermaphroditus and Salmacis is also found later in that same work.[52] Platts calls transformation a "favorite Gabriel theme."[53] This is also seen in Peter Gabriel's idea for stories about a character named Mozo that he hoped to scatter across his solo albums. Andrew Dubber says the idea took inspiration from alchemical ideas that came to Gabriel by way of the Song of Songs, as supposedly taken up by Thomas Aquinas, as taken up in turn by Carl Jung.[54] The very idea itself, it would seem, illustrates transformation. There is particular interest in gender blurring, and it is thus perhaps noteworthy that members of the band describe a significant "femininity" to their music that contrasts with the stereotypical "masculinity" associated with bluesy rock.[55]

Gabriel particularly appreciated absurdist humor along the lines of Monty Python, which he expressed by him in Harold the Barrel and Willow Farm.[56] While surrealism and absurdist humor largely departed the band when Peter Gabriel did, interest in deceitful religious leaders remained. The next major example of this is "One for the Vine." While its story of a man mistaken for the messiah might bear a superficial resemblance to the premise of Monty Python's *Life of Brian*, the song is not comical but earnest and tragic, as a man who becomes disillusioned with his people's following of a person believed to be God's chosen one and falls down the mountain, only to be hailed there as God's chosen because of how he seemingly dropped from the sky.[57] As he reluctantly embraces the role, he spots another figure following this same path, indicating the cyclicality of this phenomenon, even as that figure's disappearance perhaps hints either that the cycle can be broken or that that figure was the real divine emissary who, disillusioned by how humanity is enamored with false prophets and war, leaves Earth to return to heaven. This cyclical and typological aspect is also present in "Supper's Ready": the GESM is not merely here but "here again."

Much later, the band revisited the theme in one of their more pop radio songs, "Jesus He Knows Me," which was inspired by their puzzlement at the popularity of televangelists in the United States, these figures being seemingly omnipresent on television. The song generated a bit of controversy, as the American religious right took exception to the way the song (and, in even more obvious fashion, the video) took aim at them.[58] The song "Happy the Man" did not make it onto the studio albums of the era in which the band composed it, but its use of a biblical phrase and reference to Jesus Christ make it essential to refer to it in this context. There are other threads that connect Genesis songs with the Bible and theology that could be mentioned if space permitted. Such subjects continued to engage the band members' thinking and musical creativity, both together in the band and in their solo work.[59]

BEYOND THE BAND

Influence of the hymn "Jerusalem" can be seen in ELP's performance of the actual hymn itself, the mechanized future caught between utopia and dystopia that it depicts making a fitting introduction to the post-apocalyptic landscape of "Karn Evil 9" (on which see our chapter about ELP in this book). Tim Blake's 1978 album *Blake's New Jerusalem* also took its inspiration from the poem, which is recited on the album.[60] The poem's influence is also detectable in the reference to "satanic mills" in the lyrics to the song "Machine Messiah" on the album *Drama* by Yes, and in Sting's use of the phrase in the song "We Work the Black Seam" on the album *Dream of the Blue Turtles*.[61] It isn't clear that any of these reflects the influence of the widely known poem and hymn being mediated through "Supper's Ready." This broader context will be useful knowledge, however, to those who may not otherwise realize that Genesis was drawing on and engaging with a powerful and familiar cultural symbol.

Earlier the same year that *Foxtrot* was released (1972), Jethro Tull released its album *Thick as a Brick*, meaning that "Supper's Ready" never had a chance to be the longest rock song ever.[62] Steve Harris of Iron Maiden has indicated that those two songs are his all-time favorites.[63] We see the direct influence of "Supper's Ready" in the Iron Maiden song "Sign of the Cross," which begins with a reference to "saintly shrouded men" with another holding a cross. In "Supper's Ready" it is six plus one more to make seven, while in "Sign of the Cross" it is eleven plus one more to make twelve. Both are numbers that occur with some significance in the Bible, and both the Genesis song and the Iron Maiden one that riffs on its prototype are full of biblical imagery. What the two songs do with biblical themes and imagery is, however, quite different. Nevertheless, the reference to communion calls to mind the image of another more famous New Testament supper.[64]

CONCLUSION

"Supper's Ready" challenges us to reflect on the nature of good and evil, the flexibility and fluidity of language, and the nature of religious language and symbolism. It begins with a paranormal glimpse of something deeper in the midst of seemingly ordinary events. After a long and colorful journey, it concludes with the same image, that of a supper, drawn from the most symbol-laden book in the Bible.[65] Revelation uses supper to depict both terrestrial warfare and eschatological hope, the messianic banquet. Proclaiming supper is ready does not mean in this case a belief that the so-called "end times" have arrived. On the contrary, what is disclosed is that it has been here all along, and that "you've been here all the time." Much of it appears to recur throughout history, so that perhaps the most theologically significant words in the song's lyrics are "again" (the GESM is not here as a one-time end times villain but is here *again*) and "back" (the ignited souls are not free to go to a new home, but to get *back* home. Thus even as a major source is the apocalyptic Book of Revelation with its seemingly linear vision of history, the song's own outlook is more cyclical.

The battle of good vs. evil cannot be postponed until some final apocalypse. It is fought in the here and now, and in every generation. Doing so requires us to engage with our culture, in particular with its use of religion to manipulate and patriotism to inspire us to kill our fellow human beings. We need to look beneath its surface at its sinister underside, something that Genesis does not only in "Supper's Ready" but in many other songs as well. This particular song, however, discloses not only the depths of evil but also the power of goodness. Sometimes the greatest victories are won when a glimpse of the transcendent enables us to return to supper with a loved one and, despite all uncertainties of language and the potential for appearances to deceive us, truly love, commit, and connect nonetheless.

NOTES

1. Robin Platts, *Genesis: Behind the Lines 1967–2007*. Edinburgh: Canongate, 2007, p. 13.

2. A concept album about the Bible was not really like anything that a rock band had done before at this point. On this, see further Dave Thompson, *Turn it on Again: Peter Gabriel, Phil Collins & Genesis*. San Francisco, CA: Backbeat, 2005, pp. 18–19. On the album note especially songs like "The Serpent."

3. This detail is mentioned in many places, including Spencer Bright, *Peter Gabriel: An Authorized Biography*. London: Sidgwick & Jackson, 1988, p. 46, as well as the VH1 "Genesis Archive Documentary."

4. Thompson, *Turn it on Again*, p. 4

5. Thompson, *Turn it on Again*, p. 11. Gabriel later said that "hymn influences" were one of the things he retained after leaving Genesis (John Hutchinson, "From Brideshead to Shrunken Heads," *Musician,* 93(7) (July 1986), pp. 68–78, quoted in Platts, *Genesis: Behind the Lines*, p. 77).

6. Durrell Bowman, "Classical Styles and Sources in Early Progressive Rock by Genesis, 1969–72." https://durrellbowman.com/classical-styles-and-sources-in-early-progressive-rock-by-genesis-1969-72/; Will Romano, *Prog Rock FAQ: All That's Left to Know about Rock's Most Progressive Music*. Milwaukee, WI: Backbeat, 2014, p. 118 quotes Ed Goodgold, the band's U.S. representation on their first tour in 1972, to the effect that he viewed "Supper's Ready" as in essence a "rock and roll mass" in which "Peter performed the priestly function." He called the result "the high point of the Anglican Church."

7. Gabriel is reported to have said this in an interview with Alan Freeman, broadcast on Capital Radio in October 1982. That interview is transcribed in the *White Shadow* fanzine #3, p. 12.

8. Richard Macphail, *My Book of Genesis*. Bedford: Wymer, 2018, p. 14. Peter Gabriel says in an interview connected with the release of the remastered edition of the second Genesis album, *Trespass*, that one local paper described them as "folk-blues-mystical-rock." He goes on immediately to mention "church music." Also mentioned here: https://reverb.com/fr/news/high-tech-and-hand-made-peter-gabriel-shares-his-recording-philosophy-bacons-archive?locale=fr-FR.

9. Interview with Jeff Cramer. http://jeffcramer.blogspot.com/2017/10/a-very-candid-conversation-with-anthony.html.

10. Richard Macphail, a school friend and longtime associate of the band, mentions that there was a band at the school that took its name from a classic French novel (*My Book of Genesis*, p. 26).

11. Sarah Hill, "Ending it All: Genesis and Revelation," *Popular Music,* 32(2) (2013): 197–221 (here p. 199).

12. Steve Hackett, quoted in Macphail, *My Book of Genesis*, p. 114.

13. Platts, *Genesis: Behind the Lines*, p. 21; Macphail, *My Book of Genesis*, p. 109.

14. Bright, *Peter Gabriel*, p. 24.

15. Bright, *Peter Gabriel*, pp. 23–24.

16. Bright, *Peter Gabriel*, p. 153.

17. Bright, *Peter Gabriel*, p. 152.

18. Durrell Bowman, *Experiencing Peter Gabriel: A Listener's Companion*. Lanham, MD: Rowman & Littlefield, 2016, p. 18.

19. On the chords and their role in the song's musical structure, see Nors S. Josephson, "Bach Meets Liszt: Traditional Formal Structures and Performance Practices in Progressive Rock," *The Musical Quarterly*, 76(1) (Spring 1992): 67–92 (here pp. 84–85).

20. Mick Wall, "Supper's Ready by Genesis: The Story Behind the Song," *Classic Rock,* November 19, 2016. https://www.loudersound.com/features/the-story-behind-the-song-genesis-suppers-ready.

21. One example that may spring to mind is the Journey classic "Faithfully."

22. For more on Genesis and surrealism, see Corbett, *Pick Up the Pieces*, pp. 80–85.

23. As pointed out by Mike Barnes, *A New Day Yesterday: UK Progressive Rock & the 1970s*. New York: Omnibus, 2020.

24. On the myth of Narcissus as explored in a painting, poem, and essay of Salvador Dalí, see Eric Shanes, *Dalí*. New York: Parkstone International, 2014, pp. 134–135. The mirror that will return with Pythagoras later in the song is central to this myth. See also James C. Harris, "The Metamorphosis of Narcissus," *Archives of General Psychiatry*, 62(2) (2005): 124–125. Pythagoras features in Ovid's *Metamorphoses* and that may explain his otherwise mysterious, tantalizingly brief appearance in the lyrics.

25. Bowman, *Experiencing Peter Gabriel*, p. 31.

26. Peter Gabriel described Willow Farm as "a sort of Zen farm where the only thing that is constant is a state of change" (quoted in Platts, *Genesis: Behind the Lines*, p. 56). In many respects, that song articulated for the first time an idea he would later speak of as its real-world equivalent, the appropriately named Real World theme park (discussed in Bright, *Peter Gabriel*, pp. 3–4. On the binaries in the song, see in particular Gabriel's comments recorded in Chris Roberts' article, "Genesis on Supper's Ready: 'This is Where We Started to Become Significant'," *Prog*, March 22, 2017. https://www.loudersound.com/features/genesis-on-suppers-ready-this-is-where-we-started-to-become-significant. See also David Schwarz, *Listening Subjects: Music, Psychoanalysis, Culture*. Durham, NC: Duke University Press, 1997, pp. 94, 97–98 on gender binary as it pertains to Gabriel's song "Intruder."

27. Melting is also used in Salvador Dali's poem that he composed to accompany his painting *The Metamorphosis of Narcissus*. An egg features prominently in the painting itself. Eggs are also mentioned in several other Genesis songs across multiple albums.

28. Innsbruck EDD Online 3.0 (based on Joseph Wright's *English Dialect Dictionary*, 1898–1905). See also Bowman, *Experiencing Peter Gabriel*, p. 32; Mick Hartley, "The Delicious Talents of Gabble Ratchet." http://from-bedroom-to-study.blogspot.com/2012/07/the-delicious-talents-of-gabble-ratchet.html.

29. For those who do not have the album, the liner notes are reproduced in Hill, "Ending it All," pp. 202–203.

30. On this see, for instance Macphail, *My Book of Genesis*, pp. 25, 39, although contrast the support of the head music teacher Geoffrey Ford mentioned on p. 37.

31. One of the few authors to recognize the strong influence of Ovid on "Supper's Ready" does so in the context of an article focused on an art exhibit featuring Peter Gabriel: Tim Keane, "British Rock Meets Modernism," *Hyperallergic*, January 26, 2019. https://hyperallergic.com/480967/peter-gabriel-reflections-the-museum-of-bath-architecture-clive-arrowsmith/.

32. On the blurring of levels of interpretation, see further Martin Halliwell and Paul Hegarty, *Beyond and before Progressive Rock since the 1960s*. London: Bloomsbury, 2011, pp. 96–97.

33. Romano, *Prog Rock FAQ*, p. 117; Hill, "Ending It All," p. 201.

34. Gabriel's own vegetarianism is mentioned in Jon Pareles' article "At Lunch With: Peter Gabriel; Art, Music, Experience Unbound," *New York Times*, July 13, 1994, p. C1.

35. This is, of course, the focus of Buddhism, the seeking of a way out of the endless cycle of karma and reincarnation.

36. The Book of Revelation also features a great deal of heavenly singing, it should be noted. Macan, *Rocking the Classics*, p. 81 writes, "Genesis's epic Supper's Ready, a psychedelic recounting of the New Testament Book of Revelation, presents the New Jerusalem as the model of a perfect, fulfilled society—won, of course, after an epic struggle between the forces of good and evil."

37. The influence of Zen on Gabriel at precisely this point in his life is explored in Daryl Easlea, *Without Frontiers: The Life & Music of Peter Gabriel*. New York: Omnibus, 2018.

38. John Hick, *Faith and Knowledge*, Hampshire: Macmillan, 1988, pp. 176–179. The book was published in 1957 and issued in a second edition in 1966, the preface to which indicates that a key difference was that the author had expanded the book's treatment of this topic in particular.

39. Paul Tillich, *Dynamics of Faith*. New York: Harper & Row, 1957, pp. 50–70.

40. Tillich shared his thoughts on modern art's exploration of ultimate reality in symbolic fashion in a number of places, including an address he delivered at the Museum of Modern Art in 1959. https://www.moma.org/momaorg/shared/pdfs/docs/press_archives/2449/releases/MOMA_1959_0015.pdf.

41. The book *Genesis: Chapter and Verse* is by the band members and edited by Philip Dodd. Published by Thomas Dunne in 2007. The reference here is to p. 329.

42. Peter Gabriel has been quoted in many places as saying the following about the song, including Phil Alexander, *The Mojo Collection: The Ultimate Music Companion*. 4th ed. New York: Canongate, 2007, p. 290: "I felt like I was singing from my soul—almost like singing for my life."

43. Barnes, *A New Day Yesterday*, writes, "The very appeal of 'Supper's Ready' is how the full meaning of its apparently humdrum title is ultimately revealed as being epic on a cosmic scale."

44. Bright, *Peter Gabriel*, p. 29 mentions that the class system bothered him.

45. See further Sarah Hill, "From the New Jerusalem to the Secret World: Peter Gabriel and the Shifting Self," in Michael Drewett, Sarah Hill, and Kimi Kärki (eds.), *Peter Gabriel: From Genesis to Growing Up*. Burlington, VT: Ashgate, 2010, pp. 15–29 (here p. 16).

46. Mark Spicer, "Large-Scale Strategy and Compositional Design in the Early Music of Genesis," in Walter Everett (ed.), *Expressions in Pop-Rock Music: A Collection of Critical and Analytical Essays*. New York: Garland, 2000, pp. 77–111 (here p. 99) writes, "One can hardly imagine a more fitting conclusion for this decidedly British retelling of the story of the apocalypse."

47. Bright, *Peter Gabriel*, mentions Gabriel's interest in mythology already in his teens (p. 19) as well as his having done an O Level in Latin (p. 29).

48. See Hill, "Ending it All," p. 217 on the open-endedness of "Supper's Ready" and the continuation of the journey on subsequent albums. Barnes, *A New Day Yesterday*, contrasts the cathartic ending of "Supper's Ready" with what "Lamb" offers. Durrell Bowman (*Peter Gabriel: A Listener's Companion*, p. xix) describes "Supper's Ready" as a "semireligious epic." For more on *The Lamb Lies Down on Broadway* see further Halliway and Hegarty, *Beyond and Before*, pp. 76–79.

49. Bright, *Peter Gabriel*, p. 79.

50. On connections between gender fluidity, alchemy, and surrealism, see Arturo Schwarz, "Alchemy, Androgyny and Visual Artists." *Leonardo,* 13(1) (1980): 57–62. Milly Heyd, "Dali's 'Metamorphosis of Narcissus' Reconsidered," *Artibus Et Historiae,* 5(10) (1984): 121–131 (here p. 122).

51. Donald M. Podulska, "Classical Myth in Music: A Selective List," *The Classical World,* 92(3) (January–February 1999): 195–276 (here pp. 226–227). Tiresias also appears in another famous work that appears to have influenced "Cinema Show": T. S. Eliot's "The Waste Land" (noted by Barnes, *A New Day Yesterday*). Eliot's "The Hollow Men" is glimpsed by Halliway and Hegarty (*Beyond and Before*, pp. 97–98) behind the ending of Willow Farm.

52. The close agreement of details is highlighted in R. M. Fransson, "Ovid Rox," *The Classical Journal,* 86(2) (December 1990–January 1991): 176–182 (here pp. 180–181).

53. Platts, *Genesis: Behind the Lines*, p. 70.

54. Andrew Dubber, "Peter Gabriel and The Birth of Mozo," *Medium,* February 28, 2015. https://medium.com/@dubber/peter-gabriel-and-the-birth-of-mozo-45ef466b1339. See also Bright, *Peter Gabriel*, p. 162.

55. Martin, *Music of Yes*, pp. 61, 179–180 says the same about Yes.

56. Platts, *Genesis Behind the Lines*, p. 47.

57. On the band's shared love of Monty Python from its beginnings, see Easlea, *Without Frontiers.*

58. Thompson, *Turn it on Again*, p. 245.

59. A few examples will hopefully suffice: Noah in the whale is referred to in "Cuckoo Cocoon," wise and foolish virgins, plus candlelight, in "Carpet Crawlers," both on *Lamb*. Tony Banks's lyrics on solo albums are interesting, representing an arc that spans from "The Serpent" on the first Genesis album to "The Serpent Said" in his Strictly Inc. solo effort. Mike Rutherford sings about "turning water into wine" in his song "Moonshine," and Mike and the Mechanics' song "Seeing is Believing" affirms belief in "most everything," beginning with Jesus. When this "muddled thinking has to go," belief in love remains, despite being no more rational. Peter Gabriel's "Here Comes The Flood" is about scientific predictions of natural catastrophe rather than the biblical epic. His album *Passion* is the music he wrote for the film *The Last Temptation of Christ*. See further Bright, *Peter Gabriel*, p. 164.

60. Halliway and Hegarty, *Beyond and before*, p. 98; Barnes, *A New Day Yesterday*, ch. 7.

61. Cf. Martin, *Music of Yes*, pp. 19–20.

62. For more on this topic of the extended rock song, see Thompson, *Turn it on Again*, p. 84.

63. "Steve Harris: Genesis Was Never the Same after Peter Gabriel Left," *Prog #60.* https://www.loudersound.com/features/the-prog-interview-steve-harris.

64. The song "Seven Saintly Angels" by Cataclysm is based on Revelation and clearly reflects the influence of "Supper's Ready" in the title.

65. It is important to note that when Hill sets passages from Revelation and the lyrics of "Supper's Ready" in parallel columns (Hill, "Ending it All," pp. 204–208),

apart from in the section (Apocalypse in 9/8), whose title refers directly to Revelation, many of the purported parallels are neither close nor obvious. The proposal that there is a correspondence or similarity of genre between the song and apocalyptic literature (p. 209) is, on the other hand, more plausible, with symbolic visions in a dream state being interpretive keys to both.

Chapter 4

Jethro Tull's Songs about God
A Prog-phetic Condemnation of Idolatry

THE BAND

In every band discussed in this book, there were lineup changes at some point in their history. In the case of Jethro Tull more than perhaps any other, it is front man Ian Anderson who can be considered the defining element, which has meant that despite inevitable stylistic evolution, there has also been a significant sense of continuity.[1] Even the name the band ended up having was a rather haphazard choice, it would seem, although there has been more than one explanation as to how it came about. While a particular vocalist, instrumentalist, or lyricist has at times come to define another band, in the case of Ian Anderson and Jethro Tull, there is the clearest sense that there is a defining vision and a defining sound, whether one is listening to an album called *Thick as a Brick* by Jethro Tull or one called *TAAB2* by Ian Anderson. That defining sound is of course a merger of folk and heavy blues rock which incorporates flute. And that description, of course does not do justice to the music any more than any other verbal description could.

Ian Anderson and Peter Gabriel were both innovators in the realm of progressive rock in their incorporation of the flute (although Anderson is quick to point out that others had done so before him, particularly Ray Thomas of the Moody Blues in what is arguably their most famous song, "Nights in White Satin"). The style of each is so noticeably different that there is no mistaking one for the other. Likewise, while both Jethro Tull and Genesis incorporate strains of medieval or renaissance folk at times and both lead vocalists were storytellers, Anderson embodied the persona of the minstrel, in addition to merely singing about one, to a greater extent than anyone else in prog rock.[2] The union of musical style, vocal timbre, and stage persona makes for a (locomotive) breathtaking unity and power in performances, such that even someone who had never heard of the band or their music would soon find themselves mesmerized.

One exception to that sense of a unified sound is the intriguing solo instrumental album *Divinities—Twelve Dances with God*. It incorporates international musical styles and instruments, and the cover art features a dancing Hindu deity with iconic emblems of other religious traditions. Christianity is represented twice through the cross and the chi rho. The differences not only among religions but between Protestants and Catholics have long been a focus of Anderson's attention, as we will see in this chapter. Their similarities, both positive and negative, are also something that he has explored. Interviews with Anderson about his religious beliefs have been sparked above all else by his songs on religious topics, including those that are the focus of this chapter. His answers to questions over the years have not been entirely uniform, but there is a certain underlying consistency. Like many other prog rock musicians, he indicates that it was not classical music in general but *church* music that was a key early influence.[3]

It is worth including quotations from interviews with Anderson. Asked by *Louder Sound* in 2016 whether he believes in God, Anderson jumped immediately to answering a different question—whether he is a Christian.

> I'm not a Christian. I don't "do" Jesus. But Christianity, like most of the world's great religions, is a good, practical moral code for living. However, there are some very nasty messages in the Bible. That Moses guy—dangerous freak![4]

Even more recently in an interview with *Vintage Rock*, Anderson has said:

> I'm not a practicing Christian. I'm a huge supporter of Christianity in a very real sense of my work for the church every year. But I don't call myself a Christian because I am somewhat of a rather broader set of slightly shifting and changing beliefs. You could probably put me down as being more of a pantheist belief kind of guy. Maybe deist. I still have a huge appreciation for the Bible and the storytelling. The narrative of Christianity is compelling because unlike most other religions, it tells a story. It has a beginning, a middle and an end. And it has a particularly dramatic ending, too. When you put the whole Bible idea together, it leaves you with the prophecy of a Netflix season three, somewhere on the horizon. Christians have been waiting for 2000 years for season three, and it hasn't come yet, but never give up hope.[5]

In more than one place in recent years, he has said to the effect that he is not a Christian according to any regular definition, but he might be a "christian with a small 'c'."[6] In a 2017 interview with *Indeflagration*, Anderson says:[7]

> I'm not a Christian. I believe in the historical Jesus, Jesus of Nazareth and not Jesus "the Christ" in the sense that a Christian has to have that undying belief that Christ truly is both the Son of God and the Son of Man, as the Bible confusedly tells us, or He tells us if you believe the biblical words. I think the Bible is a very useful document, I seek reference from the Bible quite often and on a number of occasions I have included elements of biblical stories in songs. But I think that like all religions it can be very dangerous if you approach it in a literal fashion, and there are very many scary things in the Bible, most of them in the Old Testament but some of them in the New Testament too, and I have to try to keep in mind that I don't take these things too literally, I try to see the positive messages in the works of the Bible, I can see how easily people get very polarized as a result of their beliefs.

The reference to the historical Jesus is interesting. Although not otherwise couched in academic terminology, Anderson's perspective certainly reflects something of the influence of the classic quests for the historical Jesus, which sought to get behind the creeds and dogma to the human life that was tantalizingly obscured from view behind them. Today, when academic work on the historical Jesus has become more widely known, a significant number of people have come to prefer labels such as "Jesus-follower" to the more traditional one of "Christian." Anderson does not do that, and when his lyrics are considered in conjunction with his interviews, a fairly coherent picture emerges of someone whose outlook is more eclectic, open to not only less traditional Christian views but non-Christian views as well.[8] This, of course, is also true of many who happily wear the label "Jesus-follower." The focus on the "Old Testament" as the place where "most" of the "scary things in the Bible" are located is a common feature of this contemporary approach to the Bible, often veering into a neo-Marcionism. On the other hand, Anderson at least poses the distinction less starkly than others have, recognizing that "scary things" are found throughout the Bible and not only in the much older texts, which are inevitably much more foreign to most modern ears. We shall see in what follows that, in one recent song, Anderson in fact appears to be challenging the New Testament authors for toning down the frightening character of God. For now, it is sufficient if it has begun to become clear that neither Jethro Tull as a band nor Ian Anderson as an individual has ever been opposed to religion in general or Christianity in particular.

THE SONGS

The songs that are the focus of this main part of this chapter share a common focus: idolatry, the attempt to domesticate God and turn the divine into something not only more manageable but also something that serves the interests of those who, ironically, claim to serve the deity. That is the core of the problem of idolatry and the reason for its being critiqued by prophet-theologians ancient and modern, including those who do so through music. Idolatry is the creation of an image of God fashioned in one's own image—not necessarily in the sense of emulating the human physical form, but embodying human values and ideology. When one then submits to that image and dedicates oneself to serving that god of one's own making, an impenetrable circle has been created that can justify everything from minor injustices to genocidal atrocities of global proportions.

Musically, "My God" is a song that exemplifies the way Jethro Tull brings together folk and blues rock verging on heavy metal. The effect of the descent from the perfect to the flatted fifth is powerful. The notes that characterize what most clearly distinguishes the western folk and classical tradition from blues and rock become a shout of accusation and, at the same time, a cry of anguish and lament. Rather than using the flatted fifth as a passing tone that creates brief tension that is then resolved, it is the destination of the song's unifying musical motif. It does not resolve but creates tension, reinforcing the anguish and lament and almost forcing the listener to join in on a subconscious emotional level. After Anderson grew up with church and folk music in Scotland, he has said that the blues scale struck him as something of a revelation.[9] This may be the one instance in which the language used to describe what is happening musically perfectly encapsulates the meaning of the lyrics. The initial interval is a perfect fifth, and the interval created by descending a half step is a diminished fifth. The theological message of the song is about human efforts in relation to God, which take that which is perfect and diminish it.

It is astonishing how many commentators have considered "My God" to be "anti-religious."[10] Will Romano puts it more accurately when he calls "My God" "a scathing indictment of organized religion's power grab," and Anderson himself calls it "an anguished cry, a song of anger derived from my first experiences challenging religion as it was taught to me when I was fourteen years old."[11] It is interesting to consider whether we would expect the song to be at all different if it reflected a more or less devout member of the Church of Scotland. The Reformed/Presbyterian forms of Christianity are not singled out for obvious criticism in the song the way that the Anglican and Catholic churches are.[12] However, an earlier draft of the lyrics (a 1970 recording of which exists) had a clearly pluralistic outlook, emphasizing that not only do different denominations commit idolatry in their own way, but every religion does so. Those early lyrics mentioned Jews, Christians, and Muslims as all "waiting to be free," adding that each has a part of God "and so, a part of me." Different ways of thinking about God are all different ways of being human, and none is any more the only truth about God than any is the full story of humanity. That is the section that is replaced in the album version with the section on the "bloody Church of England," which plays on the use of "bloody" in the United Kingdom as a swear word as well as the literal meaning through the church's involvement in the nation's imperial military enterprise. That is juxtaposed with the serene British scene of being invited to a polite tea at the vicarage of the local parish. The song's positive message is conveyed powerfully in the contrast between the idol who "is the God of nothing if that's all that you can see" and the one whom Anderson addresses prayerfully in the second person, "You are the God of everything," before returning to the third person.

The solo section which shows off Anderson's ability to speak/vocalize while playing the flute is not just a filler of virtuoso musicianship but plays a key role in conveying the song's message. It is profoundly appropriate to have a non-verbal section as the centerpiece to a song which is not just about idolatry in the classic sense, making physical representations of God, but the making of verbal and ideological idols. The opening guitar solo and the central section featuring solo flute accompanied by chanting voices are reminiscent of religious music.[13] The ending flute and chant seeming to echo music specifically from the Sufi tradition in which the flute has played an important role both in music and as a symbol.[14] The flute also features in religious poetry from India, and many have offered the observation that in live performances, Anderson adopts a pose like one for which the Hindu god Krishna is famous. This turns out to be coincidental, however. Anderson played the harmonica standing on one leg, and when the media misreported that he played the flute on one leg, he decided to do so. The central section of "My God" does, on the other hand, seem to invite the listener to consider the sort of mystical and pluralistic spirituality associated with the inclusive religiosity of figures like Rumi, whose magnum opus *Masnavi* opens with a section whose title may be translated "The Song of the Reed Flute."

While "My God" was about God and briefly addressed to God, the song "Mine is the Mountain" from the album *The Zealot Gene* is by or from God. In other words, although the focus is on the story of Moses, it is not told from Moses' perspective but God's. Anderson has said of the song in an interview that it hangs together naturally with "My God."[15] The two are united in challenging the penchant of human beings to seek to domesticate the divine. While "My God" focused on mockery of idolatry, "Mine is the Mountain" focuses on God as one to be feared. As Moses ascends, the warnings begin. Some are the ones we might expect given the biblical source material, such as the prohibition of idols made of precious metals and the warning not to provoke God to jealousy or anger. Others are more striking and as a result, all the more poignant, in particular the demand that the one who approaches God offer "bold questions." Connecting with what we quoted Anderson as saying about the Old Testament earlier, he presents Matty and Lucas (i.e., Matthew and Luke) as toning things down, offering "something softer." Yet it is emphasized that the God of Moses is not a different deity from that of the Gospels. The use of the phrase "the power and the glory" in the song highlights that the Old Testament image of God as powerful and to be awed and feared is woven into familiar prayer language that was appended very early to the Lord's Prayer, which appears in the New Testament in different versions in precisely the two Gospels Anderson mentions, Matthew and Luke (Mt. 6:9-13; Lk. 11:2-4), although neither includes the concluding doxology in our oldest manuscripts. Ultimately, the issue of idolatry is not one limited to the Old Testament or the New, to Judaism or Christianity or indeed any religion whatsoever. Anderson allows for no division between "Old Testament God" and "New Testament God," or perhaps a better way of putting it is to suggest, if controversially, that the Sermon on the Mount and on the Plain in the aforementioned Gospels, and the Ten Commandments, both represent pointers to a fearful transcendent divine and at the same time begin the process of imaging, defining, and confining that one God. All religion seeks to domesticate the divine, and both these songs challenge that directly with a harsh prophetic edge.

It is either fitting or ironic, and perhaps both, that Anderson has said of *The Zealot Gene* that biblical language (and more specifically the classic phrasing of the King James Version) immediately evokes visual images, which he has in turn explored in words and music.[16] On the one hand, visual representation is a major component of idolatry in its most classic sense. On the other hand, as Anderson's songs elucidate with a great deal of theological insight, words, liturgy, and anything else is equally prone to becoming an idol. Yet it is impossible to think or speak about the transcendent without words, sounds, or images playing a role. Thus, as Anderson puts it, the words (or music or whatever else) can serve a non-idolatrous purpose only to the extent that they function sacramentally, as symbols pointing beyond themselves to a reality that they are incapable of capturing or doing justice to.[17]

BEYOND THE SONGS

Whole albums over the course of Jethro Tull's history have been laced with themes that are of theological interest, as well as specific songs with a particular richness for those interested in the exploration of religion. Returning to *Aqualung*, the album on which "My God" appeared, *the song* "Hymn 43," according to Marc Allan, "issued probably the most scathing overall indictment of religious zealotry." The song recommends that Jesus save himself from the "gory glory seekers who use his name in death." Allan goes on to quote Ian Anderson as having described the album as "pro- God, anti-church."[18] Also on *Aqualung*, the track "Locomotive Breath" begins with reference to the creation account at the start of Genesis, using that as a jumping-off point to an exploration of population growth spiraling out of control. The album cover features a satirical reworking of Genesis 1 that includes farcical yet poignant words such as these: "In the beginning Man created God; and in the image of Man created he him. And Man gave unto God a multitude of names, that he might be Lord over all the earth when it was suited to Man." As with other prog rock albums, and scriptural texts, there is paratextual information that accompanies them and which at times can open the door to further insights into their possible meaning.

The album *A Passion Play* is satirical, like much of Jethro Tull's output, but (despite the impression one might get in certain contexts) there is a long history of satire and theology working hand in hand.[19] The main character's name, Ronnie Pilgrim makes the story quite literally a modern Pilgrim's Progress, as it were. Ronnie witnesses his own funeral and visits both heaven and hell in the afterlife, not finding either satisfying. The point is encapsulated well in the song "Flight from Lucifer," which explores the fact that people are not entirely good or bad. There is a mention of halos, horns, and wings being swapped or dropping off. Better than either horn or halo is "the hat I once had," which presumably expresses not only the state of being human in its mixture of the heavenly and the diabolical but being human and alive rather than pigeonholed into an afterlife for the righteous or the wicked, categories into which no human being completely and perfectly fits. The final section of the album includes a plea that would fit well in a hymn: "Here am I! Roll the stone away from the dark into ever-day." This recalls the contrast in "My God" between Jesus as risen from the grave and the imprisonment of God in the idolatrous "gilded cage" of religion.

Anderson's solo album *Homo Erraticus* continues the satirical trajectory of the two prior *Think as a Brick* albums as well as *A Passion Play*, this time claiming to be inspired by a chronicle of past lives and future prophecies written by someone suffering from post-malarial delusion.[20] Not necessarily a trustworthy source, to say the least. The final track's liner note description suggests that it will offer a vision of the future that foresees a new spirituality and a new Eden after the breakdown of the old order. The actual lyrics are more somber. While it sounds as though it will involve a zombie apocalypse, the reference turns out in fact to be to humanity's penchant for consuming itself. That there "must be another Eden" is not a promise but a hope, with a call to those who get a chance to start over to forego the (forbidden) fruit next time. Its title and repeated lyric indicate that it is ultimately humanity that must "navigate this desert by our cold, dead reckoning." No magical or supernatural solution is offered to make things right, whether in the form of a miracle or a divinely revealed text. The song seems to end with a definitive bang, and yet a hopeful melody picks up after that suggesting that even after we destroy ourselves, if anyone survives, we can try to build something new from the ashes.

It would have been easy to make *The Zealot Gene* album as a whole the main focus of this chapter, as it is woven through with biblical themes and words.[21] By choosing one recent song and a couple of classic ones from decades earlier, it has allowed us to trace how this most recent offering by Jethro Tull stands in continuity with what has preceded it.

BEYOND THE BAND

Jethro Tull's influence ranges far and wide, with fans not only among fellow prog rock musicians but in punk and metal. Neal Morse, Mike Portnoy, and Randy George included a cover of "Hymn 43" on their 2020 album *Cov3r to Cov3r*. Morse has become famous for his Christian progressive rock, explored elsewhere in this book, and his vocal cover of the song indicates that he too understands it not as a criticism of Christianity but a prophetic rebuke against it. Gentle Giant's album *The Power and the Glory* (biblical words that appear twice in the lyrics to "Mine Is the Mountain" as well) focuses primarily on political power and glory but features the song "No God's a Man," whose focus is on humans recognizing their place and their limitations, but in an intriguing turn reverses the order of reasoning we might expect: no god is a man where we would more naturally have expected "no man is a god." The jarring diminished interval that features so powerfully in "My God" became a staple of heavy metal music, likely beginning with Black Sabbath's song "Black Sabbath" which was released the year before "Aqualung." The two songs share something of the same mood, walking the fine line between the lament and the eerie—both of which are appropriate responses to an encounter with divine transcendence, or with the demonic supernatural.

CONCLUSION

Jethro Tull's music has never sounded like it belonged to the present, and (as is true of Genesis) we will fail to understand not only what the band conveys but *how* they convey it if we are tone-deaf to the British tradition of comedic satire. It is precisely by recognizing that some of what is done on albums and in live shows is intended to make us laugh or simply grab our attention back when it may have wandered off, that we realize that these tactics are like the prophet Ezekiel building a model of Jerusalem or Jeremiah walking around with a yoke on his back. They are part of the performance, intended to grab our attention, but with them comes the risk that a serious prophetic message may not be taken fully seriously. In an era in which idols of nationalism and zealotry are increasing concerns, there is a need for those who can grab attention and at the same time deliver a poignant challenge. The risk is the same that faced the prophet Ezekiel millennia earlier.

> To them you are like a singer of love songs, one who has a beautiful voice and plays well on an instrument; they hear what you say, but they will not do it. 33 When this comes—and come it will!—then they shall know that a prophet has been among them. (Ezek. 33:32-33 NRSVUE)

Many have discussed Jethro Tull's songs and many more have listened to them, but few have engaged with Ian Anderson as a serious theologian, much less as a prophet. Conversely, it may be that familiarity with Jethro Tull can assist those seeking to interpret ancient Israelite prophetic literature such as that associated with Ezekiel. Might it be that his strange, attention-grabbing behavior was Ezekiel's "stage persona" and that we might be as astonished if we met Ezekiel the priest when not "performing" as some have been who have encountered Ian Anderson the "Laird of Strathaird" and salmon farmer?

NOTES

1. Cf. Robert G. H. Burns, *Experiencing Progressive Rock: A Listener's Companion.* Lanham, MD: Rowman & Littlefield, 2018, pp. 65,110.

2. Brian Rabey, *A Passion Play: The Story of Ian Anderson and Jethro Tull.* London: Soundcheck, 2013, p. 149 mentions the label "Elizabethan Rock" being applied to Jethro Tull.

3. More recently, Jethro Tull has released an album of string quartet arrangements of their songs. It is one of the testaments to the musical significance of progressive rock that they have not only borrowed from and been influenced by art music, but the influence has also run in the opposite direction as well. Other examples include Keith Emerson's Piano Concerto and Tony Banks' compositions released on the Naxos label.

4. Paul Elliott, "Jethro Tull's Ian Anderson on Politics, God, and Ritchie Blackmore's Clothing," *Louder Sound,* July 29, 2016. https://www.loudersound.com/features/jethro-tull-s-ian-anderson-on-politics-god-and-ritchie-blackmore-s-clothing.

5. Shawn Perry, "Ian Anderson & Jethro Tull: Scaling 'The Zealot Gene'." https://vintagerock.com/ian-anderson-jethro-tull-scaling-the-zealot-gene/.

6. In addition to the liner notes of the recording of his/Jethro Tull's String Quartets, see "Ian Anderson's Top Tull Clips." *Inverness Reporter,* January 10, 2014. https://www.inverness-courier.co.uk/lifestyle/ian-anderson-picks-defining-tull-clips-100988/.

7. "Interview With Ian Anderson from Jethro Tull: The Philosopher of Prog Rock," March 23, 2017. http://indeflagration.fr/in-english/ian-anderson-jethro-tull-interview/.

8. This comes across quite clearly in an interview with Derek Walker from 2017: "Ian Anderson: Winding Up the Church." http://www.tollbooth.org/index.php/past-issues/past-features/2077-ian-anderson-winding-up-the-church. See also what he says in the liner notes to *Zealot Gene* as quoted on the band's website (https://jethrotull.com/the-zealot-gene/):

> While I have a spot of genuine fondness for the pomp and fairytale story-telling of the Holy Book, I still feel the need to question and draw sometimes unholy parallels from the text. The good, the bad, and the downright ugly rear their heads throughout, but are punctuated with elements of love, respect, and tenderness.

9. Romano, *Mountains Come Out of the Sky*, p. 83.

10. So for example, Paul Stump, *The Music's All That Matters*. Chelmsford: Harbour, 2010, p. 145.

11. Romano, *Mountains Come Out of the Sky*, p. 85. Anderson has said that 2–3 songs on the album *Aqualung* hang together around the theme of organized religion, but it is not a concept album (Romano, *Mountains Come Out of the Sky*, p. 86). Elsewhere Romano uses similar terminology, calling "My God" "ghoulish" and "Anderson's personal attack on organized religion" (Will Romano, *Prog Rock FAQ*. Milwaukee, WI: Backbeat, 2014, p. 64).

12. In live performances, Anderson actually says "Catholic" while the recorded version on the album avoids doing so by substituting "you know who." Even then, the reference to the crucifix makes the meaning unambiguously clear.

13. So also Natalie Weiel, "How Jethro Tull Created Hard Rock's Most Cerebral Album – Aqualung," *Produce Like a Pro*, June 23, 2021. https://producelikeapro.com/blog/jethro-tull-aqualung/.

14. On this, see Dale A. Olsen, *World Flutelore: Folktales, Myths, and Other Stories of Magical Flute Power*. Urbana, IL: University of Illinois Press, 2013, pp. 150–162.

15. Anderson is quoted on the Spirit of Progressive Rock website (https://spirit.rocks/2022/07/26/jethro-tull-launch-video-for-mine-is-the-mountain/) as saying,

> Mine Is The Mountain is, perhaps, a late-life partner to the Aqualung album song My God. I had, as usual, a strong visual reference at the core of the lyrics. A miserable, committed trudge up Mount Sinai by Moses to face an angry maker before he must deliver the goods to his followers below is a powerful image, best imagined unless you are a wilderness trekker and much younger than I.

16. Kevin Reed, "Veteran Musician Ian Anderson Comments on Right-Wing Populism with Jethro Tull's The Zealot Gene," World Socialist Web Site, February 14, 2022. https://www.wsws.org/en/articles/2022/02/15/gene-f15.html.

17. The classic exploration of religious language as symbol can be found in Paul Tillich's *The Dynamics of Faith*.

18. Marc Allan, "Rockers Now Reveal Spirituality," *Indianapolis Star,* May 30, 1995, p. D1. See also "Good Heavens, Now Ian Anderson Wants Us to Think!," *Disc & Music Echo,* March 20, 1971. http://www.tullpress.com/d20mar71.htm.

19. Apparently, keyboardist John Evan donned devil's horns while narrating "The Story of the Hare Who Lost His Spectacles" in concert on at least on some occasions, according to Romano, *Mountains Come Out of the Sky,* p. 87.

20. Ed Masley, "Interview: Ian Anderson of Jethro Tull," *AZ Central,* September 16, 2014. https://www.azcentral.com/story/entertainment/music/2014/09/16/ian-anderson-interview-jethro-tull/15718423/.

21. On the song's inspiration beginning with emotion-laden words and proceeding from there to explore where they appear in the Bible, see Ryan Reed, "Ian Anderson Wrestles with New Jethro Tull LP's Biblical Themes: Exclusive Interview," *Ultimate Classic Rock,* January 19, 2022. https://ultimateclassicrock.com/jethro-tull-zealot-game-themes/ On the album's biblical themes, see too Bob Ruggiero, "Jethro Tull's Ian Anderson Finds His Inner Zealot," *Houston Press,* December 16, 2021 https://www.houstonpress.com/music/things-to-do-listen-to-the-zealot-gene-by-jethro-tull-and-ian-anderson-12505965

Chapter 5

Kerry Livgren's Kansas

From Syncretism to Monotheism and Complexity to Simplicity

While the first "wave" of progressive rock music (Beatles, Moody Blues, Yes, Pink Floyd, The Nice, Jethro Tull, et al., *ca.* 1965–1970) was made up of mostly European bands, as were most of the major prog bands from its second wave (ELP, Rush, King Crimson, Marillion et al., *ca.* 1970–1983), the most successful progressive rock band in terms of sales and chart position that came from the United States was Kansas. Critics have often labeled their brand of prog as a kind of country-influenced music, but Robby Steinhart's violin playing was derived from his classical training, not from any American fiddling.[1] Kerry Livgren's early, longish epic songs were influenced by European classical music and by British bands Yes and Gentle Giant more than the west coast acid rock of the Grateful Dead (who were always more country than rock) or the Doors (with whom they shared concert programs), although Kansas also retained the hard rock boogie that is a hallmark of American rock and roll. Livgren's lyrics were always incorporating larger and more diverse subjects than those of other American pop and rock songs, and even before his turn to evangelical Christianity, they were often interpreted by Christians and non-Christians alike as having trope-based subtexts about Christian topics. In a genre whose most famous adherents tended to be European and British, Kansas was the standout band from the United States of America. Over the course of Livgren's time as a primary songwriter for the band, his music moved from being more complex to simpler as he moved from someone who believed in various Eastern religions and philosophical thinking to becoming an evangelical, born-again Christian.

KANSAS AS A BAND

In early 1973, the classic lineup of Kansas came together from two earlier versions of the band with that name and the progressive rock band White Clover. The 1973 version of Kansas was comprised of Steve Walsh (keyboards, vocals, percussion), Kerry Livgren (guitar, keyboards), Rich Williams (guitars), Dave Hope (bass, guitar, vocals), Robbie Steinhardt (vocals, violin, viola), and Phil Ehart (drums). The earlier versions of Kansas had made a good name for themselves in the lower Midwest and parts of the central south—one of the demo tapes they had recorded made it into the offices of Kirshner Records and was heard by Don Kirshner's assistant Wally Gold, who traveled out to the Midwest to hear Kansas play in Ellinwood, where the band advertised that this show included free beer to draw a large crowd.[2] The ploy worked, and Gold was impressed with the band and its crowd-drawing power, signing the band to Kirshner Records shortly thereafter.

The first album recorded for the label was the eponymously titled *Kansas* album (1974)—the band's overall sound and style, a mix of progressive rock and American boogie, featured songwriting from a number of band members, not just Livgren and Walsh. Since that debut, various pieces from this album, such as "Journey from Mariabronn," "Belexes," and "Lonely Wind," would feature on Kansas shows all the way through to the present day.[3]

The differences between the two principal songwriters' styles became more concretely drawn with the second album, *Song for America* (1975); Steve Pettengill, writing for *Sea of Tranquility* webzine, describes the album as

> full tilt symphonic rock with none of the stadium rock numbers that would pop up on later albums. Comprising four lengthy intricate pieces and two very American-style romps, Kansas' second album very admirably showcases the band's trademark duality as proggers and rockers.[4]

Most often Steve Walsh would write the more straight-ahead rock songs, while Livgren would primarily write the longer, more symphonic works such as "Song for America," "Lamplight Symphony," and "Incomudro—Hymn to the Atman." This songwriting trend would continue on *Masque* (1975), although you will find longer songs on *Masque* by Walsh and Robbie Steinhardt such as "All the World," and a shortish rocker by Livgren titled "Two Cents Worth." Standout tracks include "Icarus—Borne on Wings of Steel," "Mysteries and Mayhem," and "The Pinnacle."

Leftoverture (1976) is their breakthrough album, driven by the success of "Carry On Wayward Son," which made it to no. 5 on the Billboard Hot 100 list and also propelled the album to no. 5 on the Billboard 200 list as well.

Due to a case of writer's block, Steve Walsh did not contribute any singly written songs to this album, so the bulk of the writing was accomplished by Kerry Livgren. Thus, the style of this album can be said to be nearly the quintessential Livgren-penned Kansas album. Music from this album has consistently been featured in all of their tours up to the present day, and songs such as "The Wall" and "Miracles Out of Nowhere" have consistently been listed as the best overall Kansas songs in their catalog.[5]

The follow-up album, *Point of Know Return* (1977), begins a move away from epic-length songs yet still continues to build on the prog rock formula of the previous albums. Writing credits are shared more equally than what was included on *Leftoverture*, and Walsh's "Point of Know Return" (written with Phil Ehart and Robby Steinhardt) and the instrumental "The Spider" show a progressive rock side of his writing equal to Livgren's.[6] Because of the huge success of "Dust in the Wind," *Point of Know Return* would rise to the no. 4 position on the Billboard 200 albums list, and would eventually earn a quadruple platinum record certification.

On *Monolith* (1979), the band began self-producing their work, previously having used Wally Gold and former White Clover bandmate Jeff Glixman as musical overseer's work. This release also made it to the no. 10 position on Billboard's 200 album list, but it would be the last of the Kansas studio albums to do so. "People of the South Wind," "Reason to Be," and "On the Other Side" are three of the standout tracks from this album; "A Glimpse of Home" would be cited by Livgren as being about Christ, but not the Jesus from the Bible, rather from the *Urantia Book*, which was an important text to him at the time.[7] During the tour supporting *Monolith*, Livgren became an evangelical Christian.

Audiovisions (1980) would be the last album the band would record using just the six original members until 2000's *Somewhere to Elsewhere* (which would also include longtime current bassist, Billy Greer). Songs by Livgren on this album reflected his Christian beliefs, such as the song "Hold On," which made the Billboard charts, rising to no. 40 on the singles chart. All members of the band have songwriting credits on *Audiovisions*, and Walsh is more represented on this album than Livgren; all songs on this album are shorter and simpler than those that typified Kansas records from the preceding years. Both Walsh and Livgren released solo albums prior to the recording of this record, and some critics commented on how that may have watered down available material for this album.[8]

During the band's rehearsals for their next album, a dispute over the lyrical content for the song "Crossfire" caused Steve Walsh to leave the band, leaving the group without their lead singer as well as their other primary songwriter. John Elefante was hired to replace him, and the style of his writing (like Walsh, more straightforward and pop) was incorporated into both

Vinyl Confessions (1982) and *Drastic Measures* (1983). Livgren's writing and the band's embrace of simpler structures contrasted with the progressive music of former releases. Both records produced hits: "Play the Game Tonight," composed by outside writers Rob Frazier and Danny Flower (with lyrics changed by Livgren, Phil Ehart, and Rich Williams), and "Fight Fire with Fire," written by Elefante and his brother Dino. *Drastic Measures* also only featured three songs by Livgren, who was becoming dissatisfied with this current formula for Kansas.[9] Additionally, prior to this album's rehearsal process, violinist and lead singer Robbie Steinhardt left the band as well; outside musicians would be hired to cover his parts on tour. As Livgren noted, "The violin was gone, so was Steve [Walsh]. I wasn't even sure what Kansas was any more. I completely withdrew from the group."[10]

Following the tour to support this album, both Livgren and Dave Hope (who had also become a Christian) indicated that they were leaving the band, and so Kansas ceased to be a working entity for the next few years. Phil Ehart then reformed the group, bringing Steve Walsh back to the band, who brought along his bassist from Streets, Billy Greer, and adding guitar virtuoso Steve Morse (Dixie Dregs). This version of Kansas recorded two albums, *Power* (1986) and *In the Spirit of Things* (1988), the latter of which was produced by legendary producer Bob Ezrin. Both albums have a prog rock flavor, but mostly hew to the kind of music that Walsh had written prior to his previous departure. The concept album *In the Spirit of Things* was also mostly comprised of songs that were composed by outside songwriters, following a trend in the mid-1980s by many bands who were seeking hit singles.[11] This excellent album was not well supported by the record company, who soon dropped the band.

In 1990, the majority of the original band, minus Steinhardt reformed to play a number of concerts in Europe, although this lineup did not last for long. Morse replaced Livgren, Billy Greer came back to replace Hope, and violinist David Ragsdale replaced Steinhardt. Also, during this time, the band recorded a troubled live recording *Live at the Whiskey* (1992), which illuminated the vocal issues Walsh was having when that live album was recorded. It is a pale shadow of their first live record *Two for the Show* (1978), recorded during their heyday on the Monolith tour.[12] A greatest hits box set was also released around this time (*The Kansas Boxed Set* (1994)), much like an earlier greatest hits record, featuring classic pre-Elefante Kansas songs.[13] This box set did feature a new song by Livgren, "Wheels," highlighting Walsh and David Ragsdale, which would also be included on the next full studio release *Freaks of Nature*.

Freaks of Nature (1995) would be the only studio recording the band made with Walsh, Ragsdale, Ehart, and Williams as the only guitarist, and touring keyboardist/vocalist Greg Roberts. It may be the quintessential Kansas album with Walsh as the primary songwriter, and the style of the songs reflected the change in Walsh's vocals, becoming more hard/rock and heavy metal, having lost some pureness of tone to his tense singing technique and the aforementioned substance abuse. Consequently, this album is a kind of hard rock album that embraces its uniqueness in its progressive rock flavor—angular and biting. Kerry Livgren wrote one song for this record ("Cold Grey Morning"), which contrasts with much of his earlier work in its bleakness.

The departure of Greg Roberts and David Ragsdale opened the door for Robbie Steinhardt's return; consequently, the band began adding many songs that he sang lead vocals for back into the setlist. Also, during the 1990s, many progressive rock bands such as the Moody Blues and Yes were doing orchestral arrangements of their work and performing with existing symphonies. Conductor/arranger Larry Baird collaborated with Kansas to produce a live show taking many of their most well-known hits and clothing them in symphonic garb. *Always Never the Same* (1998) is the album that resulted from this collaboration. Most of the record is music written from Kansas' 1970s time period, with three excellent new songs by Walsh, and included a striking cover of the Beatles' "Eleanor Rigby."[14]

Somewhere to Elsewhere (2000) includes all of the original band members on an album that was completely written by Kerry Livgren. Livgren had always had a standing invitation to write works for the band since his departure following *Drastic Measures*, and the songs for this album seemed to fit a Kansas record more than the kind of work he had been doing in his solo career. Consequently, there is a kind of sense of return back to an earlier era with this music, sometimes intentionally so with songs like "Icarus II." Songs of longer lengths make a return, as do song structures that are more akin to works from *Song for America*, *Masque*, and *Leftoverture*. Stylistically, some of Livgren's songs seem to combine Walsh-like topics and structures into his own language.

The band transitioned back into a touring rather than recording band after the release of *Somewhere to Elsewhere*, although a pair of live recordings were released (*Device Voice Drum* (2002) and *There's No Place Like Home* (2009), the latter of which documented one of the Baird-led orchestral hybrid concerts by the band). The band's lineup changed again due to another departure by Robbie Steinhardt, who was replaced by David Ragsdale. Steve Walsh had expressed his desire to quit recording with the group and eventually touring as well, and so left the band in 2014.[15]

The fourth version of Kansas has released two successful albums of music to date: *The Prelude Implicit* (2016) and *The Absence of Presence* (2020). New vocalist Ronnie Platt, whose voice was described as resembling a mix of both Walsh's and Elefante's, has allowed the band to cover the entirety of their oeuvre. Music from these two albums was written relatively equally by all band members, although new guitarist Zak Rizvi and Platt emerged as primary songwriters on *The Prelude Implicit*.[16] Following the recording of *The Absence of Presence*, the group traded out band members yet again, with Rizvi and keyboardist David Manion leaving, replaced by Tom Brislin, and in 2023 David Ragsdale stepped aside, with Joe Deninzon filling the violin position.

THE SONGS

Over the entirety of Kansas' catalog, all of the band's members had a hand in writing the music included on their albums; for the years 1974–1984, the majority of the songwriting was by Kerry Livgren and/or Steve Walsh. These were the years of Kansas' main impact on a large general listening audience, and the main songs that are still in the public's consciousness are ones like "Dust in the Wind," "Carry on My Wayward Son," and "Point of Know Return." As mentioned above, the primary stylistic differences between Walsh and Livgren's writing (presented in broadly reductionist terms) are that Walsh wrote more straight-ahead rock/boogie pieces, with subject matter trending toward human relationships and portraits of everyday people, often focusing on grittier portrayals. Yet Walsh's work also highlights his ability to work in typical progressive rock territory, with rhythmic twists and turns, odd meter, and virtuosic playing. Nevertheless, in comparison to Livgren's work, the listener does not find many philosophical or religious themes in Walsh's writing, whereas this kind of content is regularly contained in Livgren's lyrics.

Additionally, Livgren's love and knowledge of classical music, as noted in his autobiography *Seeds of Change,* very much influenced Kansas's music for its first six albums—indeed, in the chapter titled "Musical Influences," Livgren spends the first few pages enumerating classical composers before he begins to discuss bands such as Gentle Giant, King Crimson, the Beatles, and Procol Harum, as well as a number of more obscure bands.[17] Influences such as these naturally caused him to embrace many of the musical idioms of classically influenced progressive rock in his own work. As is typical in most pop/rock groups, the rest of the band had a very large say in how the arrangements split out for the band's instrumentation, and indeed this could be problematic for any of the band's composers (this was one of the reasons that both Walsh and Livgren left Kansas; both were tired of the battles with the group to have pieces accepted for recording). However, quite often Livgren could bring music to the band that was largely written and arranged ahead of time, with specific parts composed for each instrument in the group.[18] I suspect that Walsh did less of this, even with some of his solo material post-Kansas.

Consequently, for the purposes on this book, we have chosen to investigate how the music that Livgren wrote/cowrote for Kansas moves from more complex, classically influenced prog to more simple songs within the band as a reflection of his move from religious syncretism to evangelical Christianity. Non-religious influences also played a part, due to members of the band wanting to move to shorter, straightforward songs in an attempt to prolong their popularity with a record-buying audience. However, Livgren embraced this style shift in his own music even beyond his time in Kansas, free from interband pressure to produce shorter hits. We believe that the shift from the complexity of Eastern philosophies and religions, a combinatorial New Age-ish belief system, and the *Urantia Book* to a fairly straightforward, simpler, born-again Christianity is reflected in the music he's written and continues to write.

How is this reflected in the music of Kansas?

It is not an easy choice to only pick a pair of songs to make a comparison! There is so much music to choose from: "A Glimpse of Home" from *Monolith* (reflecting Livgren's embrace of the belief system found in the *Urantia Book,* and quoted at the beginning of this chapter), "Mysteries and Mayhem/The Pinnacle" from *Masque* (highlighting allusions to the koans from Zen Buddhism[19]), while so many songs from *Leftoverture* seem to paint a picture of Livgren's spiritual search. During this period, when he does write simpler, uncomplex songs such as "Dust in the Wind," the tone and lyrical meaning point to the yearning expressed in the longer complex works. For shorter, simpler pieces, works like "Relentless" from *Audiovisions*, "Borderline" from *Vinyl Confessions*, and "End of the Age" and "Incident on a Bridge" from *Drastic Measures*, nearly all exhibit a more terse verse-chorus-solo format. Kevin Cummings writes in *On Track . . . Kansas*:

> "Borderline" is a straight-ahead, typical rocker. . . . On *Vinyl Confessions*, for the most part, a lyric sheet is not necessary to absorb the words because the band's message has been simplified. For Kansas fans, the early 1980s were a time to put away the thesaurus and the library card. The songs appealed in a pop sense, indicative of the decade in general, and also an indication of the group's new approach: short songs with radio-friendly lyrics. Indeed, for artists in the Contemporary Christian wing of the industry such as Rick Cua and Petra, this style was the order of the day. Livgren and Elefante put considerable thought into their music, but the songs were no longer as esoteric as they had once been, giving "Borderline" no pretensions to be anything else other than a pop/rock song with a catchy hook.[20]

If need be, a quick and simple illustration could be made between an epic such as "Journey from Mariabronn" (from *Kansas*) to the minor hit "Hold

On," from *Audiovisions.* The first (cowritten with Walsh), based on Herman Hesse's *Narcissus and Goldmund,* is complex in form and structure, both musically and lyrically, while the latter song is in typical verse-chorus form with few surprises. The former is indicative of Livgren's spiritual search embracing many sources, while the latter was written to his wife as an evangelical plea to her for her to accept Christ. "Mariabronn" features many flights of instrumental virtuosity from all of the players in the band, whereas "Hold On" is more restrained and focused. A better example can be drawn from two other songs: "Incomudro-Hymn to the Atman" from *Song for America,* and "The Coming Dawn (Thanatopsis)" from 2000's *Somewhere to Elsewhere.* The latter album was released long after Livgren had become a born-again Christian, and so his songwriting incorporating his faith was more settled and mature. Both of these songs feature a lyrical consideration of death, though it is treated differently in each.

"Incomudro-Hymn to the Atman" is the longest recorded song by Kansas, at just over twelve minutes, released on *Song for America* in 1975. The title is a combination of a made-up word that Livgren saw in a dream and a hymn to the individual self using a term found in both Hinduism and Buddhism. In *Seeds of Change,* Livgren writes:

> This song illustrates the syncretistic approach I took to religion as it seeks to combine elements of Hinduism with those of Zen Buddhism. "The man is not alive who knows the value of his soul"—this is the atman, valuable because it can be merged, according to Eastern thought, with the universal soul, the all-that-is.
>
> The concept of reincarnation is most obvious in the line, "For growing old is only going back to where you're from." Zen thought stresses our need to "pass beyond the years" and break away from the bounds of time, space and desire ("Time is lost in stillness, where there are no hopes and fears"). The "void" is a reference to satori or nirvana, the same nothingness sought in all Eastern religions. It can only be achieved by inward illumination—"everything you seek is waiting patiently within."[21]

The structure of the song fits this statement: syncretistic elements such as stylistic mixing (art music/classical music juxtaposed with hard rock), inclusion of mixed meter/time signatures, large sections of instrumental solos and chamber music, multiple key areas, use of Eastern-flavored scales such as the Phrygian mode, as well as the imagery and concepts of the religions cited in the lyrics.

This song opens with a kind of triumphant processional featuring the whole band, led by a harmonized keyboard melody using a synthesized string preset.

This introduction moves into a short, quasi-Eastern tinged violin solo, which is initially quiet and tentative-sounding, lifting briefly out of the initial D minor key before settling into the first two verses. These first two verses, simply sung by Steve Walsh, present the listener with what I might describe as "humankind faced with unsurety," especially if one is facing the end of life. Rather than illustrating a sense of doom and loss, Livgren's lyrics attempt to comfort the listener, pointing them forward to the cycle of life through reincarnation. These lyrics are set to a sparse yet quietly busy accompaniment, where the bass and guitar provide commentary to the vocalist's melody, yet the instrumental lines do not intrude. This vocal melody consistently moves toward the short refrain—briefly the instruments rest, focusing the listener on the vocals ("I wonder what you'd think . . ." which are affected with a strange echo effect) before being added back into the texture, the music building through these two lines of lyrics to underscore the answer to the unease stated in the verses. This build-up is masterfully accomplished, moving back into the processional music from the song's introduction.

Instead of moving into another set of verses, *Incomudro* now moves into an extensive instrumental section comprising the largest part of the song. Here, the kind of syncretism described by Livgren is displayed. The band moves through no fewer than seven separate subsections, each one varied in tone and mood, before the last section highlights drummer Phil Ehart in a 1.5-minute-long drum solo. Each section changes character, not unlike a person or the listener walking through a series of differently furnished rooms.

The first of the solo sections is similar in tone and instrumentation to the verses, but uses a different chord progression and features a solo synth line counterpointed with piano flourishes. Steve Walsh follows this with an organ solo, which is more typically "art music-esque" than his usual rock-infused Hammond C3 playing. The next transitional section features solo violin, then organ, and then some electric piano, landing on the most classically influenced section. This divertimento-style section seems quite formal and composed, as opposed to improvisational or spontaneous—it too functions like a transition, landing on a short arrival section utilizing a guitar solo. This moves into a long section punctuated by a rhythmic ostinato driven by the rhythm section and violin, cycling through a variety of tonal centers and highlighting an extended composed synthesizer solo using various synth patches. Its end is punctuated by a triumphant arrival point, suspended in the air (foreshadowing the song's ending) and landing on the gong hit that begins the expansive, constantly moving and shifting drum solo, which eventually moves back into the song's introductory string synth processional.

This whole section gives the listener a sense of a journey, almost as if the narrator has presented them with an aural illustration of that "glimpse of all the life that is around" mentioned in the second verse. Like the implication of the verses' lyrics, the music shows a wealth of depth and a feeling of what the possibilities of moving forward can be. The journey is not one of dread or a fatalistic ending, but a kind of "show of wonders," building on each preceding section/cycle in rebirth, moving to a triumphal procession.

The return to the last two verses and outro begins much as the song began, although the violin solo that concludes the introduction is now longer and more confident, as if all we've moved through in the preceding section has provided a way forward—the verses are no longer accompanied by the back-and-forth bass and guitar commentary but by the synth string keyboard sounds that are used for the intro's confident processional. The lyrics in these verses provide the solution to the (implied) dissolution from verses 1 and 2; this "core of gold," this "Master Plan" (capitalized in the lyrics by Livgren), is the practice of Zen's thought of embracing the stillness and breaking away from the bounds of time, space, and desire, which Livgren states is the same nothingness sought in all Eastern religions.[22] The music for this section's refrain is similar to that of the first and second verses, but the vocal effect is less pronounced (or changed), and so the message is clearer: "Everything you seek is waiting patiently within; For growing old is only going back to where you've been." This refrain also increases the tempo, moving into the outro.

The last section of *Incomudro* begins with a fairly typical Kansas rock-out guitar solo over a descending chord progression but soon moves into a series of swirling arpeggiated and/or sequenced chords, over which a repeated upward-moving Phrygian melody builds in pitch and instrumentation, ending suspended up in the air and landing on an explosion with wind sounds fading away. The effect here is a kind of running toward nirvana, with increased excitement until you reach enlightenment, and then poof! You have achieved your goal.[23]

"The Coming Dawn (Thanatopsis)" was written in 2000 for *Somewhere to Elsewhere*, an album written entirely by Kerry Livgren, and for the first time since *Audiovisions*, featuring all of the original members of the band. Much of this album was recorded at Livgren's studio on his farm in Berryton, Kansas, while Steve Walsh's vocals were recorded at his home in Georgia, due to him also working on his masterful album *Glossolalia* at the same time while Kansas was working on *Somewhere to Elsewhere*. While a fair amount of this album shows Livgren writing in a musical language familiar to longtime Kansas fans, a very different approach is illustrated in "The Coming Dawn (Thanatopsis)."

The word "thanatopsis" refers to a consideration of death and is probably most familiar to us as a poem by William Cullen Bryant. That poem, although filled with a great deal of dark imagery as is typical of many works on the subject of death, nevertheless turns in the final dozen lines, pointing the reader to approach death not as a feared journey, but:

Thou go not, like the quarry-slave at night,
Scourged to his dungeon, but, sustained and soothed
By an unfaltering trust, approach thy grave,
Like one who wraps the drapery of his couch
About him, and lies down to pleasant dreams.[24]

It's not known if Livgren was referencing this poem in "The Coming Dawn," but his consideration of death is also a hopeful one, rather than dreaded. Confident in his faith, Livgren writes as one who is hoping that the choices he made in this lifetime will carry on into the next one. Each verse illustrates an aspect of Christian belief, including doubt. The first verse expresses a hope that "what was lived and won't be lost," but then continues that thought, wondering if that past "which was lived" matters much at all. Verse two expresses that surety in his faith allows him to hold on, but he will die for a "lifetime that will last." Verse three expresses a knowledge of God's nearness and love, although the singer cannot see, he does not doubt that God's presence is near. Lastly, the choruses which follow each verse describe what the singer foresees at the moment of passage:

When my world, starts to fade, I can only hope that every choice I made
Will endure, and carry on . . . . . . into the coming dawn[25]

Rather than subsuming his faith or the meaning of these lyrics in more figurative language, the illustrative word choices and metaphors selected are simply presented.

Unlike so many previous songs, "The Coming Dawn" begins simply and directly, with bell/chime-like piano chords which then accompany the singer into the first verse with a very straightforward I–vi–IV–V chord progression. The transition between verse one and two adds the violin with string synth and chimes (foreshadowing the middle solo section). For the second verse, the entire band joins the music, but is always supportive rather than featured.[26] All musical support is based on the quality of the simple musical materials (especially the beauty of the melody) rather than subtextual, more complex musical elements. It's as if the faith of the lyrics is presented with a sense of joy and warmth, real and solid, and without taint or with very little doubt—with patience and calm.

The song's instrumental section, consisting of a two-minute-long violin solo accompanied by the whole band, also exhibits simplicity in its construction. For nearly two-thirds of its duration, the violin plays whole or half-note chord tones, sometimes including occasional non-harmonic passing tones. Again, there is very little noticeable counterpoint other than what naturally occurs from voice leading, relying on the changing and sequenced chord progression to provide much of the focus. There are no meter changes throughout the whole piece, even in this instrumental section, and all of the dissonance is mild and most often part of the underlying chord rather than serving as a non-chord tone. An interesting musical choice happens in the middle of this solo: much of the rhythmic accompaniment falls away, and the violinist continues, underpinned by choral synth and acoustic guitar—this might be a nice musical illustration of the lyrics of the chorus (" . . . every choice I made/will endure, and carry on . . . ."), the current world fading away before moving into the new life. The last section of this solo features a shifting sense of tonality with pairs of fully-diminished leading-tone seventh chords moving to their tonics in a sequence, as if real movement or moving forward happens here in this interlude rather than in the simplicity of the chord progressions of the verses.

As the solo concludes, the song returns to the music of the introduction, and the third verse begins much as the first verse did with its bare accompaniment of the singer. Unlike the first verse, however, the band rejoins on the chorus and continues until the final fadeout. The outro begins on the deceptive cadence of the last word of the chorus, and the music feels suspended in the air rather than landing on a solid final cadence chord. The cyclical chord progression moving from A minor down to F major and then back and forth from F major to G major gives the listener a sense of "music without end" which fades beyond sight: beginning with simplicity and ending simply.

BEYOND THE SONGS

Kerry Livgren's autobiographical testimony *Seeds of Change*[27] traces his spiritual journey from his Lutheran beginnings, moving through questioning these roots, and traversing through various religious viewpoints that were quite common to many who were in their late teens and early twenties in the late 1960s. In the chapter titled "The Quest Leads to the East," Livgren lists the number of authors, their books, and movements which influenced him. The first paragraph is telling:

> The period from 1970–77 was a particularly turbulent time for me. During these years I went from one philosophy to another, from friend to friend, from band to band, and from rags to riches. Propelling myself through diverse life-styles, I seemed to ping-pong back and forth between different gurus, authors and conflicting religious philosophies. All of these elements combined to shape my evolving musical style and world view.[28]

The next paragraph's first sentence is also telling:

My highly impressionable mind kept trying to make sense out of this heterogeneous input, and I actively looked for different levels of validity in otherwise opposing viewpoints. *I started to develop an amalgamation of all of the things I took in. . . . I became a real syncretist, fusing elements from many sources, convinced that all of this revelation ultimately sprang from one source.* (italics mine)[29]

This chapter lists Hermann Hesse (whose *Narcissus and Goldmund* influenced "Journey from Mariabronn"), Claudio Naranjo's *The One Quest*, *Autobiography of a Yogi* by Paramahansa Yogananda, *The Gospel of Zen* and D. T. Suzuki's *Essays in Zen Buddhism*, the Taoist *I Ching* and *Tao Teh Ching* of Lao Tzu, and Hinduism. Throughout this chapter, Livgren repeatedly quotes and discusses how these and other authors/books assemble a theology that borrows from each other and both Western and Eastern religious thoughts, seeking to both reveal God within yourself and paradoxically illustrate that there is no personal God.[30]

Looking for a deeper, moral, and personal connection, Livgren became disenchanted with the Eastern religions and by 1976 was following none of the above, but rather had formed a worldview by assembling bits and pieces of what he wished from each of them. In 1977, he was introduced to the *Urantia Book* by one of the recording engineers who thought that its themes would resonate with Livgren, based on the lyrics of his that he had heard. Livgren wrote:

The most attractive thing about this book was the way it synthesized all the diverse elements I had been studying into a coherent picture of reality. Unlike Eastern religions that played down the person of Jesus or wrote him off as another avatar, *The Urantia Book* stressed him as the central figure of our planet. But it also included the best of the Eastern concepts that Christianity could not incorporate. I really thought I had found the handle.[31]

The Urantia Book, whose author is unknown, originated in Chicago in the middle of the twentieth century.

The text introduces the word "Urantia" as the name of the planet Earth and states that its intent is to "present enlarged concepts and advanced truth."[32] The book aims to unite religion, science, and philosophy. Its extensive content on topics of interest to science sets it apart among documents said to have been received from celestial beings.[33] Among other topics, the book discusses the origin and meaning of life, mankind's place in the universe, the history of the planet, the relationship between God and people, and the life of Jesus.[34]

Reading *The Urantia Book*, it is easy to see how it formed a critical link for Livgren between belief in Eastern religions and his eventual born-again

Christianity. So many of its religious concepts are close to orthodox Christianity: Deity in three persons/parts (God the Father, God the Son, and God the Spirit, known as Universal Father, Eternal Son, and Infinite Spirit). God the Father guides each individual through a Thought Adjuster, who is compared to the Egyptian *ka* or the Hindu *atman*.[35]

Jesus is central to the book, and while many of his deeds and attributes are similar or the same as written in the New Testament (both human and divine, son of God and born of Mary, performed miracles, led twelve disciples, crucified and rose from the dead), *The Urantia Book* also presents some differences as well (He was born of a natural human conception, His crucifixion is not considered atonement for sin, nor is He considered to be the Eternal Son).[36]

Livgren's "A Glimpse of Home" from the *Monolith* album reflects his study of this book; in his autobiography, he prints the lyrics from this entire song, and with the portion of the lyrics that began this chapter, it would be easy for a listener unfamiliar with *The Urantia Book* to confuse these words with an embrace of the biblical Christ. However, Livgren writes: "this song was about Christ, but it was the Christ of *The Urantia Book*, not the Bible."[37]

Unlike the Eastern religions and the worldview presented by *The Urantia Book*, evangelicalism does not require a large amount of study or training to become an adherent; at first, all you must do is believe. Thus, "At its most basic level, evangelical Christianity is characterized by a belief in the literal truth of the Bible, a 'personal relationship with Jesus Christ,' the importance of encouraging others to be 'born again' in Jesus and a lively worship culture."[38]

David Babbington in his book *Evangelicalism in Modern Britain: A History from the 1730s to the 1980s,* posits four central aspects of evangelical belief: conversionism (a "born-again" experience), biblicism (a high regard for biblical authority, often solo scriptura), crucicentrism (the central tenet of atonement by Jesus' death and resurrection), and activism (evangelism and proselytization).[39] These can be practiced in many varied ways by a large number of congregations and denominations, some quite fundamentalist and conservative, others much more liberal and much less legalistic. Different denominations will focus on one aspect or another when organizing their worship services or mission; for example, Missionary Baptist churches may focus on evangelism or missions, whereas an Apostolic church may focus on utilizing 'gifts of the Spirit' with an emphasis on glossolalia or prophecy. However, whatever complexities arise from these variations on these four central tenets, these variants of practice are individual to each denomination as individual matters of worship and are not the fundamental basis for belief. There is a graceful simplicity in evangelical Christianity reflected in the Apostles Creed (or the Old Roman Creed upon which the Apostles Creed expands) which is direct, and while it is not used in many evangelical congregations' worship services, it is often embraced by the evangelical church as a simple set of belief statements.[40]

Livgren's spiritual and religious life changed when he underwent his conversion experience in an Indianapolis hotel room in 1979. Rather than having to rely on a large number of disparate sources and training, having to earn or empty himself to reach nirvana to construct his syncretic religious worldview, his acceptance and belief in Christ simplified his spiritual life. Doing so via evangelical Christianity rather than through other more liturgically based denominations, it colored his thinking and music-making in such ways as to make his music more direct, less conflicted, and easier to understand by a greater audience.

When Livgren and Dave Hope left Kansas in 1983 to begin their careers in contemporary Christian music (CCM), there were hardly any progressive rock bands within that genre of pop music. Most music for this format was purposefully written to be simple and direct and was often an offshoot of simple, acoustic guitar-based folk music. Larry Norman and others brought a harder edge and more ties to contemporary pop/rock into CCM, but often this was viewed with a critical eye from the churches, who viewed all rock music (including rhythm and blues, soul, disco, metal, hard country, et al.) as "the devil's music." By the mid-1980s, groups like Petra, The 2nd Chapter of Acts, DeGarmo and Key, and others were beginning to be more widely accepted, but the music most often employed simple forms, easy-to-understand lyrics, and rare instrumental virtuosity, in short songs.[41] Consequently, as a means to try and be successful in this format and to be supportive of his Christian audience, much of Livgren's later work either adopted more direct or simpler parameters and constructions.[42] Livgren himself mocked this attitude in the song "Mainstream" from the *Drastic Measures* album:

Just crank turn'em out on the assembly line and chart turn'em higher (higher, higher)
Just keep it simple boys it's gonna be alright as long as you're inside the
  Mainstream . . .[43]

However, even with some of his post-Kansas music featuring influences from classical music (such as his instrumental New Age-esque *One of Several Possible Musiks* or his cantata based on Lazarus), the vast bulk of his work outside of Kansas has continued to be simpler, musically less complex (e.g., using fewer key changes, fewer odd time signatures, less virtuosic instrumental breaks, et al.), but albeit beautiful, well-constructed, and made with great craftsmanship.

BEYOND THE BAND

By definition, *all progressive rock is syncretistic*—it is a borrowing of styles and genres, a blend and mix of many styles and genres within rock music, and an embrace of many of the complex aspects of those musical combinations. Not all prog rock had to be complex—many of the most prominent prog bands had songs that could be simple, and often these were slow songs or ballads: Yes's "Wondrous Stories"; Emerson, Lake & Palmer, "From the Beginning"; Rush, "Tears"; Spock's Beard, "June." Indeed, some bands made a switch to simpler songs as a career move without theological intent: Genesis did so: "Turn It On" et al. as did Asia featuring many prog stalwarts. ELP did this disastrously with *Love Beach*, before breaking up for a short time.

Livgren's post-Kansas music began with a poorly received solo album (*Timeline*, 1984), which was recorded with the band that later became AD. Formed shortly after he and Dave Hope left Kansas, Livgren faced a legal hurdle from the moment they left: because of the way their initial management and record company contracts were written, they discovered that they could not really record for a general audience outside of Kansas. A waiver was granted to them to work in the contemporary Christian format, and their first album as a band, *The Art of the State*, was released in 1985 on Sparrow Records. In total, AD recorded three officially released albums. These and follow-up records continued to feature shorter songs with occasional sophisticated instrumental interludes, but most of these songs are under five minutes and provide excellently crafted melodic writing as a vehicle for the words.

The follow-up solo album *One of Several Possible Musiks*, is an odd outlier, whose nature is a return to progressive rock and employs the kind of complexity that is missing from his non-instrumental songs. While strongly melodic and employing traditional rock music harmonic progressions, much of the music is a fusion of classical elements and rock, strongly borrowing from Renaissance dance music and some new age musical elements (such as what a fan of the radio program Hearts of Space might hear). Much of what is contained on this record is highly reminiscent of the middle instrumental sections of a number of Kansas songs, but minus the bite or edge that that group could bring to such music. However, the albums recorded in the 1990s as solo records return to embrace straightforward songwriting whose lyrical themes reflect his faith, albeit with occasional glimpses of sophistication.

In the early part of this century, following the Kansas album *Somewhere to Elsewhere,* Livgren reformed the second version of Kansas, which was now called Proto-Kaw. The recordings he made with Proto-Kaw are excellent examples of a return to that musical language he employed with Kansas. However, the work on these more modern albums is quite different from that which was part of the 1970s-era group heard on the album *Early Recordings from Kansas 1971–1973*. Those songs are very much a product of their time and can be compared to slightly-earlier contemporaries such as the Amboy Dukes' "Journey to the Center of Your Mind" and Syd Barrett-era Pink Floyd.[44] However, that earlier album is much more complex and experimental than the three more recent Proto-Kaw albums, again reflecting Livgren's more direct songwriting since he became an evangelical Christian.

In recent decades, his output of new work has slowed due to health issues, and much of his work has centered on reissues of various records and some new pieces of instrumental music titled *Several More Musiks*, as well as a reissue of *One of Several Possible Musiks* with extra tracks and partially rerecorded ones from the prior album. A new album of a work that was long in gestation, titled *The Resurrection of Lazarus*, was released in 2021 and is akin to a musical or a cantata similar to those composed for Easter services in larger churches. This piece features every singer that worked with Livgren in Kansas and AD. Since this piece is so reliant on text, the simplicity of the musical language and structure is still in evidence, albeit cast in the form of a cantata.

While Kansas is highly successful as a band, their influence on progressive rock music is not often recognized in view of the many bands from the United Kingdom such as Yes, Genesis, ELP, and Pink Floyd. Even in North America, critics and other music writers tend to overlook the band while focusing on the Europeans. However, many of the new wave of prog bands that arose in the 1990s and 2000s, especially those with Christian underpinnings, very much looked to Kansas as a primary influence. Bands such as Spock's Beard, The Neal Morse Band, Fringe, Thank You Scientist, Bent Knee, and others all benefited from the classical plus hard rock music combination with strong vocals. As of 2023, Kansas is still a successful recording and touring group attracting large audiences.

CONCLUSION

There is a musical parallel of complexity to a kind of simplicity in the music of Kansas that reflects principal songwriter Kerry Livgren's journey from syncretism to evangelical Christianity. In the group's first six albums, there is a noticeable difference between his writing style and that of the other band members. Livgren's use of classical music, more philosophical lyrical content, and other complex structures typically, if not always stand over against a more straight-ahead rock/boogie with more typical lyrics. When Livgren became a born-again Christian, much of his music changed to reflect the simplicity of that branch of Christian thought in contrast to his earlier restless spiritual search through a number of Eastern religions. In the world of progressive rock music, some might find his later works to be musically diffuse and not as worthy as some of his music that is more complex. Not so! It is just another facet of his excellent craftsmanship reflecting his change from one belief system to another. All of his work with Kansas as well as that of his solo career continues to influence the progressive rock musical landscape, then as well as now.

NOTES

1. Malcolm Dome, "Robbie Steinhardt Obituary," *Prog*, September 20, 2021. https://www.pressreader.com/uk/prog/20210910/281496459388916.

2. Chris Callaway, "How Free Beer and Lies Earned Kansas its First Record Deal," *Westword*, April 11, 2017. https://www.westword.com/music/forty-years-later-kansas-is-celebrating-the-past-and-conquering-new-goals-8854982.

3. See a variety of Kansas's setlists, both historical and current, at Setlist.fm. https://www.setlist.fm/setlists/kansas-bd6b5ea.html.

4. https://www.seaoftranquility.org/reviews.php?op=showcontent&id=1553.

5. Dave Ling, "The Top 10 Best Kansas Songs," *Classic Rock. Louder Sound*, July 14, 2016. https://www.loudersound.com/features/too-10-best-kansas-songs.

6. This was a stressful time for the band in relation to its songwriting—Kevin Cummings writes in his book *On Track . . . Kansas* (pg. 39) about their record deal with Kirshner that paid the band a very small royalty rate and owned the band's publishing, which still paid the songwriters their royalties. This meant that the non-songwriters in the band made less money than those who composed. Naturally, tensions arose once the band became successful—the money that was earned was unequally distributed. Additionally, at this time, Walsh temporarily left the band because he thought he should go out as a solo artist; rumors told to me by Kevin Silva (who is close to the band) indicate that Walsh was placated by being given co-songwriting credit on a few songs composed by Livgren on *Point of Know Return*, which also strained relationships within the band. (author interview with Silva) See also: https://www.loudersound.com/features/kansas-an-everyday-story-of-success-failure-drugs-booze-and-jealousy.

7. Kerry Livgren, *Seeds of Change*. Sparrow, 1991,Word Publishing (UK) LTD, Milton Keynes, England, p. 124.

8. William Ruhlmann, *Audio-Visions*. https://www.allmusic.com/album/mw0000311539.

9. Author Kevin Cummings in *On Track . . . Kansas* writes that the last two songs that end this album, both by Livgren ("End of the Age" and "Incidents on a Bridge") were felt by Livgren to be misplaced on this Kansas album. Indeed, they sound out of place and might have been better suited to a previous Kansas record, or with Livgren's post-Kansas group, AD.

10. Dave Ling, *Kansas: An Everyday Story of Success, Failure, Drugs, Booze, and Jealousy*, https://www.loudersound.com/features/kansas-an-everyday-story-of-success-failure-drugs-booze-and-jealousy.

11. Bands such as Heart, Aerosmith, Chicago, and REO Speedwagon.

12. An additional live record from the Steve Morse era was released in 1998 as part of a set of recordings from the King Biscuit Flower Hour show. *The King Biscuit Flower Hour Presents Kansas* (1998) is an excellent contrast to the *Live at the Whiskey* record.

13. *The Best of Kansas* (1984) was a great success commercially and included a new song ("Perfect Lover") by John Elefante when it was originally released. When the record was released on compact disc, Elefante's song was replaced by Livgren's "The Pinnacle."

14. The record also includes some introductory and transitional material credited to Larry Baird.

15. Prior to Walsh's departure, much of the rest of the group recorded and toured as the band Native Window, often opening for Kansas (?!!).

16. This album also contains two bonus tracks, cover versions of the traditional songs "Home on the Range" and "Shenandoah."

17. Livgren, *Seeds of Change*, pp. 55–62.

18. Kerry often wrote specific things for folks to play, evidenced by the counterpoint of "Mysteries Out of Nowhere" from *Leftoverture*, or the incredibly intricate bass guitar parts in "Song for America." This is quite different from Walsh's music for Kansas, which seems to have largely been arranged by the band ("The Spider" from *Point of Know Return* is a notable exception).

19. Livgren, *Seeds of Change*, pp. 93–94.

20. Cummings, *On Track . . . . Kansas,* p. 67.

21. Livgren, *Seeds of Change*, pp. 86–87.

22. Livgren, *Seeds of Change*, p. 87.

23. "Incomudro" (along with "Belexes") was originally recorded by the second version of Kansas and can be found on the album *Early Recordings from Kansas 1971–1973*, released in 2002—the song is very similar to the well-known version on *Song for America*, although there are some differences with the middle section. Because of the use of flute in this early iteration of the band (and containing no violin), this differing instrumentation sounds quite psychedelic at times, and the middle section sounds much like the middle section of Pink Floyd's "Echoes."

24. William Cullen Bryant, *Thanatopsis*. https://www.poetryfoundation.org/poems/50465/thanatopsis.

25. Kerry Livgren, "The Coming Dawn (Thanatopsis)," in *Somewhere to Elsewhere,* Magna Carta Records, NewYork, 2000.

26. Contrast this with the music for the verses in "Incomudro"—here, some of the main musical interest in the first two verses comes from the background contrapuntal material by the guitar and bass guitar—there is nothing like this in "The Coming Dawn."

27. Cowritten with Kenneth Boa; originally published in 1983; updated in 1991 by Word Publishing.

28. Livgren, *Seeds of Change*, p. 33.

29. Livgren, *Seeds of Change*, p. 33.

30. An excellent quote is this one: "The final meaning of negative theology, of knowing God by unknowing, of the abandonment of idols both sensible and

conceptual, is that ultimate faith is not in or upon anything at all. It is complete letting go." (Robert Sohl and Audrey Carr, editors; *The Gospel According to Zen: Beyond the Death of God.* New York: New American Library, 1970, p. 11)

31. Livgren, *Seeds of Change*, p. 119.

32. Partridge, Christopher, *UFO Religions.* New York: Taylor & Francis, 2012, p. 138.

33. Gardner, Martin, *Urantia: The Great Cult Mystery.* Amherst, NY: Prometheus, 2008, p. 181.

34. Wikipedia article on Urantia Foundation, *The Urantia Book*, 1955. https://en.wikipedia.org/wiki/The_Urantia_Book.

35. Ibid, p. 1459.

36. House, H. Wayne, *Charts of Cults, Sects, and Religious Movements.* Zondervan Publishing House, Grand Rapids, MI, 2000, pp. 262–264, p. 273.

37. Livgren, *Seeds of Change,* p. 124.

38. https://crcc.usc.edu/topic/evangelicals-and-evangelicalism/.

39. Bebbington, David W., *Evangelicalism in Modern Britain: A History from the 1730s to the 1980s.* New York: Taylor & Francis, 1933.

40. Typically, this creed is not used in many evangelical services due to the lack of liturgy used in their worship settings, whereas it is common in many mainline Protestant churches, as well as Catholic and Orthodox ones.

41. An exception would be guitarist Phil Keaggy (formerly from the 1970s progressive rock band Glass Harp), whose abilities as a guitarist were often best often displayed on his instrumental works. He and Livgren both contributed to The 2nd Chapter of Acts' Narnia concept album *The Roar of Love.*

42. Exceptions would be the work he did with reformed versions of the earliest Kansas band named Proto-Kaw.

43. Livgren's "Mainstream" from *Drastic Measures*, 1983—ironically, the song structure and lyrics *are* simple and straightforward—what *does* make the song more critical of the record industry is the song's length, made longer by the minute and a half instrumental section in the middle and the longish solo at the end of the song, and therefore too long for easy radio play.

44. However, the experimentation on this record is fantastic—outbursts of noise and a laid-back Chicago-style horn section move into a 60s-style melody and lyric on "Nactolos 21." The sax solo in the middle moves back and forth from static to frenetic, and the whole is a great example of Livgren trying many things within the confines of one song.

Chapter 6

Rush's "Freewill"

Beyond Election to Choice as a Theological Anthem

RUSH AS A BAND

Rush was formed in 1968 in Toronto, originally with Alex Lifeson on guitar, Jeff Jones on bass, and John Rutsey on drums. Jones was soon replaced by Geddy Lee, and for the next six years, they began to make a name for themselves in the club scene in Ontario. The release of their first eponymously named album in 1974 brought greater recognition, including from some DJs and record executives in the United States, leading to a distribution deal from Mercury Records as well as a national tour in the United States. At this point, Neil Peart replaced Rutsey in the band, just as the band was to begin their first U.S. tour.[1]

At this time, the band's influences were Led Zeppelin, Blue Cheer, The Who, and the Yardbirds, and their music had a stylistic quality not unlike those bands or a harder-tinged Humble Pie. Starting with Fly by Night and Caress of Steel, the group began to incorporate more progressive rock influences into their music, and the lyrics from this time forward would most often be written by Neil Peart, whose autodidactic education was highly informed by a large, highly varied reading list. Turning away from themes on the first album, which had previously embraced the regular working-class Joe anthems ("Working Man") and come-hither songs ("In the Mood," "Finding My Way"), both *Fly by Night* (1975) and *Caress of Steel* (1975) would embrace longer song structures and styles along with songs whose topics were more fantastical, historical, worldly, and philosophical. Songs such as "By-Tor and the Snow Dog," "Bastille Day," "The Necromancer," and "The Fountains of Lamneth" all display a search for ever-growing musical sophistication, including extended tonalities, rhythmic and metric complexity, and fantasy, historical, and science fiction–based lyrics.

While their constant touring built up their fan base, their musical eclecticism was causing concern with their record company, which began to pressure them to write more commercial music since sales of *Caress of Steel* were disappointing. At this time, the band chose to ignore those directives and wrote and recorded their breakthrough album *2112* (1976), whose like-named suite (influenced by Ayn Rand, who is thanked in the liner notes for this album) is a full-length side of the original LP, a multi-movement suite or cantata united by a single story. The rest of the album consisted of shorter songs unrelated to the *2112* concept but still with a wide variety of topics. While longer concept pieces such as "Xanadu," "La Villa Strangiato," and "Cygnus X-1/Hemispheres" would be a feature of the next two albums—*A Farewell to Kings* (1977) and *Hemispheres* (1978)—there would always be a collection of unrelated songs on each of them; Rush would not release a full concept album until 2012's *Clockwork Angels*.[2]

2112's success allowed them to write and record whatever they musically wished to do in the future, and so each successive album finds the band exploring and indulging in whatever styles or lyrical themes that interest them. This would lead them to incorporate new wave (*Permanent Waves*, 1980), reggae (*Signals*, 1982), rap (*Roll the Bones*, 1991), a great deal of sophisticated production (choirs, orchestra, etc., on *Power Windows,* 1985, and *Hold Your Fire*, 1987), and to a certain extent on *Presto,* 1989, before stripping it all back to include grunge (*Counterparts,* 1993, and *Vapor Trails,* 2002), and back to a heavy, sophisticated three-piece rock group influenced by the heavy, dark metal of Tool and like-minded groups with *Snakes and Arrows* (2007) and *Clockwork Angels* (2012). Indeed, Peart says:

> We didn't have any protective nature of what Rush was that could never be influenced by new wave music, or could never use an African rhythm. There is no such thing as "that doesn't suit Rush"; those words have never been uttered.[3]

However, as Peart and others would acknowledge, *Moving Pictures* (1981) became their quintessential album, where all of those prior influences melded together and became their own, and it has become the record for which they are most known.[4]

As mentioned above, during the middle 1970s and into the 1980s, the band's expanded instrumentation beyond the power trio allowed them to become conversely more progressive and less hard rock/metal. Their music from the 1990s until their last studio release, *Clockwork Angels*, refocused on the power trio model, occasionally augmented by additional instrumentation.

Rush was never perceived as a critical wonder; indeed, their success was completely built via word of mouth and their ever-growing fan base, many of whom would become successful rock musicians working in genres as diverse as straight-ahead pop, comedy, nu-metal, neo-prog, grunge, hair metal, thrash, and industrial rock. Indeed, thanks to Sam Dunn and Scott MacFadyn's documentary *Beyond the Lighted Stage*, the band enjoyed newfound fame and acceptance beyond the oft-stated declaration that Rush was the biggest cult band in the world.[5] Due to this increased visibility and because of insistent pressure and polling from their listeners, Rush was inducted into the Rock and Roll Hall of Fame in 2013.

Part of the Foo Fighters' Dave Grohl's intro to the Hall of Fame induction read:

> Their influence is undeniable, and their devoted fanbase only rivalled by The Grateful Dead.

Geddy Lee responded to this and the fan's tireless advocacy in his acceptance speech, acknowledging that:

> I have to thank the most passionate, most dedicated, incredible fanbase around the globe, for not only supporting and encouraging our musical progress over the years, but for the insistence of their voices, which has most certainly led us to this evening.

Up until they played their last concert in August of 2015, they continued to be a progressive hard rock band, writing and performing new music, and embracing whatever influences interested them.

As a group, none of the members of Rush were Christian, although both Lifeson and Peart grew up around the faith, and Lee is Jewish. By the time that Rush was successful, all three had become disenchanted with religion. Lifeson, answering a question in Louder as to whether he believed in God, said:

> No. When I was younger I did. My mother is not super-religious but she has a belief. My father was the total opposite. He thought religion was a crock. In my early teens I started to question it all. I had friends who were Jesus freaks, others were just very spiritual, and we had these great long discussions about these things. But as I get older it just becomes a less and less sensible thing to think about.[6]

Geddy writes in his autobiography *My Effin' Life:*

> When I was young I ran away from the obligations of the religious household in which I was raised. I felt like I was exercising my free will, but because I was headstrong I didn't fully understand the implications of my actions.[7]

In 1994, Peart wrote about his Christian grandmother in an article for the St. Catherines Standard:

She was a classic Puritan grandmother: wiry and iron-hard, a stern disciplinarian—her chosen instrument was the wooden spoon, applied to my backside with enough force to break more than a few of them—but I also remember a million acts of kindness. And if she believed the injunction against sparing the rod, she could still "spoil the child" in other ways, and we also knew her innate softness, her pure gentleness of heart.

I remember staying at her house when I was small, and at bedtime she would emerge from the bathroom totally transformed: leaving behind the severe cotton dress, the hard black shoes, and the strict hairnet, she tiptoed into the dark room on bare feet, wearing a long white nightgown, her hair down in a rope of grey braid. She seemed so frail and girlish as we knelt beside the big wooden bed to say our prayers: "Now I lay me down to sleep."[8]

Later in this chapter we'll read about Peart's eventual worldview, that of a "linear thinking agnostic."

THE SONG

Because of their three-piece, multi-instrumental, essentially hard rock group, Rush became the forerunners of a type of music known as progressive hard rock or metal.[9] Their longer songs, coupled with fantasy or historically based lyrics, lent them a fair amount of footing in the world of progressive rock. However, toward the end of the 1970s, they wished to try new things, incorporate new song structures, and not necessarily continue to write the longer prog songs for which they were becoming well-known (although "Natural Science," the closing track on *Permanent Waves,* clocks in at eleven minutes in length and also embraces a kind of science-as-religion worldview in its lyrics). The title of the album was originally to be *Wavelength,* but the band found the title had already been used too many times. The eventual title of *Permanent Waves* was a commentary on the music industry, constantly announcing new waves in music (as indeed the music of the early 80s by The Police, Ultravox, The Phones, Talking Heads, and Greg Kihn were all called New Wave).[10]

Permanent Waves pivoted from epics (creating new or fantastical worlds) to showing more of a reflection of our own natural world (also seen in that record's "epic," "Natural Science"). This album was a big step away from *Hemispheres* in its six tracks' topics and points of view—still oblique at times, but often very focused and human. "The Spirit of Radio," while a critique of commercial radio, is also an embrace of the magic that a good station's music brings to us. "Jacob's Ladder" is nothing short of a colorful description of cloud formations tied to the poetic phrase "weave the fabric of their (men's) dreams";[11] "Entre Nous" is a love song, "Different Strings" is cast in a similar vein as many of the songs from *A Farewell to Kings*, but is also a love song, and the album closes with "Natural Science," whose focus is a casting of nature viewed through the religion of science, which could be a cautionary tale.

"Freewill" is the darkest music on this record, and lyrically it is meant to ask us to beware of giving up that precious ability of choice for other avenues of thought, religion, or worldviews which highlight predestination. Geddy writes in *My Effin' Life:*

> In 1979, when he [Peart] handed me the lyrics for "Freewill," I instantly loved the song. It was a powerful expression of the way Rush was taking control of its own destiny, and echoed my own refusal of religious dogma, of subjection to the hand of God, or, more abstractly, fate.[12]

Peart would return to this point of view frequently in other songs such as "Roll the Bones," "Faithless," and "Far Cry." While it is musically an up-tempo rocker, various aspects of its construction are put together in a way that suggests an interpretation of a restless, frantic, unsettled, and somewhat angry piece of music.

Much of the music labeled progressive rock features more contemporary-classical music elements such as non-typical forms, frequently changing meters and key centers, and non-typical instrumentation. "Freewill" embraces most of these, although with sometimes more subtle application than earlier works from the previous two albums. However, coupled with the subject matter of the lyrics, the music underscores the text, keeping the listener on their toes by shifting away from expectations or familiar landing points.

Peart's first verse and pre-chorus portray a type of person who thinks that fate, or a supreme "power" has already determined what the future might hold:

The stars aren't aligned or the gods are malign,
blame is better to give than receive[13]

Each successive verse lays out an implied negative portrayal of those who are adherents or believers in predeterminist world views. Indeed, the second verse spells out an angrier, more violent example. However, Peart's chorus provides another point of view, that choice always presents an option, you do not have to select a heavenly option, and making no choice is still indeed a choice.

The texts for the verses are rhythmically set in such a way to both embrace a pattern and simultaneously break it; the opening of each measure begins with a quarter note followed by an eighth-dotted quarter pairing (sometimes just two eighths), followed by a changing descending line in quarter notes—sometimes three, sometimes four, or five of them. (The vocal part is doubled by the bass guitar part, also unusual.) Coupled with the drum part, the listener's sense of downbeat and afterbeat common to so many rock songs is shifted and changed, and a sense of unease results.[14]

Additionally, the verses' accompaniment is set to single melodic lines, not chords, underlining a sense of hollow points of view. Fuller harmony, along with more clarity and simpler time signatures, is used in the pre-chorus and choruses. The vocalist moves to a higher tessitura, but still incorporates some of the motivic material in augmentation, followed by a descending stepwise pattern. The pre-chorus also begins in B minor, slipping back toward the opening tonic of F, before landing on the key of D major to move into the choruses. Even with the repeated loop-like phrases (common in much of rock music), there is a tonal sense of restlessness in both of the verses and pre-choruses.[15]

The chorus presents the listener with more stability and clarity—each line consists of more regular time signatures (three 4/4 measures followed by a 3/4 bar), a melody which begins and ends on the tonic pitch, and a major key tonality. Additionally, the melody, while still descending in stepwise motion (like the pre-choruses), flips (or inverts) the hook's leap direction, providing a nice contrary argument to the melodies of the verse/pre-chorus. The drumming here is much less complicated, as are the majority of the fills/melodic elaboration of the bass guitar part.[16]

The guitar solo in the midst of the piece is the most complex part of the song. While the key, chord progression, and time signature do not deviate through the whole of this section, each of the instruments plays against them. After affirming the key of D major, this solo section's change of mode to D minor hints that the choruses' winning argument has not been settled—bass guitar and drums begin this section with the bass working against the compound meter of 12/8 by dividing each measure (except the last of each phrase) into a 3/4 + 6/8 subgrouping against the drums' support of the overall 12/8 feel, moving around a harmonic loop of Dm (2 bars), F major, then one bar of B-flat major to E-flat major chords. The guitar solo begins with more technically simple material, based on a number of single-line string-bending pinched harmonics, becoming more and more virtuosic, with faster and more frantic figures. This culminates in a section where sliding eighth-note chord figures similar to the introduction's alternate with single-line motives and figures, while the bass and drums fully align with the 12/8 time signature. It's an excellent aural spotlight, the music coalescing into a kind of agreement after so much argument. So much of this solo seems to be delivered as someone repeatedly arguing, trying to make their point in more and more intense ways. Eventually, a seeming consensus is reached. Following this, an abbreviated (and slower) portion of the first measure of the introduction leads us into the pre-chorus, sans vocals.

The following pre-chorus features that portion of the lyrics which seems to be a rationale for being human, regardless of choice vs. election, delivered by Geddy Lee singing in his highest register:

Each of us, a cell of awareness,
imperfect and incomplete

Reinforced by the notion that genetics (one of the primary determiners of being human) produces an element of randomness rather than deterministic certainty, Geddy sings this in a strained, high register, doing his utmost to catch our attention and convince the listener—Peart's lyrics spin it thusly:

Genetic blends with uncertain ends
on a fortune hunt that's far too fleet

Rather than surety, it seems that to be human is to be spun into a short life, searching for meaning and fortune with no guarantee.

The change in point of view here is interesting, especially following the solo. It functions more like a bridge, whose role in most pop/rock songs is a change of view, movement to a different key area, or preparation to return to familiar music and key areas. Here, that change back to B minor has already been accomplished and feels like a relief from the intensity of the solo. However, the repeat of this pre-chorus section serves to underscore a failure to end in D major, with the implication being that in this object lesson, there is more to wrestle with. Because of the change in tessitura, this portion of the song sounds like an almost desperate attempt to convince the listener that all of us are "imperfect, incomplete on a fortune hunt." To question and embrace the choice *of* choice makes the most sense. A return to the chorus and its affirming D major key center affirms this.

The outro becomes a curious thing—beginning with the initial motive from the intro and verse in D major. Over the next four measures, it is sequenced to begin on F, B-flat, and then E-flat major, before moving into the opening two-measure descending scale (underscored by B-flat and F, one bar each[17]), before landing on a G major triad in the last measure. From a purely musical standpoint, this is very odd. This chord does *not* function as any sort of strong harmony in any of the keys from this song, and for a song with such a strongly argued position to end here detracts from the certainty of the argument, from a purely tonal music theory point of view.

However, the central argument of the song is that choice is better than predetermination or determinism. If the song were to follow expectation, the outro would be solidly in D major, and the four measures of the motive from the verse could easily be scored and harmonized that way. That is not how Lee and Lifeson chose to score it—rather, with full understanding of Peart's text, they end the song with an excellent musical illustration: they chose to end it, not as we expected, but as they *chose*.

BEYOND THE SONG

Many writers have noted that "Freewill" is likely is a criticism of the certainty of religion, especially those worldviews that hold that destiny or fate as immutable, and the outcome of our lives as predestined, whether through social, economic, educational, or other means.

Predestination as a theological tenet is most expressed through Calvinism, most notably in its Five Points, which were distilled as a defense against Arminianism, a theological movement in Protestant Christianity that arose as a liberal reaction to the Calvinist doctrine of predestination. The movement began early in the seventeenth century, *ca.* 1610, and asserted that God's sovereignty and human free will are compatible.[18] Calvinist codification into its Five Points cannot be dated precisely, but they are listed in *The Counter-Remonstrance of 1611* along with two additional points.[19]

The first of the Five Points of Calvinism is Total Inability or Total Depravity, which counters the first Arminianist Five Points, that of Freewill.

> 1. Total Inability or Total Depravity
> Because of the fall, man is unable of himself to savingly believe the gospel. The sinner is dead, blind, and deaf to the things of God; his heart is deceitful and desperately corrupt. His will is not free, it is in bondage to his evil nature, therefore, he will not—indeed he cannot—choose good over evil in the spiritual realm. Consequently, it takes much more than the Spirit's assistance to bring a sinner to Christ—it takes regeneration by which the Spirit makes the sinner alive and gives him a new nature. Faith is not something man contributes to salvation but is itself a part of God's gift of salvation—it is God's gift to the sinner, not the sinner's gift to God.[20]

Its remaining points are Unconditional Election, Limited Atonement, Irresistible Grace, and Perseverance of the Saints.

The first point of Arminianism (formulated earlier than those of Calvinism), that of Free Will, is set forth in the Five Articles of Remonstrance:

1. Free Will or Human Ability
Although human nature was seriously affected by the fall, man has not been left in a state of total spiritual helplessness. God graciously enables every sinner to repent and believe, but He does not interfere with man's freedom. Each sinner possesses a free will, and his eternal destiny depends on how he uses it. Man's freedom consists of his ability to choose good over evil in spiritual matters; his will is not enslaved to his sinful nature. The sinner has the power to either cooperate with God's Spirit and be regenerated or resist God's grace and perish. The lost sinner needs the Spirit's assistance, but he does not have to be regenerated by the Spirit before he can believe, for faith is man's act and precedes the new birth. Faith is the sinner's gift to God; it is man's contribution to salvation.[21]

The remaining points from the Five Articles of Remonstrance are: Conditional Election, Universal Redemption (or General Atonement), Resistance to the Holy Spirit, and Falling from Grace.

By contrast, Calvinism presents that humankind does not possess the ability to choose due to total depravity. Coupled with the second point of Unconditional Election (and indeed the other three points), Calvinism lays responsibility for salvation completely on God, implying that human responsibility plays little or no role. Both schools of thought support their points of view with scripture.[22] "Freewill" in both lyric and music challenges this point of view, clearly supporting the Arminianist point of choice. The second verse's lyrics cast a dark eye toward predestination, likening life to be "all pre-ordained, a prisoner in chains, a victim of venomous fate." The music is ever-changing, choosing new paths, new futures, denying the conventional and predictable choices of more common pop music.[23]

Those denominations and their resident theologians who embrace either Calvinism or Arminianism today still argue for their strongly held viewpoints. Calvinists from many of the Reformed Presbyterian congregations will go so far as to parse the differences between free will and choice, whereas most folks would not find many differences between the two. Many evangelical denominations hold to the prompting of the Holy Spirit, and that the individual has a choice in front of them, exercising their free will to accept the gift of salvation from God.

Indeed, the paradoxical nature that both election by God and choice of the person play into division between believer and unbeliever, illustrating the fourth point of both Arminianism and Calvinism: can the Holy Spirit be resisted, or is Grace irresistible?

Arguably, the most famous convert from nonbeliever to believer may be that of Saul of Tarsus, whose confrontation with Jesus on the road to Damascus made him into an apostle (Acts 9:3-9). Considering that Saul persecuted the early church, it may safely be assumed that he did not want nor choose to convert[24] (see Gal. 1:13-14). Yet, additional reading in Acts 9 further underscores God's irresistible choice of Saul:

> Then Ananias went to the house and entered it. Placing his hands on Saul, he said, "Brother Saul, the Lord—Jesus, who appeared to you on the road as you were coming here—has sent me so that you may see again and *be filled with the Holy Spirit.*" Immediately, something like scales fell from Saul's eyes, and he could see again. He got up and was baptized, and after taking some food, he regained his strength. (Acts 9:13-19—New International Version)

However, so many folks who have worked as missionaries, pastors, et al. can tell stories of folks who have resisted the call of the Holy Spirit; one of those who grew up with Christian relatives and who has read the Bible extensively was . . . Neil Peart. Many of his lyrics to songs such as "Faithless," "Roll the Bones," "Ghost of a Chance," "Stick it Out," or "The Watchmaker" reflect this: a disbelief in any religion, but someone who respected anyone's search as genuine. As he wrote in *Masked Rider*: "I'm a linear-thinking agnostic, but not an atheist, folks."[25] He later went into a great amount of detail about his views in a February 2013 interview with Jim Ladd on Sirius XM, where he discussed his reaction to religion and faith in more depth.

In the interview, Peart said:

> I went to Sunday school as a little kid and when they'd tell us to sing the song about god watches each sparrow fall and all of that, and I said well no, I don't really think so. When you look at the world now, I saw the comic and the great writer Stephen Fry the other day talking about that, he said people would say "what if you went to heaven and met God?" And he said oh, that wouldn't be a pleasant meeting. I'd say why did you create those parasites that grow behind babies' eyes and destroy their vision on the way out and all of that. That's not any kind of a god to be worshiping, is it?

> And I always say too, if I'm going to go up to heaven and meet St. Peter and Jesus and God and Allah and Buddha, whichever one you wanna pick, I'm gonna be okay, because I have lived a life based on that and I believe in generosity and charity and kindness and courtesy, those are things that just seem good to me anyway, I don't need a threat to make me behave that way and I don't need a reward."[26]

Peart's personal stance, however clearly implied by these interviews and the lyrics of "Faithless" and "Ghost of a Chance," is expanded to contain an additional layer of interpretation; the lyrics and music of "Freewill" lend themselves to the argument beyond the more obvious critique of religion, arguing the nature of predestination and choice. Peart has embraced the gift to choose his own path and embodied free will in his worldview. That last pre-chorus section of "Freewill" emphasizes *his* reasons for keeping his options open—all humans are merely a small part of the whole but are missing so much and are on a treasure hunt for truth that is too short to be certain.

Christian Rush fans over the years and on many online forums have discussed this to great lengths, acknowledging Peart's secular humanist/agnostic point of view, but have been grateful to find that this song from *Permanent Waves* extends to their belief systems as well. And when they've applied the lyrics of "Freewill" in their discussions of Christian theology, the topic of this chapter is nearly always the center of those posts and talks. And always, the conversations come back around to the central lyric based around choice. It is deliciously ironic to note that many will point out to their Calvinist brethren that to believe in that first point requires a choice to do so.

Peart would agree.

BEYOND THE BAND

While there are numerous examples of progressive rock musicians wrestling with existentialism, far fewer have worked through the ideas of determinism versus choice. Existential albums can be found from bands such as Pink Floyd's *Wish You Were Here* (1975), "A New Machine, Pts 1 & 2" from *A Momentary Lapse of Reason* (1988); Radiohead's *OK Computer* (1997), *Kid A* (2000), and *In Rainbows* (2007); King Crimson's *In the Court of the Crimson King* (1969); and Yes's *Close to the Edge* (1972), along with many others. Songs or albums that wrestle with freewill versus determinism are hard to come by.

A poll posted in The Prog Archives (www.progarchives.com) set an interesting question: "Which lyrics better express your thoughts on free will?" comparing the Rush song and Robert Wyatt's (Soft Machine) "Free Will and Testament"[27] which elicited a number of responses both for and against determinism.[28] Much of Wyatt's lyrics seem to push for a stance of 'soft-determinism,' yet the last lines of the song's lyrics state:

Had I been free, I could have chosen not to be me.
Demented forces push me madly round a treadmill.[29]

Other musicians might illustrate this dualism better; music by avant-garde classical composer John Cage in his works featuring indeterminacy as a compositional tool can illustrate the question, especially when considering those works of his employing chance operations *and* determinism. He often used the *I Ching* for his chance pieces composed since 1951. However, the 'free will' of these works was often based on predetermined musical elements. James Pritchett writes that works from *Music for Piano* were based on paper imperfections: the imperfections themselves provided pitches, and coin tosses and *I Ching* hexagram numbers were used to determine the accidentals, clefs, and playing techniques.[30]

Oddly enough, an article on the website *Thinking on Music* written by Jonathan L. Friedmann muddies the waters a bit more. He asserts that in general, a listener's basic music choices are governed by a kind of determinism, and our freedom of choice is illusory. Friedmann writes:

> critics (known as incompatibilists) hold that free will cannot exist in a universe governed by cause and effect. This means that, try though we might, our choices can never truly be unimpeded by prevailing factors.

And

> The sensation of free choice results from a "moment-to-moment ignorance" of the accumulating factors leading up to it. Third, free will can only exist if we are in control of all the variables that determine our thoughts and actions, including physical and emotional states, genetic traits, cultural conditioning, personal experiences, environmental settings, and so on.

> Musically, this suggests that we have little say in our choices: we like what we hear before we even hear it. Short-term choices—like playing a CD while doing laundry—and long-term affinities—like a favorite piece or recording artist—are not entirely rational or voluntary.[31]

CONCLUSION

It is perhaps a bit disingenuous[32] to use a band whose members' theological beliefs embrace agnosticism (at best) or atheism to illustrate a central tenet of Christianity, but Rush's "Freewill" points out that choice is the initial and possibly most fundamental arbiter in matters of faith, regardless of denomination, culture, or worldview. Free will (or choice) vs. election has been a long-standing argument within Christianity for centuries, and we live today in a world where this duality is diffused or watered down into many tints of theological possibilities. Yet, this argument still proves to be an ongoing one in many discussions about a central understanding of Christianity: are all saved by Christ's death and resurrection (by choosing to accept the truth of that sacrifice), or are only a portion of humanity saved because God 'elected' them or predetermined that they would be saved, leaving the remainder to be cast out?[33] The quote of the song's lyrics which begins this chapter provides an interesting perspective, one which many Christian fans of Rush have espoused: a very real gift from God to humanity is that of choice, not merely predestination. "Freewill" musically illustrates this theological argument of election vs. choice in a challenging, fast, loud, virtuosic, ever-changing song which confronts its listeners with their own choices. How will you decide?

NOTES

1. https://www.rush.com/band/.
2. https://www.rush.com/band/.
3. Interview with Neil Peart, *Beyond the Lighted Stage,* Sam Dunn, Scott MacFadyen, Banger Films/Zoe Records, 2010.
4. Peart interview, *Beyond the Lighted Stage.*
5. Heller, Jason—*An Introduction to Rush, the biggest cult band in the world*—AV Club—2013—There is a fair amount of controversy in this statement—after all, the band earned twenty-four gold, fourteen platinum and three multi-platinum albums over the course of their career, and is ranked fifth (behind the Beatles, The Rolling Stones, Kiss, and Aerosmith) on the all-time list for most consecutive gold or platinum studio albums by a rock band. (from the Canadian Music Hall of Fame)
6. Paul Elliott, "Alex Lifeson on Grilled Octopus, Police Brutality and Disco Biscuits," *Classical Rock,* August 27, 2022. https://www.loudersound.com/features/interview-alex-lifeson-on-grilled-octopus-police-brutality-and-disco-biscuits.
7. Geddy Lee, *My Effin' Life.* New York: HarperCollins, 2023, p. 289
8. Neil Peart, "A Port Boy's Story," *St Catherines Standard,* June 24 & 25, 1994—quoted on the Power Windows website.http://www.2112.net/powerwindows/transcripts/19940624stcatharinesstandard.htm.
9. Jeff Wagner, *Mean Deviation: Four Decades of Progressive Heavy Metal.* Bazillion Points, Brooklyn, NY, 2010, pp. 21–31.
10. Martin Popoff, *Limelight: Rush in the '80s.* ECW Press, Toronto, Ontario, 2020, p. 21
11. Neil Peart, *Entre Nous, Permanent Waves.* Core Music Publishing Mercury, Nashville, TN, 1980, 822, 548, 2.
12. Geddy Lee, *My Effin' Life,* p. 289
13. Peart, "Freewill."
14. Time signatures in the verses constantly change: 6/4, 4/4 (x2), 6/4, 7/4, 6/4, 7/4, 6/4, 4/4 (x2) following the melodic rhythm—the drum parts can be more simply explained by breaking all of the 6/4 and 4/4 measures into 2/4, with the 7/4 comprised of two 2/4 bars with a 3/4 measure. However, these drum patterns work at cross purposes at times with the vocal/guitar/bass parts, providing some of the cognitive dissonance of these parts of the song.
15. Peart creates a highly anxious mood around "those who think that life has nothing left to chance," the notion that all of the bad things in life are mere fate or destiny.

16. The constant change from line to line, chorus to chorus, becoming more and more complex over the course of the song—a possible nod to the notion that at the end of the day choice vs. predestination can be more complex over the alternative.

17. The opening two measures would be F lydian and C major scales, with F and C major harmony implied, one bar each.

18. Arminianism, Encyclopedia Britannica Online.

19. Peter DeJong, *"The Opinions of the Remonstrants (1618)"*. *Crisis in the Reformed Churches: Essays in Commemoration of the Great Synod of Dordt, 1618–1619 (PDF)*. Grand Rapids, MI: Reformed Fellowship, 1968.

20. David N. Steele and Curtis C. Thomas, *Romans: An Interpretive Outline*. Presbyterian & Reformed Publishing Co, 1963, Appendix D Pages 144–147.

21. Ibid.

22. See: *Calvinism & Arminianism: Controversial Passages* by Dennis McCallum and Gary DeLashmutt.
    https://dwellcc.org/learning/essays/calvinism-arminianism-controversial-passages.

23. Peart's dark imagery does, however, lend itself to an illustration of total depravity . . . .

24. Many New Testament scholars avoid the language of "conversion" in relation to Paul. Paul clearly represents a conversion from disbelief to belief, but because there has been a penchant for understanding him as a convert from Judaism to Christianity, many do not use this word. (cf. Acts 11:26 "And it was in Antioch that the disciples were first called Christians;" The author of Acts often refers to "The Way" throughout this book, including quoting Paul who says "But this I confess to you, that according to the Way, which they call a sect, I worship the God of our fathers, believing everything laid down by the Law and written in the Prophets"

25. Peart, *The Masked Rider*. Pottersfield Press, Lawrencetown Beach, Nova Scotia, 1996, p. 116, this passage is quoted several times in articles and obituaries, and so on, but *no one* lists a page number. On p. 116 of this book, this sentence reads: "The music of Vespers still wandered through my thoughts, and two epiphanies in one day had been too much for a linear-thinking agnostic like me." The discrepancy may be due to revisions put into place during a 2002 reprinting, or else it is just wishfully misquoted and repeated.

26. Ed Brayton, *Neil Peart on Religion*. Patheos, December 2017, this is part of a transcription from the interview with Jim Ladd—cf. with an interview Peart did with MacCleans.ca with Mike Doherty on August 13, 2012.

27. First recorded by Hugh Hopper & Kramer on the *A Remark Hugh Made* album, 1994.

28. Free Will, poll found in Progarchives.com. https://www.progarchives.com/forum/forum_posts.asp?TID=47173.

29. Robert Wyatt, "Free Will and Testament," Tess Music, ASCAP, BMI, GEMA.

30. James Pritchett, *The Music of John Cage*. Cambridge: Cambridge University Press, 1993, p. 94.

31. Jonathan L. Friedmann, "Music and the Myth of Free Will," *Thinking on Music,* November 6, 2014. https://thinkingonmusic.wordpress.com/2014/11/06/music-and-the-myth-of-free-will/.

32. Geddy would agree—in *My Effin Life* (p. 289) he writes "Even if some of Neil's concepts were a bit of a stretch for me, I sang it every night with confidence and pride, offering it to our audiences as a contribution to the time-honoured discussion about existentialism, determinism, and faith. It was, in fact, indeterminism that I believe was at the heart of it—the idea that our lives are not predetermined—and I hoped that would come across; but in the four decades since, I've seen people play fast and loose with the interpretation of the last lines of the chorus."

33. Echoes of the song from *Signals*: *Subdivisions:* "Be cool or be cast out;" Does your predetermined/Calvinistic salvation make you cool?

Chapter 7

Neal Morse's *Similitude of a Dream*
A Recasting of Pilgrim's Progress

Throughout the late 1980s, those bands that were venerated as the movers and shakers in progressive rock from its beginning days and into their dominance were not as popular as they once were. Bands such as Yes, Genesis, Kansas, and Pink Floyd had all broken up, shed and replaced primary members, or gone into hibernation. However, up-and-coming groups who named these initial bands as influences were just beginning to emerge in the early 1990s and become known as neo-prog. Bands such as Dream Theater, Opeth, Fates Warning, Porcupine Tree, the Flower Kings, and Spock's Beard led the way, reviving the genre even as grunge, new country, and hip-hop were ascendant in all of the record charts. As a member and principal songwriter for Spock's Beard, Neal Morse was a tireless and busy part of this renaissance, eventually becoming part of a number of other prog-related groups including Transatlantic and Flying Colors. Morse's music incorporates much of prog's language, combining styles and musical languages from many hard rock, pop, and classical works. His embrace of Christianity in 2002 put a pause to his work with a number of his successful collaborations with Spock's Beard and Transatlantic, albeit temporarily; he would work with both again. As a Christian, Morse has been vocal about his faith in nearly all of the music he has written since he embraced Christianity, whether through his solo records, Spock's Beard, or with Transatlantic or Flying Colors. He is restless and prolific as a songwriter and recording artist.[1] Since 2014, one of Morse's primary groups is his eponymously named group, the Neal Morse Band (now often known as NMB, since the release of *Innocence and Danger* in 2021). Their album from 2017, *The Similitude of a Dream*, is an adaptation of the great Puritan allegorical novel *A Pilgrim's Progress* written by John Bunyan, first published in 1678, including musical devices such as melody, form, and orchestration to expand its allegorical elements.[2] In what follows, we shall bring the wider subject of religious allegory to bear on this album with particular attention to how Morse utilizes, adapts, and at times diverges from his allegorical source material.

THE BAND

The Neal Morse Band (NMB) as a Recording Artist

This group consists of keyboardist/guitarist/vocalist Morse, drummer/vocalist Mike Portnoy, guitarist/vocalist Eric Gillette, bassist Randy George, and multi-instrumentalist/vocalist Bill Hubauer. All sing and write the music on their records, although Neal Morse is the principal lyricist and conceptualist. This group originated out of Morse's solo career after he left Spock's Beard and Transatlantic in 2002 to focus on more readily integrating his Christian faith into his musical career.

As mentioned above, Neal Morse has been a tireless musician who has written and recorded a lot of music, whether as part of a group or as a singer-songwriter. His first recording was *The Light* (1995), originally released on SynPhonic records. This record established a number of Morse's characteristic trademarks: long-form song structures (especially on the title track, one of Spock's Beard's most played works[3]), lyrical depth and whimsy, and an amalgamation of musical styles. He would write and record five more albums with the Beard—*Beware of Darkness* (1996), *The Kindness of Strangers* (1998), *Day for Night* (1999), *V* (2000), and *Snow* (2002)—along with two solo albums that were less progressive rock and more straight-ahead singer-songwriter style pop-rock—*Neal Morse* (1999) and *It's Not Too Late* (2002). During this period in his career, he was also part of the progressive rock group Transatlantic, recording two albums with them during the early part of this century: *SMPT:e* (2000) and *Bridge Across Forever* (2001).[4]

After the album *Snow*, Morse released the *Testimony* album in 2003, made with a large number of collaborators, including Kerry Livgrin from Kansas, but featuring Mike Portnoy, with whom he had collaborated in Transatlantic and who would become a mainstay in most of the rock or progressive rock music he would make from this point onward. Quite a few prog albums follow this record: *One* (2004, featuring Randy George on bass), *?* (2005), *Solo Scriptura* (2007), *Lifeline* (2008), *Testimony 2* (2011), *Momentum* (2012, featuring Eric Gillette and Bill Hubauer), and *Sola Gratia* (2020). Morse's recording career includes non-progressive rock music with straight-ahead singer-songwriter albums, worship music for churches, compilation albums, and musicals. As of early 2024, he has recorded an astonishing forty-eight studio albums, forty-three live albums, and sixteen compilation and rarities albums, along with a large number of video and fan-centered "Inner Circle" exclusive recordings.[5] While he has made his way as a solo artist under his own name for many years, he continues to collaborate with most of the musicians he's worked with over the years, including Spock's Beard, with whom he reunited during the 2016 Morsefest, performing all of their album *Snow* for the first time.[6]

Of all the musicians he has worked with, Morse has most often collaborated with drummer Michael Portnoy, working with him in many of Morse's solo records as well as in groups such as Transatlantic and Flying Colors. Portnoy is a very well-known virtuosic musician who also shares Neal's relentless urge to perform and collaborate.[7] He is best known as the drummer and cofounder of Dream Theater, one of neo-progressive rock's seminal bands. In that group, he was also one of the principal songwriters and later, coproducer (along with guitarist John Petrucci) of many of their albums. He left Dream Theater in 2010 and has only recently (2023) returned to that group. In the interim, he worked with a number of groups, most notably Avenged Sevenfold, Adrenaline Mob (which he cofounded), Winery Dogs, Sons of Apollo, Metal Allegiance, BPMD, and others, as well as Transatlantic and Flying Colors with Neal Morse.

He is a very highly regarded musician who can be heard on albums like Dream Theater's *Images and Words* (1992), *Metropolis 2: Scenes from a Memory* (1999), *Six Degrees of Inner Turbulence* (2002), and *Systematic Chaos* (2007); Liquid Tension Experiment's three albums (with Dream Theater's Petrucci and keyboardist Jordan Rudess, along with master bassist/stick player Tony Levin); Sons of Apollo's *Psychotic Symphony* (2017), the Winery Dogs' eponymous first album (2013); and any of the three Cover to Cover records he has done with Morse, Randy George, and a host of guests, along with the works he's done with Transatlantic, Flying Colors, and other Neal Morse projects.[8]

Randy George connected with Neal Morse shortly after he had recorded *Testimony* and became part of the touring band for that album's tour.[9] Known primarily as the bassist for the Morse band, he is a multi-instrumentalist, arranger, and producer, who also cofounded the progressive rock band Ajalon.[10] This trio formed in Seattle and released three albums: *Light at the End of the Tunnel* (1996), *On the Threshold of Eternity* (2005, including guest performances from keyboardist Rick Wakeman, along with some additional vocals by Neal Morse), and *This Good Place* (2023). One reviewer wrote of Ajalon:

> Imagine that born again Christian and songwriter extraordinaire Kerry Livgren (of Kansas fame) would have formed a new band in the present millennium together with Rick Wakeman, Phil Keaggy and Neal Morse and you have a pretty good idea of what the music of Ajalon is like.[11]

He has also done a number of solo records: *In Light of the King's Countenance* (2004) and *Action Reaction* (2012) are instrumental works, and *Beyond Words* (2023). This most recent recording includes collaborations with Morse, guitarist Eric Gillette, and his wife Pamela George, with whom he regularly collaborates in the Phoenix, Arizona, area.

Guitarist and vocalist Eric Gillette is a prominent member of the Neal Morse Band—his first professional record was with the Swon Brothers for their debut album in 2010. Like all members of the Morse band, he is a multi-instrumentalist and has been featured as a drummer during several Morsefests. He has also performed numerous cover songs where he plays and sings all of the parts, including Queen's "Bohemian Rhapsody." He has released four solo recordings: *Afterthought* (2013), *The Great Unknown* (2016), *Covers Vol. 1* (2022), and *A New Day* (2020), which is a New Age-esque electronic orchestra recording. He has also recorded with Tree of Life, Lazleitt, Patema, and others. In 2023, he formed the progressive metal band TEMIC with former Haken keyboardist Diego Tejeida and released the album *Terror Management Theory*.[12]

Like Mike Portnoy, keyboardist, vocalist, and instrumentalist Bill Hubauer began his musical career at Boston's famed Berklee School of Music but became a full-time software engineer with Adobe. However, music has always been a large part of his life. Prior to his audition with Morse, Hubauer cofounded Ten Point Ten, recording *Blue* (2007), *Cartography* (2000), and the albums *Eleven* and *12 25* in 2003. After touring with Ten Point Ten supporting the Christian parody group the ApologetiX in 1997, he then joined that group in 2000. He initially played keyboards and guitar for their tours, but eventually became more involved with the group, producing their frequent record releases.[13] He has also toured and recorded with Joe Deninzon & Stratospheerious (Deninzon is the newest violinist with Kansas), and cofounded the band We Came From Space and recorded *How to Be Human* (2013), *While You Were Away* (2018), *Reasons in the Rhyme* (2020), and *Overlords* (2023) with them. Hubauer has played many different instruments within the Neal Morse Band, playing saxophone and clarinet, mandolin, keyboards, and singing with the group.

The Neal Morse Band's beginnings lie in the recordings that Morse did featuring some of the aforementioned players. In 2012, he decided to put together a more established group that was separate from his solo progressive rock releases (such as *Sola Scriptura* and *Solo Gratia*). He began to hold auditions, first by soliciting videos from performers, and then by holding in-person auditions at his Radiant Studios in Nashville, Tennessee.[14] Brazilian guitarist Adson Sodre was originally part of the band (which was to tour behind Neal's solo album *Momentum*), but was not retained due to visa issues.[15] He was replaced by that tour's second guitarist, Eric Gillette.

As of the beginning of 2024, the band has recorded four studio albums—*The Grand Experiment* (2015), *Similitude of a Dream* (2016), *The Great Adventure* (2019), *Innocence and Danger* (2021)—and eight live albums. Four of those live records were recorded at various Morsefests in Tennessee, and three of them were recorded (all in Europe) after the last three studio albums were released and toured. Of the four albums, two are concept albums using the same source material that is discussed in this chapter: *The Similitude of a Dream*, covering the first part of John Bunyan's *A Pilgrim's Progress*, and *The Great Adventure*, covering part two of that story. The remaining two studio albums were written as collections of unrelated songs, some more progressive than others, some shorter than long, and containing one or two cover songs as well as material by the group.

Songwriting is shared by all of the members of the band, although Neal Morse is held to be the main conceptualist and principal lyricist. While a number of secular songs are part of the band's repertoire (especially the cover songs), four of the five band members are Christian and have extensive work in the CCM industry; Mike Portnoy is Jewish. Consequently, the overall tenor of the group's spiritual output is Christian, mostly evangelical in nature. In the Catholic World Report, Bradley J. Birzer characterizes Morse in this way:

> With the zeal of the convert, all of Morse's releases have dealt with Christianity in one form or another, and Morse, using every skill he learned before and during his time in Spock's Beard, has done his best to baptize and sanctify the genre of progressive rock. If Wilson is a bit of a mischievous trickster figure, Morse is the Chestertonian fool, the man who gives his all to God, indifferent to the standards of the world and content to be judged only by his Maker. The world sees him as the fool, but he is, in actuality, a sort of Jeremiah.[16]

THE ALBUM

Work on the album that became *The Similitude of a Dream* began in December 2015—Morse discussed the album's genesis in an interview with Michael Young, conducted while the NMB was touring the album:

> Funny story, it actually started with a Facebook post, that led me to the 1670's book "Pilgrim's Progress" by John Bunyan. I'd never read it, so I really didn't give it a second thought at the time, but for some reason it popped into my mind around December of 2015. I was writing some ideas and thought I needed some direction and I remembered it, so I took my phone out and googled—*Pilgrims Progress SparkNotes*—I started jotting things down, reading more, there just seemed to be something there, that's how it started for me.[17]

Writing with the full band began the following month, with everyone in the group contributing to its music and Morse writing all of the lyrics.[18] Prior to the adoption of *Pilgrim's Progress*, the band had sought to release a single disc's worth of music, but the scope of the project seemed to dictate that a double disc was required. This caused some dissension between Mike Portnoy and the rest of the group. During this period of his career, Portnoy had left Dream Theater and was working with a number of groups. Dream Theater had recently released a double-disc concept album, *The Astonishing* (2016), and Portnoy did not want to be seen as actively competing with them for this NMB record. However, after the initial disagreement, the longer recording was made and was fully embraced by the whole band, with the release of *Similitude* occurring in November of 2016.

The Similitude of a Dream is an adaptation of what is Part One of the Bunyan novel, necessarily condensing 162 pages (as printed in 1678) of material into roughly 9 pages of lyrics and 106 minutes of running time spread over two compact discs. While the double-disc recording is divided into twenty-three tracks, Morse views the whole of this album as one piece.[19] Indeed, with many of the ends of one track leading directly into the next track, it is sometimes hard to determine when one "song" ends and the next one begins.

The record opens with "Long Day," which isn't how the novel begins, but seems to be a rumination by the first-person singer of the album, exhausted and haunted, sung by a modern-day version of Christian. Instead of stepping into the rest of the novel, this album moves into the "Overture," which introduces musical themes from many upcoming songs: "A Road Called Home," The Ways of a Fool," Slave to Your Mind," "Slough," "Confrontation" and "The Battle" and "Broken Sky/Long Day (Reprise)." This track moves directly into "The Dream," which does match the beginning of the *Pilgrim's Progress*. The second half of this song's lyrics and its musical setting may be equated to the evangelistic call experienced by many Christians at the beginning of their journey, a call that tugs at one's very soul.

The next four tracks illustrate Christian (as written and mostly sung by Morse) wrestling with the idea that he must leave the City of Destruction. He initially seeks guidance from his wife (who chooses not to accompany him, setting up the follow-up album, *The Great Adventure*, based on Part Two of *Pilgrim's Progress*), leaving the City and the attempts by Christian's neighbors[20] to bring him back to the City. The protagonist sings to himself in "City of Destruction," the music strident, argumentative, and pushing forward and falling into "We Have Got to Go." This plea to his wife is folk-like, simple, and earnest. The instrumental solo which ends this track changes the scene into the beginning of the journey itself. Both "Makes No Sense" and "Draw the Line" portray the beginnings of that journey, the first of these songs illustrating an internal monologue describing how Christian feels about the arguments his neighbors are presenting (labeling them "the awakening dead!"). "Makes No Sense" ends with a lyrical and musical sense of light and hope following the confusion felt by Christian. "Draw the Line" is a mocking yet hard-rocking portrayal of the arguments presented by Christian's neighbors, along with Christian's counterarguments. This track ends with what seems to be the character of Pliable (again, not named[21]) agreeing to join Christian on the journey. The music shifts to "Something So Beautiful," before using a lounge-like bluesy-jazzy instrumental coda to move into "The Slough."

Following the novel, the next few tracks illustrate Christian meandering from the path to the Wicket Gate, bogged down in "The Slough," a kind of keyboard-led traveling music, by turns adventuresome, hopeful, but pulled in many directions, and kind of aimless. The music is pulled back into focus by a short bass solo playing one of the main themes from the Overture before segueing into "Back to the City." Here, Pliable makes a U-turn and verbally strikes out at Christian, calling him a liar; Christian's reply is heartbroken but still pleads with Pliable to trust in him who will "wipe every tear from your eyes." While the end of this song changes direction, representing Christian's encounter with Help who pulls him out of The Slough, "The Ways of a Fool" presents The Worldly Wiseman's pitch to Christian, who is seduced by this rascal's arguments. This track stylistically covers a lot of ground, with its Beatles/Beach Boys vocal harmonies, coupled with instrumental breaks that borrow from Genesis and Kansas, followed by a sinister guitar version of the main tune in this song which culminates in a Queen-like frenzy of harmony. It ends with Christian singing a version of the hopeful section of "The Dream," substituting the word "Life" for "Love," twisting the meaning of hope/love from the original dream to simple worldly experience.[22]

> Forget all about that dream, I'll find a place in between, and just take a turnabout tomorrow.[23]

This track ends with a return of the sinister guitar, played on a scratchy LP record on a cheap record player, which is followed by a very wistful keyboard solo, again echoing a theme that is featured in many places on the record—here, a veiled vision of hope.

Christian soon repents his choice, and the last two tracks before the intermission correspond to the portion of the novel where Evangelist helps Christian back to the path to the Wicket Gate. The rocker "So Far Gone" seems to be sung to the Evangelist, and within this song, Morse (as Christian) doubts his ability to continue due to his waywardness and sin, just "too far gone." However, in a foreshadowing of the ending to this album, the Evangelist sings back to him that you can turn and you are not "too far gone." In one of the best lyrics from the album, he sings

The King loves you with all his heart
And every lie can be made true, for I have seen the broken sky turn blue[24]

Christian then returns to the path and the Wicket Gate, changing the earlier lyric about the arguments of his neighbors ("It makes zero sense to me"), and recasting its music from "Makes No Sense" to the words "It now makes sense to me." At this moment, Christian moves securely toward the Wicket Gate, eventually moving to the end of his journey. "The Breath of Angels" is an initial climactic musical moment where Christian realizes what the reward will be for his faith and persistence on this journey, putting aside fear and breathing in the breath of angels that casts out every fear and dries every tear. The music builds into a state of ecstasy, and the guitar solo in the midst of this track prefigures the ultimate end of the whole. However, while this initial climax sounds like the end, it's only a pause. This song corresponds to the section of the novel where Christian comes to the Wicket Gate and is admitted by Good, the gatekeeper; there is still more to the journey and some tribulations yet to endure. This song (the last on disc one of the two-CD set) ends with a pulsing repeated guitar chord which abruptly stops.

In a live concert presentation of this piece, this is where the intermission occurs—up to this point, *The Similitude of a Dream* has been fairly faithful to the novel in terms of one scene following another, and major characters and places are represented, although not always named as such. This will change in the pieces for the second half. In this part of the piece, many scenes and characters from the book are omitted, changed, condensed, or presented out of order.

Disc two (or Act Two, if it is performed live) opens with "Slave to Your Mind," set in the House of the Interpreter with Christian describing what he sees, being instructed by the Interpreter on Christian grace. Characters shift in this track, from Christian to the narrator, then (for a bit) to Satan, and back to Christian describing the wonders of God in this house. Much from this location in the novel is left out or rearranged—missing sections include the two children Passion and Patience, and the Stately Palace, while The Man in the Iron Cage is moved to its own track. Yet The Dusty Parlor, the Woman with Water (the Gospel), the Wall of Fire and vision of God feeding that fire are all present and presented as if in a fever dream—fast, aggressive, with Satan still battling for Christian's soul. There is some excellent aggressive musical interplay at the end of this piece—virtuosic single beat tradeoffs between all of the instrumentalists, culminating in a keyboard solo which segues into the next song.

By way of contrast, "Shortcut to Salvation" follows (out of order from the novel—see below), and it's a complete change from what precedes it. Sung by Formalist and Hypocrisy, they try to tempt Christian to follow their shortcut in a breezy, carefree manner that really echoes some of Supertramp's musical language (especially the saxophone break in the middle), only to be turned away by Christian singing the music that will become the record's apotheosis—it is a nice touch that Christian (here sung by Gillette) and his two detractors sing the last part of this song in counterpoint, in two utterly oppositional points of view.

In contrast to the novel's running order, "The Man in the Iron Cage" is moved away from its original place, which was in the House of the Interpreter; musically it makes a huge contrast, taking the cheerful waywardness of the last track and destroying it. In the novel, this character may be one of the most fundamentally lost, simply because he no longer believes in the forgiveness that is given to him that he once preached as a minister. His music is angry, bleak, and despairing—even when Christian (sung by Morse) offers to him that "you are never too far gone," turning his own words and music (from "So Far Gone") into a message of hope, The Man in the Iron Cage rejects him out of hand, again refusing the proffered forgiveness. Much of the music in this track is reminiscent of "Black Dog" by Led Zeppelin, a kind of call and response between the main subject of this song and the dark rage of his fate. Moving directly into "The Road Called Home," the opening of this song moves forward and shifts, still somewhat aggressively, moving back and forth with music that turns back on itself, twisting, modulating, trying to pull itself out of the gloom of the previous track. This morphs and changes, culminating in a keyboard solo that is very Dennis DeYoung/Styx like—but then shifts and changes again and again before falling into the lyric, which is sung by the Narrator, introducing the characters of Simple and Sloth. (Again, the running order here is changed—if the NMB were to follow the book, the next three tracks would have "Freedom Song" and "I'm Running" follow the events from the House of the Interpreter followed by "Sloth" and then followed by the events of "Shortcut to Salvation.")

"Sloth" begins with a nice example of text painting in its flexible tempo and out-of-time vocal entry. (There's also a nice use of solo voice in a first-person point of view, changing to a vocal chorus to ask questions of Christian.) The song then shifts to Christian's point of view, singing a reprise of "A Long Day" (accompanied by a very Beatles-like guitar line). This reprise is very much like what we'll get in the last track; it's as if the journey is approaching its glorious end, and the protagonist is growing more confident in his faith, and that confidence is reflected in the music he sings. Here it ends with a high, simple bass solo playing the first theme of the "Overture," echoed by the same music on guitar—mellow, not challenging, as if affected by Sloth a little bit.

"Freedom Song" is a joyful, almost Eagles-like country rock song—again, as mentioned above, out of order according to Bunyan's novel. (This and the following track should come after the Interpreter's house.) It nonetheless makes a good musical contrast after Sloth, expressing the delight of releasing one's burdens. Sung by the narrator (Morse), the choruses are covered by all of the singers in the NMB voicing the Three Shining Ones from the novel. Multi-instrumentalist Bill Hubauer shines with some excellent mandolin here. Where this track provides the offer and promise extended to Christian, "I'm Running" presents the reaction to that burden's release from Christian himself—the lyrics here portray the goofy, Southern California quasi-hippy that reflects Morse's youth in that state. George plays the track's initial interlude, a joyous, flashy bass solo which is answered by a flurry of horns that reflect the lyrics' "GTO engine gunning . . . " The joy keeps spinning for the song's ending, with the vocalists repeatedly singing:

Can there be more? (but wait there's more)
More, more, more (More in store...)[25]

Yet the song ends somewhat wistfully with another plaintive bass solo, then segues into "The Mask."

At this point, the recording and the novel diverge: "Shortcut to Salvation's" scene happens here, and the NMB leave out many of the scenes and quite a number of plot points and details that follow it. Missing are the Hills of Difficulty, the Arbor (Christian falling asleep and losing his scroll[26]), the characters Timorous and Mistrust, the Palace Beautiful and the discussion within it with Prudence, Discretion, Piety, and Charity, who also take Christian to its armory.

"The Mask," following the keyboard segue from "I'm Running," begins with a piano cadenza, morphing into a heavily effected piano part where the figure is spread over a great part of the keyboard—uneasy, broken. This song serves as the intro and transition to the confrontation with Apollyon portrayed in the next track. Christian (now in the Valley of Humiliation) discusses what is really in his heart, hidden by the mask that he (like everyone) wears, and describes the approach of Apollyon. This song is very illustrative in its text painting: even the synth sounds are ugly and aggressive. This song moves directly into "Confrontation." As one would expect, this is a hard-rocking, confessional/confrontational song sung by Christian (Morse) and Apollyon (Portnoy), with the demon accusing Christian and claiming him as lawful prey due to the former's sin. However, Christian counters with his faith in God. Musically, there are a couple of excellent quotations from previous songs: Apollyon twisting the lyrics sung by the Evangelist in "The Man in the Iron Cage": "You are never too far gone" becomes "You are surely too far gone" as sung by the demon. The instrumental section that follows quotes from the "Overture" and leads to Apollyon's demand for Christian to return to the City of Destruction, using that song's music to hammer his message home. The music twists and turns, followed by a back-and-forth, line-by-line taunting between the two characters, before the physical battle erupts, initially portrayed by an angry organ solo accompanied by a fast double-bass drum pattern.[27]

"The Battle" is a turbulent, constantly changing instrumental piece, full of shifting musical gestures and odd time signatures—two hard-hit chords open this piece, moving into odd keyboard spindrifts, then shifting into a whirlwind of instrumental figures. The music always pushes forward, moving with lots of juxtapositions and instrumental tradeoffs, using material that was previewed in the "Overture," "Slough," and other places. Strangely, this material seems less battle-like and less scary than some of what has been featured in previous instrumental breaks—in some ways, it's more of a flight of virtuosity instead. All of the instruments normally played by the NMB are effectively used, sharing space with some additional instruments including marimba, which lends a kind of Frank Zappa color to the orchestration. The track ends after an instrumental climb to a solid high-note cadence followed by a moment of pause.[28]

The final track is a combination of two songs: "Broken Sky/Long Day Reprise" opens quietly, with material from the "Overture" played on piano. Christian (sung by Neal) sings a shortened summary of the whole piece, beginning with the emotions and tribulations that he faced, moving into how he was able to overcome his fear and move into the chorus of "Broken Sky," whose music was first sung by the Evangelist in "So Far Gone:" "Where I have seen and I have known/By setting down the road called home."[29] The second verse returns to the opening introspection, asking four questions ("Why go through all of the trouble . . . "etc.[30]) before answering them and moving into the chorus (sung by Eric Gillette) with growing confidence. The music of the bridge repurposes the ending of "City of Destruction," transforming that track's lyrics from one of fear and flight into a vision of light, song, an open door, and ultimately coming home. The last line is an invitation to all listeners—the lyrics here are no longer inward-facing but address *us*: "There's so very much more/As together *we* (emphasis mine) seek to come home."

The instrumental interlude which follows is the first of three increasingly ecstatic bursts, featuring music from the first theme of the "Overture," here played with confidence and joy, leading into the last chorus, which is sung with great certainty.[31] The second instrumental interlude features keyboard work reminiscent of Dennis DeYoung's work in Styx and functions as the transition leading into the second track "Long Day (reprise)," transforming the album's first song from weariness and despair to the discovery of salvation and its protagonist's move from exile in the City of Destruction to coming home to the Celestial City. The music is big and open, and using material from the first track, now cast into a higher key, D-flat major, up a perfect fourth from G-flat major, and as mentioned above, sung by Eric Gillette, who typically sings those songs due to his higher vocal range. His last lyric before the last instrumental interlude again includes an invitation to the listeners, in a final invitation to join him ("c'mon").

This last interlude is the final culmination of ecstasy, each building on the intensity of the previous ones, and so very reminiscent of highly emotional music one can find in evangelical (especially Pentecostal) worship music: additional instruments are added to the band, the keys rise higher and higher in pitch, and the progression moves from understandable lyrics to wordless or instrumental music. Once this interlude cadences, the music shifts to a simple coda sung by Morse and accompanied by a very restrained organ and piano, which move upward and are open-ended and up in the air, rather than presenting a final authentic cadence. The music is an adaptation of the last part of "Makes No Sense" and presents the listener in this last part of the album's last track with the fulfillment of hope and the encouragement to take the seemingly daunting journey: you're just one step away. Lyrically, the words all tie up various themes from prior songs with a positive outlook: "to be the completed man, to love and understand, to change everything I am, it now makes sense to me . . . ."[32]

Morse's adaptation transforms the language into contemporary American vernacular, whose tone veers from poetic to pop culture everyman.[33] There is little change to Bunyan's narrative, although the necessary condensation causes some of the characters from the novel to be omitted or combined. While the essential story is preserved, it can be hard to discern what characters are present and from whose point of view the lead vocalist is singing. Indeed, in some songs, differing characters are singing from a first-person perspective, and the switch is not always easily perceived. Even in the printed lyrics, no character is named, and so the listener must determine whether the current singer is merely the narrator, Christian, Pliable, a neighbor, Christiana (Christian's wife), the Worldly Wiseman, et al., and often changing point of view within the same song, occasionally sharing the same melodies/harmonies.[34]

The biggest conflation about characters might be between a narrator and the main character of Christian (who is never named within the context of the album). In songs such as the opening tracks "Long Day" and "The Dream," it is clear that the narrator is singing, but in "Slave to Your Mind" (which opens the second CD), Christian begins the song but switches to the narrator's point of view for a brief moment with the lines, "I saw in my dream, the interpreter and the man, behind a wall of flame, He took him by the hand."[35] This is the place on this album where there seems to be an implication that the narrator *is* Christian, blurring the separation that has been shown in other songs, both prior to this and following this track.

Along with editorial trimming of various scenes, situations, chapters, and characters from Bunyan's novel, the ordering of songs on *Similitude* differs from *Pilgrim's Progress*. While this makes good musical sense based on the feel and musical content of the album's tracks, some of this ordering is extreme when compared to the novel. The most noticeable of these happens in the second half of the album (disc 2), where the placement of "Shortcut To Salvation" precedes "The Man in the Iron Cage." In the novel, the Man in the Iron Cage is found in the House of the Interpreter, which is the subject of the song "Slave to Your Mind." If placed in proper *Pilgrim's Progress* running order, the songs should go "Slave to Your Mind," "The Man in the Iron Cage," "Freedom Song" (reflecting Christian's burden falling from his back), followed by "The Road Called Home," "Sloth," and "Shortcut to Salvation."[36] Morse addresses some of this in his Pop Matters interview with Jordan Blume:

> We skip a bit ahead after that to get to the happy ending. I did the same thing on *Testimony*, actually. It just felt like it was the right thing to do at that point. You want to get to the satisfying place and end on a positive note. Sometimes you have to skip a bit of the story. It reminds me of that Monty Python thing: [imitates English accent] "Let's skip a bit, brother! Let the people just feast upon the lands and the orangutans and the sweets"[37] [laughs]. Yeah, so it just felt like the right thing to do.[38]

Additionally, the opening track "Long Day" is unique to Morse's adaptation of *Pilgrim*, because it jumps into the main narrative of the story; the novel's version begins with the material in *Similitude's* third track "The Dream." "Long Day" is followed by the instrumental "Overture," more typically an opening of a concert, opera, or piece of musical theater. However, Morse's ordering has logical musical underpinnings since "Long Day" is reprised at the end of the whole record to be followed by the ecstatic instrumental break and its peaceful ending, recasting the doubt of "Makes No Sense" into a coda of completion and making a nice set of bookends between the first and last tracks.[39]

Bunyan's text has been transformed and condensed into a more personalized tale, and characters have been reduced and shifted so the whole of the tale is less about the multitude of characters and their related, allegorical roles (Hopeless, Ignorance, Patience, Purity, Evangelist, et al.). Morse's text describes interactions with many of these players, but often elides past who they are. This lack of characters' names from the novel also makes the allegory contemporary to each member of the audience, rather than casting it back to the original, medieval, unsubtle naming device such as Pliable or Obstinate. Exceptions are Sloth, the Man in the Iron Cage, Apollyon, and the Worldly Wiseman. A good example of how the lyrics slip past the change of character happens in the song "Draw the Line," where Christian has sent his neighbors and Obstinate back to the City of Destruction (those characters not named in the song), to be joined by Pliable for the last third of this track, who sings, "I think I see your way/I'd really like to know/If only for one day/ something so beautiful"[40] A listener may be confused by not knowing which character sings this part; this is continued by the move into "Back to the City" where the first sung lines contain, "You said all would be well/But you lied!/ Yeah, you lied/So I'm going back/I'm going back, yeah/ I'm going back to the City"[41] Since Neal Morse sings both of these parts, it would be easy to believe that the character of Christian sings both since Neal most often sings the parts of that character, resulting in confusion. However, the original's Puritan tone as translated into a modern evangelical dialect is not obfuscated by these omissions.

Much of the original novel's point of view is cast as a typical story,[42] with characters speaking their lines and the omniscient narrator filling in the details of place, situation, and providing descriptions of every kind. *The Similitude of a Dream* is different; many (if not most) of the lyrics are in first person, even if the character is not the protagonist. This makes the audience become quite intimate with the tale, almost as if we're hearing it for the first time, person-to-person, without the distance of a piece of art, a novel, or a film, three steps removed. This is quite similar to the way many Christians present their personal testimonies, and very similar to the title of Morse's own autobiography: *Testimony, the Inspirational and Spiritual Journey of a Prog Rock Musician*.[43] In his interview with Morse, Derek Walker notes:

> Looking across the ideas that Morse has used for his concept albums, it becomes clear how often he takes a fairly esoteric theme, such as the glory of God or the Fall, and personalises it, so that listeners can relate to it. By putting it into people's personal perspectives, listeners can hear it being sung from the inside. Add his own biography in the two *Testimony* albums, and you can see how Morse is a born storyteller.

Morse: "I try to do that," he concurred. "I'm excited about that. It gets me up in the morning, trying to take deep spiritual matters and put them in hopefully, poetic ways, but ways that people can feel and relate to. That was the challenge with *Similitude* lyrically: wanting to take the concepts in this very old book and make it relatable today. I really enjoyed working on *Similitude*, because it fell together in such a great flow."[44]

As mentioned elsewhere in this book, progressive rock music is often characterized by its use of many different styles and the fusion of many of those into a polyglot of musical languages; this album displays that over and over. Given the backgrounds of the individual musicians who wrote and performed this album, it should not be a surprise. Morse, George, and Portnoy's involvement with the Beatles tribute band Yellow Mallow Custard, along with their three Cover to Cover albums, and Gillette's frequent release of cover tunes on YouTube and on disc, show their intense interest and commitment to music by their influences and contemporaries. Hubauer's membership and producing duties with the Christian parody band the ApologetiX cause him, by the very nature of that group, to become quite intimate with the style and musical languages of those bands the ApologetiX appropriated. All of that is on display here. There are shades of the Beatles ("City of Destruction," "The Ways of a Fool"), Kansas ("The Ways of a Fool," "Overture," "The Battle," "The Slough"), Supertramp ("Shortcut to Salvation"), Emerson, Lake, and Palmer ("Ways of a Fool"), Styx ("The Road Called Home" intro, "We Have Got to Go"), and others. In many ways, this has always been a musical fingerprint of Morse, who will often quote small bits of text or name-drop in many of his pieces (cf. the mention of the Genesis album *The Wind and the Wuthering* in Spock's Beard's "All on a Sunday" cast as "the wind and the weathering were on channel 14"[45]). In an interview with Jordan Blume, Morse acknowledges this stylistic borrowing in answering a question about self-borrowing when the NMB writes:

> Well, the band will toss out ideas or say, "Well, is that too much like something else you did, or like some Yes song, or whatever." A lot of times when you're writing, you have those concerns; sometimes you'll be really inspired about something and you'll really feel it, but then you'll think, like, *Oh, wow. That's exactly like this Supertramp song*. It definitely happens. I try not to worry about it too much because I'm just kind of moving forward in God, and I try not to worry so much about what people think and just trust in God.[46]

Like many progressive rock concept records (and indeed the operas, oratorios, and cantatas they're modeled after), there is much musical sharing of themes between various tracks, some introduced in the "Overture," much like the large-scale classical pieces after which an album such as this is modeled. Portnoy is given credit for insisting on this practice (having done it before with other double-disc albums such as Dream Theater's *Metropolis, Scenes from a Memory 2*[47]), and the strength and quality of the thematic material throughout *Similitude* make this musical technique shine.[48]

Taken as a whole, the allegory of Bunyan's *Pilgrim's Progress* is masterfully transformed by the NMB on this album, and the whole group stretches out musically to portray this more intimate reading of the story. Indeed, while the whole of this adaptation hews fairly close to the overall story of the novel, the allegorical nature of Bunyan is not portrayed by the lyrics as much as the music, especially when they can expand in the various interludes or instrumental pieces. In this way, this album presents a unique allegorical representation, one that exists in the musical language more so than the personal lyrics of Morse. It's not a one-to-one correlation, like the concept of leitmotiv in Wagner's operas, where ideas and characters are portrayed by a musical snippet or a particular instrument, but often an emotional one, with the shared musical themes between various songs recast, reordered, and presented with new lyrics displaying new allegorical relationships along Christian's journey.

Lastly, *The Similitude of a Dream* represents the high-water mark in the Neal Morse Band's career both in its critical and popular response. Along with excellent reviews, it also won a number of fan polls and other awards, including album of the year from Prog Radio, the Prog Report, The Fire Note, and Rock at Night.[49] This enthusiasm was shared by the band; shortly after the album was completed, Mike Portnoy said:

> "I honestly think this is THE album of my career," declares Portnoy. "Neal and I have now made 18 studio albums together, and I consider THE SIMILITUDE OF A DREAM the absolute creative pinnacle of our collaborations together. I've always had a soft spot for double concept albums such as Pink Floyd's THE WALL and The Who's TOMMY, and I can bravely say that I think we've created an album here that can sit side by side with those masterpieces. Bold words, I know, but after a career of almost 50 albums, I honestly consider this to be one of the defining works of my career."[50]

Because of the success of *Similitude,* the Neal Morse Band followed up this record with another concept album, The Great Adventure, which applied the same kind of musical recasting to Part 2 of *Pilgrim's Progress,* which was also quite successful with their fan base and critics.

BEYOND THE ALBUM

The essential nature of both *Pilgrim's Progress* as a novel and *The Similitude of a Dream* as a musical adaptation of that book is that they use allegory to communicate their message beyond the story itself. The use of allegory in theological works is common but often misunderstood or misapplied, so it is helpful to recognize what is truly allegorical and what might be merely symbolic, especially in religious art.

Allegory has long been a useful genre and tool in religion and philosophy as well as storytelling. Plato's Allegory of the Cave is one of the most famous, and the Bible is full of its use in various parables and dreams. *Baker's Evangelical Dictionary of Biblical Theology* defines it thus:

> A popular form of literature in which a story points to a hidden or symbolic parallel meaning. Certain elements, such as people, things, and happenings in the story, point to corresponding elements in another realm or level of meaning. The closer the resemblances between the two realms, the more detailed is the allegory. The best allegories are interesting, coherent stories in their own right and through the story provide new insight into the realm they depict (e.g., *Pilgrim's Progress* and *The Narnia Chronicles*). Semitic parables, including the Gospel parables, have varying amounts of allegorical elements. Those with many corresponding elements in both realms are properly called allegories.[51]

The most common examples of biblical allegory are both Jewish and Christian, found in both the Old and the New Testaments; much of the symbology of the first eleven chapters of Genesis is frequently argued to be allegorical, and much of the Book of Proverbs uses similar figurative language to the parables of the New Testament. The church father Origen thought that much of the Bible could be interpreted allegorically, writing that if they are interpreted in the literal or fleshy sense, they would be impossible or nonsensical.[52]

Most of the parables of Jesus told to his disciples involve allegory, so much so that they required explanation of the literal meaning to be understood. Indeed, during the Last Supper, its symbolism in the gospels was quite rich. As Jesus taught about the bread and wine—what Christians now celebrate as the Eucharist—the Jewish disciples were also eating the Pascha, the Passover meal of unleavened bread and bitter herbs, whose symbology was dictated in the Law by Moses who witnessed the first Passover in Egypt.

For many, the most talked-about allegory in the Old Testament would be the *Song of Solomon*. Due to its sensual poetry, bordering on the erotic, many interpreters have striven to portray this book as an allegory. The entry on this book from *The Encyclopedia Britannica* states:

> The book, whose author is unknown (Solomon's name is a later addition), is a collection of love poems spoken alternately by a man and a woman. There is no coherent story in the book. A number of the poems systematically describe the beauty and excellence of the beloved. The Song of Solomon has received various interpretations, the most common being allegorical, dramatic, cultic,

and literal. Among Jews, the allegorical interpretation regards the book as an allegory of God's love for the Israelites, with whom he has made a sacred covenant. Among Christians, the book is interpreted as describing the covenantal love of Christ for his church. In medieval mysticism, the Song of Solomon was construed to apply to the love between Christ and the human soul.[53]

Many modern scholars hold that the book is a set of secular love poems instead of an allegory.

Of course, not all allegory is religious; for instance, *The Wizard of Oz* has been described as a parable on populism by Henry Littlefield, and in George Orwell's *Animal Farm*, the animals are analogues of figures from the Russian Revolution.[54] Personification in literature and poetry (going as far back as Homer) can sometimes be viewed as a type of allegory, and often allegorical interpretations of texts are offered where the author may not have intended them to occur. This is a common issue in that many viewers and critics identify a piece of film, literature, or music as allegory: part of a piece may use trope or symbolism, but the whole of the work is not based on a large-scale metaphor or other kind of symbolic device. The blogger Michelle Maiellaro provides a good contrasting description of the two: "an allegory is a complete work of art, whereas most figures of speech are the building blocks of a story's foundation."[55] One example of a novel that was thought to be allegory and is not is *The Lord of the Rings,* by J.R.R. Tolkien.[56] His famous quote following a number of reviews that listed the novels as such reads:

> I cordially dislike allegory in all its manifestations, and always have done so since I grew old and wary enough to detect its presence. I much prefer history—true or feigned—with its varied applicability to the thought and experience of readers. I think that many confuse applicability with allegory, but the one resides in the freedom of the reader, and the other in the purposed domination of the author.[57]

This novel and others by him use mythological tropes and other literary devices to communicate the story, but the whole of the story (and indeed his whole legendarium) is fictional historical high fantasy. Yet he wrote allegory on occasion—his novella *A Leaf by Niggle* is allegorical and somewhat autobiographical in nature, where the main character is a creator of a great work of art and he is forever tweaking the piece, and is found to be unprepared for death and must work his way through purgatory.[58]

Christian allegory is often the subject of many writers, especially pastors writing sermons, but it seems that many times writers are trying to enclose works whose main characters, subject matter, and so on. are not Christian. Consequently, along with *The Lord of the Rings* (and Gandalf), you will find that there are writers who claim that the Harry Potter novels are allegorical, as are Ernest Hemingway's *The Old Man and the Sea, Beauty and the Beast, The Lion King*, and others. These do contain Christian symbolism, but only as a small part of their story or characterization. The film *The Matrix* contains a lot of Christian symbolism, but its central story is much more syncretistic and more heavily influenced by semiology than Christianity.[59] For literature and poetry, better examples exist: along with Bunyan's *Pilgrim's Progress* (far and away the most often cited example of Christian allegory) are C. S. Lewis' *The Chronicles of Narnia, The Pilgrim's Regress*, and *The Great Divorce*, Dante's *Divine Comedy*, and Hannah Hurnard's *Hinds' Feet on High Places*. Current authors and poets including the Neal Morse Band continue to add to this list, and a number of artists, composers, playwrights, and filmmakers continue to adapt their works in the present day.

BEYOND THE ARTISTS

Due to the fame of John Bunyan's novel, there have been a number of artworks derived from its stories and characters, including literature, poetry, film, and fine art, especially in paintings. One can find any number of websites that list artworks by professional or amateur artists. Some pieces are notable: *The Moving Panorama of Pilgrim's Progress* was conceived in the mid-nineteenth century by Edward Harrison May and Joseph Kyle and involved a number of their contemporary illustrators and painters such as Frederic Edwin Church, Jasper Cropsey, and others. Two versions of this painting were made, one that stayed in a particular gallery and another that toured the country.[60]

Many literary works take themes and characters from *Pilgrim's Progress*: *The Celestial Railroad* by Nathaniel Hawthorne, *Innocents Abroad* by Mark Twain, and others; a blogger only identified as Janie wrote an excellent article in *The Redeemed Reader* titled "The Pilgrim Travels on: Literary References to The Pilgrim's Progress" that lists a number of them, plot points that are borrowed, characters lifted, et al. *Little Women* by Louisa May Alcott brims with references to Bunyan, with chapter headings based on places and characters from the novel: "Playing Pilgrims," "Amy's Valley of Humiliation," "Meg Goes to Vanity Fair," and others.[61] Works mentioned earlier in this chapter such as C. S. Lewis's *The Pilgrim's Regress,* and "The Wizard of Oz" also borrow characters and plot points as well.

As of 2024, there are at least ten films or television programs listed on the Internet Movie Database titled "Pilgrim's Progress": one from the silent period (1912), some of which are live action, and others which are animated. Some films riff on the title such as *Miss Pilgrim's Progress* from 1949, but have nothing to do with anything from the novel. Many films adapting some of the literature mentioned prior also contain elements of the story, and a great number of quite disparate films (allegorical or not) featuring a lone pilgrim in despair setting out on a journey seeking spiritual enlightenment can be said to be influenced by *Pilgrim's Progress*, even films such as *Easy Rider* (1969) or *Wild* (2014). Additionally, a number of live theater works have adapted the Bunyan, such as Tom Key's from 2014.

In music, there are many adaptations, from single songs which only borrow the name, such as Procol Harum's "Pilgrim's Progress" (from *Salty Dog*, 1969), to full works. Because of the mention in a number of interviews or reviews when the album was released, Genesis's *"The Lamb Lies Down on Broadway"* is named as a piece of music that is influenced by *Pilgrim*. The singer and principal lyricist for Genesis is quoted for saying:

> "'The Lamb' was intended to be like a 'Pilgrim's Progress,' said Peter, "an adventure through which one gets a better understanding of self—the transformation theme. I was trying to give it a street slant, and that was before punk happened. I felt an energy in that direction, and it seemed that prancing around in fairyland was rapidly becoming obsolete."[62]

Inspired by the story of *Pilgrim*, *The Lamb Lies Down on Broadway* does not follow Bunyan's plot or reuse any of its characters.

Because of the Puritan/conservative Christian nature of the original novel, many contemporary Christian albums/soundtracks and musicals that are mostly produced by evangelical church choirs and orchestras have been composed. Music by Michael Dooley, Chris LeDoux, and *PILGRIM the Musical* by Bob Kauflin, Mark Altrogge, and Janice Landry, are representative, with numerous performances and tours of *PILGRIM the Musical* listed around the United States.

The most well-known opera is by the English composer Ralph Vaughan Williams, whose adaptation is similar to *The Similitude of a Dream* in that it only uses Part 1 of *Pilgrim's Progress*. Premiered in 1951, Vaughan Williams initially thought about a number of pieces based on the novel before settling into the opera.[63] While this piece has not been as successful as other vocal works by him, it was a piece that the composer loved and worked to perfect. Gereint Lewis writes about the opera in the BBC Music Magazine, tracing that long history and the pieces Vaughan Williams produced that refer back to music he had written incorporating elements of Bunyan, including incidental music for a play of *Pilgrim* in 1906. Works derived in some fashion from that music include *The Shepherds of the Delectable Mountains* (1922) and others. Gereint writes that the opera was worked on from 1925 up to the time of its premiere in 1951, with a concerted effort to complete it made during the late 1940s.[64]

The opening of the opera also mirrors Morse's opening, not beginning with Bunyan's dream, but with Bunyan himself in gaol, singing to the audience from the novel. Differences from the novel include renaming the main character Pilgrim instead of Christian as well as some contraction of events; however, it is a very faithful adaptation, and Vaughan Williams masterfully sets it to music. It has not completely disappeared from the modern stage, although it is not often performed, partially due to its very large cast list. Two recent performances (from 2012 and 2019) were mounted in England by the English National Opera and the Royal Northern College of Music, and two standout recordings exist: the 1971 HMV recording with John Noble as Pilgrim, played by the London Philharmonic and Philharmonic choir conducted by Adrian Boult; and a 1997 Chandos recording with Gerald Finley as Pilgrim, performed by the Orchestra of the Royal Opera House and Royal Opera Chorus, conducted by Richard Hickox.

CONCLUSION

While allegory as an artistic form was most popular during the late Middle Ages, artists in many styles and genres continue to use it even today. In particular, Christian allegorists continue to find it attractive, and John Bunyan's *The Pilgrim's Progress* is the model that is held as the most well-known of that subset of allegory. The whole of the Neal Morse Band's *The Similitude of a Dream* transforms Bunyan's *Pilgrim,* casting it into a largely first-person narrative, utilizing contemporary language which includes idioms common to anyone who is familiar with West Coast American speech patterns, and setting it to music that is a brilliant example of modern neo-progressive rock music. This is achieved by the band's songwriters and their vast knowledge of progressive rock history, employing a large array of musical languages, techniques, and styles to produce a *Pilgrim's Progress* that is incredibly relatable and intimate to the listener, yet often giving in to virtuosic yet meaningful instrumental flights that propel the narrative along. Oftentimes, this music itself communicates the principal allegorical content and provides the shift from lyric to lyric, especially in how previously heard music is changed from earlier in the album and redeemed along the journey. And what a journey it becomes in *The Similitude of a Dream*! It is an impressive adaptation of the most famous of all Christian allegorical artworks, molded into a new reality, and yea verily, closer to the heart.

NOTES

1. Very much like my co-author, James McGrath, who writes quickly and publishes a lot of high-quality blogs, articles, and books.

2. The original title page reads: The Pilgrim's Progress from This World, to That which is to come: Delivered under the Similitude of a DREAM Wherein is Discovered, the manner of his setting out, His Dangerous journey; And safe Arrival at the Desired Countrey (sic).

3. SetlistFM—the Setlist WIKI. https://www.setlist.fm/stats/spocks-beard-5bd6b3ac.html.

4. Transatlantic is comprised of Roine Stolt (guitarist, vocals, from the Flower Kings), Neal Morse (keyboard, vocals, guitar), Pete Trewevas (bass guitar, vocals; from Marillion), and Mike Portnoy (drums and vocals, from Dream Theater).

5. The most complete source for this is the Wikipedia discography page. https://en.wikipedia.org/wiki/Neal_Morse_discography— other sources include AllMusic and Neal's page on his record company, Radiant Records. Radiant Records has made much of his work possible, with a large online presence, delivering much content to a very engaged fan base that has been very supportive of Morse's work, as well as Morse's collaborators through the Inner Circle and the yearly Morsefest concerts, which have recently expanded to concerts in Europe as well as here in Tennessee.

6. This performance included nearly all of the present and past members of Spock's Beard.

7. The number of collaborations that Portnoy is involved with is staggering—while talking with Portnoy, I discovered that he has played and/or recorded approximately 900 songs by various artists (author interview with Portnoy, February 2022)—some of this information can be found here: https://mikeportnoyforum.com/f/how-many-songs-has-mike-covered.

8. Portnoy's discography, like Morse's, is huge. https://en.wikipedia.org/wiki/Mike_Portnoy_discography.

9. MusicPlayers.com interview, Scott Khan: Randy George: Nothing Basic about Neal Morse's Bassist. https://musicplayers.com/2019/04/randy-george-nothing-basic-about-neal-morses-bassist/.

10. Jon Liebman – interview in For Bass Players Only. https://musicplayers.com/2019/04/randy-george-nothing-basic-about-neal-morses-bassist/.

11. Reviewer's nom de plume is SouthsideOfTheSky – posted on the Prog Archives website.https://www.progarchives.com/album.asp?id=7961.

12. Eric Gillette's website. https://www.ericgillettemusic.com/.

13. From Hubauer's first involvement in 2000, the band has released thirty-nine albums (!). See the list at the Wikipedia ApologetiX discography. https://en.wikipedia.org/wiki/ApologetiX#Studio_albums.

14. These are detailed in a set of three videos on YouTube. https://www.youtube.com/watch?v=KROmGAOJ2jc.

15. In a maddening set of hardly-existing internet posts, this is a bit of info that once seemed available but has been taken down after being quoted quite a lot by various fans of the band. It is still mentioned on the Wikipedia site for Neal Morse.

16. Bradley J. Birzer, the Catholic World Report, September 11, 2012. https://www.catholicworldreport.com/2012/09/11/sola-gratia-the-prog-foolishness-of-neal-morse/.

17. Michael Young, "Interview: The Neal Morse Band—Behind the Scenes of 'The Similitude of a Dream'," *Artist Waves*, February 6, 2017. https://artistwaves.com/interview-the-neal-morse-band-behind-the-scenes-of-the-similitude-of-a-dream/.

18. Roie Avin, *Essential Modern Progressive Rock Albums, Images and Words Behind Prog's Most Celebrated Albums 1990–2016.* Royal Avenue Media, Cooper City, FL, 2017, p. 273.

19. Ibid, p. 274.

20. Including the character Obstinate, who is not named here but present in the novel.

21. Hardly anyone is named on the record! Only the Man in the Iron Mask, Satan, the Worldly Wiseman, and Apollyon are so identified.

22. Unlike the novel, there is no sense that this takes place in the village of Morality.

23. Morse, "The Ways of a Fool," *The Similitude of a Dream*, Radiant Records 3984-15477-2, 2016 – music by Eric Gillette, Randy George, Bill Hubauer, Neal Morse, and Michael Portnoy; lyrics are available at many sites online, I used DarkLyrics.com. http://www.darklyrics.com/lyrics/nealmorse/thesimilitudeofadream.html.

24. Morse, "So Far Gone," *The Similitude of a Dream.*

25. Morse, "I'm Running," *The Similitude of a Dream*, Radiant Records, 2016 - When performing this live, Neal goofs the last chorus' vocals, repeating the GTO line in the *Live from Tilburg* video.

26. The Scroll given to Christian by the Three Shining Ones plays a very important role in the book but is never mentioned in the album—in the novel, its gift to Christian happens shortly after leaving the House of the Interpreter and coming to the Cross and sepulcher. Eventually, this scroll is Christian's passport into the Celestial City—he would not have been allowed to enter without it.

27. Musically, the "battle" seems to begin at this moment, but as happens on other tracks throughout this record, the new track does not begin here but after the organ solo.

28. In comparison/contrast to the Bunyan novel, *many* scenes and characters are omitted here: The Valley of Shadow, Vanity Fair, the stoning of Faithful, the Doubting Castle (and the Giant Despair), the character of Hopeful, The Delectable Mountains, Enchanted Ground, the River of Death, and the character of Ignorance, who is denied entrance to the Celestial City. If they (and previous plot points and scenes) were included, this album could have reached a very unwieldy length.

29. Morse, "Broken Sky," *The Similitude of a Dream.*

30. Morse, "Broken Sky."

31. I am reminded of the end of that great C. S. Lewis allegory, "The Last Battle" from *The Chronicles of Narnia*, where Aslan leads a great romp and race to his Father's country and exhorts those around him to follow him "farther up and further in!" (cf. George MacDonald *Lilith* "But why ask? for time had nothing to do with me; I was in the land of thought—farther in, higher up than the seven dimensions, the ten senses" from chapter 43).

32. Morse, "Broken Sky/Long Day" (Reprise), *The Similitude of a Dream.* When performed live, the band joins in on the final chord, swelling in volume with a final hit of the chord.

33. This reflects Morse's youth in California and can be seen in most of his writings and lyrics, especially his self-published autobiography *Testimony* (2011, written with Paul Broudakis). His lyrics can sometimes slip into a kind of 'surfer-dude' language, even in the midst of weighty or sublime topics, jarring the listener back to reality out of the moment.

34. Listeners can find this to be confusing; in musical theater or opera, different singers play different roles, and so the differentiation between roles is more easily discerned. However, that is not true of *Similitude*, even though there are four lead vocalists on this record. This is not the first time this happens on a Morse recording—it is also an issue for Spock's Beard's album *Snow*. On that album, Morse sings lead vocals most of the time, yet he sang different characters. He eventually moves away from this kind of confusing characterization in the musicals that he's recorded, *Jesus Christ the Exorcist* (2019), *The Dreamer: Joseph Part One* (2023), and *The Restoration: Joseph, Part Two* (2024).

35. Neal Morse, "Slave to Your Mind," *The Similitude of a Dream*, 2016, 1.

36. This numbering reflects track numbers as if the whole of the album were one piece on a single disc instead of two. No. 13 "Slave to Your Mind," is track 1 on disc 2.

37. Terry Gilliam, Terry Jones, Eric Idle, John Cleese, Graham Chapman and Michael Palin, *Monty Python and the Holy Grail*, EMI Films, 1975.

38. Jordan Blume, "The Similitude of Dreams: A Conversation with Neal Morse," *Pop Matters*, January 16, 2017.
https://www.popmatters.com/the-similitude-of-dreams-a-conversation-with-neal-morse-2495406011.html.

39. And serving as a springboard into the NMB's follow-up album, *The Great Adventure*, which covers part 2 of *Pilgrim's Progress*.

40. "Draw the Line," *The Similitude of a Dream*.

41. "Back to the City," *The Similitude of a Dream*.

42. I often read that *Pilgrim's Progress* is a candidate for the very first novel ever written, although since it is an allegory, it may be disqualified as the first – see J. Chapman, *The Westminster Review, 138*, pp. 610–1892.

43. c.f. Morse's earlier concept albums *Testimony* (2003) and *Testimony 2*.

44. Derek Walker, WalkerWords, July 2, 2017.https://walkerwords.wordpress.com/2017/07/02/the-neal-morse-interview-pt-2-deeper-into-the-music/.

45. "All on a Sunday," *V*, Spock's Beard, music and lyrics by Neal Morse, Metal Blade Records, 2000.

46. Blume, "The Similitude of Dreams: A Conversation with Neal Morse."

47. Ibid.

48. By contrast, this technique unfortunately hampers the NMB's follow-up album, *The Great Adventure* – much like a film sequel telling similar jokes or lines from the initial film, there are quite a few places where incredibly special moments from *Similitude* are hit too often in the second record.

49. Joel Barrios, "Progressive Rock Extravaganza 2016: A Look at My Favorite Albums of the Year 2016," *Rock at Night*. https://www.rockatnight.com/2016/12/progressive-rock-extravaganza-a-look-at-my-favorite-albums-of-the-year-2016/.

50. Blabbermouth.net, "The Neal Morse Band to Release The Similitude of a Dream in November," September 10, 2016. https://blabbermouth.net/news/the-neal-morse-band-to-release-the-similitude-of-a-dream-in-november.

51. *Baker's Evangelical Dictionary,* ed. Walter Elwell, Baker Books, Ada, MI 1996.

52. Origen, (G. W. Butterworth, trans), *On First Principles*, in *Readings in World Christian History* (Andrea Sterk and John Coakley, ed.), Orbis Books, Maryknoll, NY, 2013, p. 75.

53. Song of Solomon, *Encylopedia Brittanica Online.* https://www.britannica.com/topic/Song-of-Solomon.

54. Littlefield, Henry, "The Wizard of Oz: Parable on Populism," *American Quarterly*, 16 (1964): 47–58.

55. Michelle Maiellaro, "10 Allegory Examples from Literature, Film & Music (+ Definition)," *Smart Blogger*, September 2023. https://smartblogger.com/allegory-examples/

56. Indeed, *The Lord of the Rings* is often called a Christian allegory (as opposed to the more common allegory on the Second World War that many contemporary reviewers asserted), simply because of the angelic nature of Gandalf and his death and resurrection after his defeat of the Balrog.

57. Tolkien, JRR – The Fellowship of the Ring, Introduction p. xv – see also: https://medium.com/@rich.thomas.e/tolkiens-drift-4167d41c03c4 and https://ask-middlearth.tumblr.com/post/93871332606/tolkien-wrote-i-cordially-dislike-allegory.

58. See also: "Save the Allegory!" an article in *Slate* written by Laura Miller that discusses the trend to label so many things allegorical when they are not – the subtitle for the article is excellent: "An entire literary tradition is being forgotten because writers use the term *allegory* to mean, like, whatever they want." https://slate.com/culture/2016/05/an-allegory-is-not-the-same-as-a-metaphor-in-praise-of-the-medieval-literary-tradition.html.

59. In *The Matrix*, the protagonist hides some of his software code disks in a hollowed-out copy of Jean Baudrillard's *Simulacra and Simulation*, a central text for semiologists.

60. *The Moving Panorama of Pilgrim's Progress.* https://panoramaofpilgrimsprogress.wordpress.com/history/ - the interior artwork of the NMB album "The Pilgrim" by Paul Whitehead is similar in style to this panorama.

61. Janie, "The Pilgrim Travels on: Literary References to "the Pilgrim's Progress" *Redeemed Reader*, May 16, 2019. https://redeemedreader.com/2019/05/the-pilgrim-travels-on-literary-references-to-the-pilgrims-progress/.

62. Spence Bright, *Peter Gabriel: An Authorized Biography.* Sidgwick & Jackson Ltd, London, England, published 1989.

63. Hugh Ottaway, "Vaughan Williams: Symphony in D and *The Pilgrim's Progress.* A Comparative Note." *The Musical Times*, 94(1328) (1953): 456–458.

64. Geraint Lewis, "Pilgrim's Progress Opera: How Vaughan Williams Turned John Bunyan's Allegory into an Opera," *BBC Music Magazine*, December 27, 2022. https://www.classical-music.com/features/works/pilgrims-progress-opera-vaughan-williams.

Conclusion

In many ways, it might seem to make little sense to offer an overall conclusion to this book. Yet if this were a book about major theologians of the second half of the twentieth century or the religious views of key fiction authors in that period, this would seem an obvious thing to do. The same is no less true in the present case. It is all too rare for rock musicians, even those who demonstrate a technical proficiency that equals that of musicians in other genres, to be treated with the intellectual seriousness one might afford poets, filmmakers, authors of fiction, and other artists. This includes not only a failure to engage with them at the level we have in the individual chapters in this book, offering close studies of particular works, but also when it comes to the level of comparison between songs and between artists. As educators as well as researchers in religion and music, we also note that many progressive rock musicians have provided an accessory to their audience's musical education, as well as expanding their listeners' grasp on the humanities due to their incorporation of classical, jazz, and folk musical elements and exploration of, or at least reference to, religious and philosophical worldviews from diverse European and other global sources.

The 1960s, which gave birth to the musical and religious counterculture that eventually produced progressive rock as its grandchild, also produced key critical theorists who challenged the dominance of the European narrative about "Western civilization."[1] It might thus seem natural to ask why this music and those musicians who made it continued to challenge the establishment in so many ways (including the developing rock music establishment), yet nevertheless drew deeply on the European musical heritage in the way that it did. If we consider the musical influences from beyond the sphere of earlier rock and R&B, we find that they are not consistently representatives of the establishment, and even when they were, to at least some extent, they too pushed boundaries and flouted norms. It is all too easy for those who only listen to the music of composers of the Romantic and modern eras to assume that their popularity in our time is anything but a recent phenomenon. (Indeed, musical popularity has always been in a cycle of reacting to or rebelling-against the previous generation's aesthetic or stylistic norms.) Critical and popular acclaim aside, however, we must also consider their relationship to musical and, in our context, religious establishments. If we think of the British composers that influenced these bands, Ralph Vaughan Williams' religiosity was at best vague and unconventional, in keeping with the spirit of his age, while Gustav Holst set Sanskrit and Gnostic texts to music.[2] Turning to other composers whose music was not merely an influence on but was performed by ELP, Bartók and Ginastera, if not at the absolute cutting edge of the avant-garde, certainly pushed boundaries and represented cultures (Hungarian and Argentinian) that were not the dominant voices in traditional European art music. Bartók was as much, if not more, avant-garde in his religious views as in his music, as first an atheist and then a convert to Unitarianism. Yet he also worked to document folk songs, which influenced him as much as traditions of European art music.

J. S. Bach has obviously become a household name and his religious faith has been much studied, but that could easily not have occurred were it not for the revival of interest in him by Mendelssohn.[3] On the other hand, the pieces by Mussorgsky, Prokofiev, and Copland that ELP popularized and adapted had yet to become as widely known as they have in the intervening decades. Musically, the frequent reference to prog rock being influenced by *classical* music obscures the fact that the most direct influences were more recent and even living composers whose works were not yet established as classics or part of the repertoire. Even to the extent that not only musically but literarily there were influences on prog bands that were classical in the strict sense, we should consider the fact that rediscovery of the old, when the old has been neglected, can be as revolutionary as the creation of the new. The Latin literature that influenced Peter Gabriel's lyrics and the Sanskrit works that Jon Anderson claimed as a source of inspiration were not merely traditional but ancient. Neither set of texts was widely known and appreciated in the mainstream of popular culture in the United Kingdom in the twentieth century, when these artists were active. Consider how the rediscovery of Christianity's long history has served as a challenge to many evangelical Protestants who grew up thinking that nothing happened between the end of the Book of Revelation and the start of the Protestant Reformation. Those who have challenged the fire and brimstone judgmentalism of their own theological heritage have often not simply rejected present and older voices dominant in their tradition but have rediscovered neglected voices from the history of theology that have embraced or at least allowed for the possibility of universalism.

Thus, if some elements of the counterculture were genuinely new or recent, such as the discovery of Lysergic acid diethylamide, others were archaic in other cultures but relatively new to the English-speaking world. The sitar is a classical Indian instrument whose use by the Rolling Stones, the Beatles, and others was an innovation in their own cultural and musical contexts. This is important to note since progressive rock is sometimes viewed as a shift away from the radical character of the early days of rock music. This book has shown that, far from being less radical, prog was every bit as radical, if not indeed more radical, even if at times in different ways. To be sure, there is, in many ways, a greater historical and cultural significance when white musicians drew on elements of black music in an era of racial segregation and intense discrimination. While it may have begun as something that today might be labeled as "cultural appropriation," even so, it represented a challenge to social divisions, both inasmuch as this idiom of an oppressed minority was found attractive by some among their oppressors and as black music essentially took over (or one might even say colonized) white popular music. Hence, as we emphasized in the introduction and at various points throughout this book, cultural boundaries are never as rigid as they are in the imagination, either of those who define themselves over against an "other" or the theorists who attempt to define and label in the interests of clarity. Returning to prog, in an era of social stratification in which art music is felt to be the cultural property of a socioeconomic elite, integrating it with popular music for everyone also represents a transgression of prevailing norms.

This book has only scratched the surface of the potential for serious academic study of the religious aspects of specific songs and of specific artists within the genre of progressive rock. Our difficulty choosing from among the works of the artists included is perhaps best illustrated by the fact that the chapter about Yes includes two "songs" that actually span two and a half LPs. The decision not to include a major focus on songs like "2112" and "Roll the Bones" by Rush and "The Fountain of Salmacis" by Genesis, to say nothing of many others by these artists, as well as songs too numerous to list by Peter Gabriel, Pink Floyd, Gentle Giant, Queen, Arcade Fire, Dream Theater, and Glass Hammer. The list could go on. Even if we had included more in the present book, there would still be much benefit to offering book-length studies of specific groups or songwriters.

This book has hopefully shown the way prog rock, past and present, has given expression to, pushed back against, and shaped prevailing cultural trends not only in music but in religion. Much of this music has become classic in its own right, and much of it certainly has become popular. Just as there is a coolness factor in rejecting traditional religion, the irony is not to be missed that someone who then bucks the anti-religious trend may be set upon by defenders of anti-religious dogmatism with all the zealotry that they would claim is the reason they rejected religion in the first place, with arguments that they themselves had previously used mirrored back to them and used against them in surprising ways. This music that stands at odds in some ways both with culture and with counterculture deserves attention as an example of how artists, theologians, and human beings in general navigate cultural shifts. Both individuals and eras navigate between past and future, between elaborate and simple, and between childhood belief and cynicism.[4]

If at the moment some of these artists may seem to be out of fashion (so that one might quip about the appropriateness of a volume on progressive rock being part of a series on *popular* culture), Johann Sebastian's Bach's music was neither widely popular in its own time nor immediately celebrated in the century that followed his death. Those of us who love music and work as educators have been surprised as music streaming services have led the latest generation of students to know music that a few years earlier was unfamiliar to most of our students. In the same way, theologians known for a long time only to those who researched archaic church history and thought have seen a resurgence, and neither the authors nor detractors of the various Gnostic texts rediscovered at Nag Hammadi in the twentieth century could ever have guessed they would become globally influential more than a thousand years later. That is perhaps the key takeaway point from our book—not that these specific songs and artists are guaranteed to be viewed as having made a lasting contribution to either music or theology when viewed with hindsight many years or even centuries from now, but that we never know in advance where our musical and spiritual explorations may lead us, and so it behooves us to listen closely to the voices of our time and the recent past as well as those at a further remove from us. Both in seeking the ineffable and in seeking to understand human cultural products that reflect that search, attention to music is crucial—not only formally religious music but popular music as well. So much of what has attained the status of classic has done so by building on popular currents and ephemeral creations that are not recorded for us. When we have the privilege of historical moments being preserved, they deserve our attention. We hope that this book in some small way helps to shed more light on the important and multifold intersections of theology and progressive rock.[5]

NOTES

1. See, e.g., Frantz Fanon, *The Wretched of the Earth*. New York: Grove Press, 1965.

2. The ELP song "Touch and Go" quotes from Vaughan Williams' "Fantasia on a Theme of Thomas Tallis," and the album *Emerson, Lake, and Powell* included a

cover of Holst's "Mars, Bringer of War" from his suite *The Planets*. Vaughan Williams attended the school at which the founding members of Genesis met, and they were undoubtedly aware of his music.

3. See, for instance Jaroslav Pelikan, *Bach among the Theologians*. Minneapolis, MN: Fortress, 1986; John Eliot Gardiner, *Bach: Music in the Castle of Heaven*. New York: Knopf, 2013; Michael Marissen, *Bach & God*. Oxford: Oxford University Press, 2016, as well as the opening chapter of Patrick Kavanaugh, *Spiritual Lives of the Great Composers*. Grand Rapids, MI: Zondervan, 1996.

4. Echoing here the lyrics of the Genesis song "In the Cage."

5. The allusion to a song on Pink Floyd's second album is also intentional.

Bibliography

Alexander, Phil, *The Mojo Collection: The Ultimate Music Companion.* 4th Edition. New York: Canongate, 2007.

Allan, Marc. "Rockers Now Reveal Spirituality." *Indianapolis Star*, May 30, 1995, D 1. See also "Good Heavens, Now Ian Anderson Wants Us to Think!," *Disc & Music Echo,* March 20, 1971. http://www.tullpress.com/d20mar71.htm.

Allen, Liam, "The Stories of the Christmas Hits," *BBC News,* December 26, 2010. https://www.bbc.com/news/entertainment-arts-12049738.

Avin, Roie, *Essential Modern Progressive Rock Albums, Images and Words Behind Prog's Most Celebrated Albums 1990–2016,* Cooper City, FL: Royal Avenue Media, 2017.

Barnes, Mike, *A New Day Yesterday: UK Progressive Rock & The 1970s.* New York: Omnibus, 2020.

Barrios, Joel, "Progressive Rock Extravaganza 2016: A Look at My Favorite Albums of the Year 2016," *Rock at Night.* https://www.rockatnight.com/2016/12/progressive-rock-extravaganza-a-look-at-my-favorite-albums-of-the-year-2016/.

Baudrillard, Jean. *Simulacra and Simulation.* Ann Arbor, MI: University of Michigan Press, 1994.

Bebbington, David W., *Evangelicalism in Modern Britain: A History from the 1730s to the 1980s.* New York: Taylor & Francis, 2003.

Billson, Charles James, "The English Novel," *The Westminster Review,* 138 (July–December 1892): 602–620.

Birzer, Bradley J., "Solo Gratia: The 'Prog' Foolishness of Neal Morse," *Catholic World Report*, September 11, 2012. https://www.catholicworldreport.com/2012/09/11/sola-gratia-the-prog-foolishness-of-neal-morse/.

Blake, Mark, Joe Boyd, Victoria Broackes, Anna Landreth Strong, Howard Goodall, Jon Savage, and Rob Young, *Pink Floyd: Their Mortal Remains.* London: Victoria and Albert Museum, 2017.

Blume, Jordan, "The Similitude of Dreams: A Conversation with Neal Morse," *Pop Matters*, January 16, 2017. https://www.popmatters.com/the-similitude-of-dreams-a-conversation-with-neal-morse-2495406011.html.

Bond, Helen, *The First Biography of Jesus*. Grand Rapids, MI: Eerdmans, 2020.

Bosso, Joe, "Interview: Keith Emerson Talks ELP's Tarkus Track-by-Track," *Music Radar,* October 8, 2012. https://www.musicradar.com/news/guitars/interview-keith-emerson-talks-elps-tarkus-track-by-track-565038.

Bowman, Durrell, "Classical Styles and Sources in Early Progressive Rock by Genesis, 1969–72." https://durrellbowman.com/classical-styles-and-sources-in-early-progressive-rock-by-genesis-1969-72/.

Bowman, Durrell, *Experiencing Peter Gabriel: A Listener's Companion*. Lanham, MD: Rowman & Littlefield, 2016.

Brayton, Ed, "Neil Peart on Religion," *Dispatches from the Culture Wars,* December 18, 2017. https://www.patheos.com/blogs/dispatches/2017/12/18/neil-peart-religion/.

Bright, Spencer, *Peter Gabriel: An Authorised Biography*. London: Sidgwick & Jackson, 1989.

Bryant, William Cullen, "Thanatopsis." https://www.poetryfoundation.org/poems/50465/thanatopsis.

Burns, Robert G. H., *Experiencing Progressive Rock: A Listener's Companion*. Lanham, MD: Rowman & Littlefield, 2018.

Carey, Benedict, "A Neuroscientific Look at Speaking in Tongues." *New York Times,* November 7, 2006. https://www.nytimes.com/2006/11/07/health/07brain.html.

Chambers, Stuart, *Yes: An Endless Dream of '70s, '80s and '90s Rock Music: An Unauthorized Interpretative History in Three Phases*. Ottawa: General Store Publishing House, 2002.

Cheaney, Janie, "The Pilgrim Travels on: Literary References to "the Pilgrim's Progress," *Redeemed Reader,* May 16, 2019. https://redeemedreader.com/2019/05/the-pilgrim-travels-on-literary-references-to-the-pilgrims-progress/.

Corbett, John, *Pick Up the Pieces: Excursions in Seventies Music*. Chicago, IL: The University of Chicago Press, 2019.

Cummings, Kevin. *On Track... Kansas: Every Album, Every Song*. Tewkesbury: Sonicbond, 2020.

Däniken, Erich von, *Chariots of the Gods*. New York: G. P. Putnam's, 1970.

DeJong, Peter, *"The Opinions of the Remonstrants (1618)"*. Crisis in the Reformed Churches: Essays in Commemoration of the Great Synod of Dordt, 1618–1619. Grand Rapids, MI: Reformed Fellowship, 1968.

Dodd, Philip (editor), *Genesis: Chapter and Verse*. New York: Thomas Dunne, 2007.

Dome, Malcolm, "Robbie Steinhardt Obituary," *Prog,* September 20, 2021. https://www.pressreader.com/uk/prog/20210910/281496459388916.

Dome, Malcom, "Touching the Face of God: Jon Anderson on Religion," *Louder,* October 25, 2016. https://www.loudersound.com/features/religion-jon-anderson.

Dubber, Andrew, "Peter Gabriel and The Birth of Mozo," *Medium,* February 28, 2015. https://medium.com/@dubber/peter-gabriel-and-the-birth-of-mozo-45ef466b1339.

Easlea, Daryl, *Without Frontiers: The Life & Music of Peter Gabriel*. London: Omnibus Press, 2018.

Eisenbaum, Pamela, *Paul Was Not a Christian: The Original Message of a Misunderstood Apostle*. New York: HarperCollins, 2009.

Elliott, Paul, "Alex Lifeson on Grilled Octopus, Police Brutality and Disco Biscuits," *Classical Rock*, August 27, 2022. https://www.loudersound.com/features/interview-alex-lifeson-on-grilled-octopus-police-brutality-and-disco-biscuits.

Elliott, Paul, "Jethro Tull's Ian Anderson on Politics, God, and Ritchie Blackmore's Clothing," *Louder Sound,* July 29, 2016. https://www.loudersound.com/features/jethro-tull-s-ian-anderson-on-politics-god-and-ritchie-blackmore-s-clothing.

Ewing, Jerry, *Wonderous Stories: A Journey Through the Landscape of Progressive Rock.* London: Flood Gallery Publishing, 2018.

Eyl, Jennifer, *Signs, Wonders, and Gifts: Divination in the Letters of Paul.* Oxford: Oxford University Press, 2019.

Fanon, Frantz, *The Wretched of the Earth.* New York: Grove Press, 1965

Ford, Peter T., "Compositional Style of Keith Emerson in Tarkus (1971) for the Rock Music Trio Emerson, Land and Palmer." Master's Thesis, Indiana State University, Terre Haute, IN, 1994.

Forrester, George, Martyn Hanson, and Frank Askwe, *Emerson, Lake, and Palmer: The Show That Never Ends. A Musical Biography.* London: Helter Skelter, 2001.

Fransson, R. M., "Ovid Rox," *The Classical Journal,* 86(2) (December 1990–January 1991): 176–182.

Friedmann, Jonathan L., "Music and the Myth of Free Will," *Thinking on Music,* November 6, 2014. https://thinkingonmusic.wordpress.com/2014/11/06/music-and-the-myth-of-free-will/.

Gallant, David, *Asia: Heat of the Moment.* New York: Asia Music Limited, 2007.

Gardiner, John Eliot, *Bach: Music in the Castle of Heaven.* New York: Knopf, 2013.

Gardner, Martin, *Urantia: The Great Cult Mystery.* Amherst, NY: Prometheus, 2008.

Gilman, Lawrence, *Stories of Symphonic Music: A Guide to the Meaning of Important Symphonies, Overtures, and Tone-poems from Beethoven to the Present Day.* New York: Harper & Brothers, 1907.

Ginsberg, Allen, "On Burroughs' Work," in *Reality Sandwiches.* San Francisco, CA: City Lights Publishers, 1963.

Grady, B., and K. M. Loewenthal, "Features Associated with Speaking in Tongues (Glossolalia)," *The British Journal of Medical Psychology,* 70(2) (1997): 185–191.

Halliwell, Martin, and Paul Hegarty, *Beyond and before Progressive Rock since the 1960s.* London: Bloomsbury, 2011.

Harris, James C., "The Metamorphosis of Narcissus," *Archives of General Psychiatry,* 62(2) (2005): 124–125.

Harris, Steve, "Genesis was Never the Same after Peter Gabriel Left," Prog #60 .https://www.loudersound.com/features/the-prog-interview-steve-harris.

Heggarty, Paul, and Martin Halliwell, *Beyond and Before: Progressive Rock across Time and Genre* (Updated and Expanded Edition). London: Bloomsbury, 2021.

Heller, Jason, "An Introduction to Rush, the Biggest Cult Band in the World," *AV Club,* August 1, 2013. https://www.avclub.com/an-introduction-to-rush-the-biggest-cult-band-in-the-w-1798239702.

Heyd, Milly, "Dali's 'Metamorphosis of Narcissus' Reconsidered," *Artibus Et Historiae,* 5(10) (1984): 121–131.

Hick, John, *Faith and Knowledge.* Hampshire: Macmillan, 1988.

Hill, Sarah, "Ending It All: Genesis and Revelation," *Popular Music,* 32(2) (2013): 197–221.
Hill, Sarah, "From the New Jerusalem to the Secret World: Peter Gabriel and the Shifting Self," in Michael Drewett, Sarah Hill, and Kimi Kärki (eds.), *Peter Gabriel: From Genesis to Growing Up.* Farnham: Ashgate, 2010, pp. 15–29.
Holm, Randall, "Pulling Back the Darkness: Starbound with Jon Anderson," in Michael J. Gilmour (ed.), *Call Me the Seeker: Listening to Religion in Popular Music.* New York: Continuum, 2005, pp. 158–171.
Horst, Dirk von der, "Precarious Pleasures: Situating 'Close to the Edge' in Conflicting Male Desires," in Kevin Holm-Hudson (ed.), *Progressive Rock Reconsidered.* New York: Routledge, 2002, pp. 167–182.
House, H. Wayne. *Charts of Cults, Sects, & Religious Movements.* Grand Rapids, MI: Zondervan Publishing House, 2000.
Howe, Steve, *All My Yesterdays.* New York: Omnibus, 2020.
Jacobsen, Martin, "Analyze it to Life: Yes – Close to the Edge." May 21, 2015. http://www.deathmetal.org/article/analyze-it-to-life-yes-close-to-the-edge/.
Josephson, Nors S., "Bach Meets Liszt: Traditional Formal Structures and Performance Practices in Progressive Rock." *The Musical Quarterly,* 76(1) (1992): 67–92.
Kavanaugh, Patrick, *Spiritual Lives of the Great Composers.* Grand Rapids, MI: Zondervan, 1996.
Khan, Scott, "Randy George: Nothing Basic about Neal Morse's Bassist," *Musicplayers.com,* April 10, 2019. https://musicplayers.com/2019/04/randy-george-nothing-basic-about-neal-morses-bassist/.
Keane, Tim, "British Rock Meets Modernism," *Hyperallergic,* January 26, 2019. https://hyperallergic.com/480967/peter-gabriel-reflections-the-museum-of-bath-architecture-clive-arrowsmith/.
Lambe, Stephen, *Citizens of Hope and Glory: The Story of Progressive Rock.* Gloucestershire: Amberley Publishing, 2011.
Lee, Geddy, *My Effin' Life.* New York: HarperCollins, 2023.
Lewis, Geraint, "Pilgrim's Progress Opera: How Vaughan Williams Turned John Bunyan's allegory into an opera, " *BBC Music Magazine,* December 27, 2022. https://www.classical-music.com/features/works/pilgrims-progress-opera-vaughan-williams.
Liebman, Jon, "Interview with Randy George." *For Bass Players Only.* https://forbassplayersonly.com/randy-george/.
Ling, Dave, "Kansas: An Everyday Story of Success, Failure, Drugs, Booze, and Jealousy," *Louder Sound.* https://www.loudersound.com/features/kansas-an-everyday-story-of-success-failure-drugs-booze-and-jealousy.
Ling, Dave, "The Top 10 Best Kansas Songs," *Classic Rock. Louder Sound,* July 14, 2016. https://www.loudersound.com/features/too-10-best-kansas-songs.
Littlefield, Henry M., "The Wizard of Oz: Parable on Populism," *American Quarterly,* 16(1) (1964): 47–58.
Livgren, Kerry, *Seeds of Change.* Brentwood, TN: Sparrow Books, 1991.
Lorde, Audre, *Sister Outsider: Essays and Speeches.* New York: Penguin Books, 2020.

Lucky, Jerry, *Progressive Rock*. Burlington, VT: Collector's Guide Publishing, 2015.

Lynch, Danielle Anne, *God in Sound and Silence: Music as Theology*. Eugene, OR: Pickwick, 2018.

Macan, Edward, *Endless Enigma: A Musical Biography of Emerson, Lake, and Palmer*. Chicago, IL: Open Court, 2006.

Macan, Edward, *Rocking the Classics: English Progressive Rock and the Counterculture*. Oxford: Oxford University Press, 1997.

MacDonald, George, *Lilith: A Romance*. London: Chatto & Windus, 1896.

Macphail, Richard, *My Book of Genesis*. Bedford: Wymer, 2018.

Maiellaro, Michelle, "10 Allegory Examples from Literature, Film & Music (+ Definition)," *Smart Blogger*, September 2023. https://smartblogger.com/allegory-examples/.

Marissen, Michael, *Bach & God*. Oxford: Oxford University Press, 2016.

Martin, Bill, *Music of Yes: Structure and Vision in Progressive Rock*. Chicago, IL: Open Court, 1996.

Masley, Ed, "Interview: Ian Anderson of Jethro Tull," *AZ Central,* September 16, 2014. https://www.azcentral.com/story/entertainment/music/2014/09/16/ian-anderson-interview-jethro-tull/15718423/.

McParland, Robert, *Science Fiction in Classic Rock Musical Explorations of Space, Technology and the Imagination, 1967–1982*. Jefferson, NC: McFarland, 2017.

Miller, Laura, "Save the Allegory!," *Slate,* May 3, 2016. https://slate.com/culture/2016/05/an-allegory-is-not-the-same-as-a-metaphor-in-praise-of-the-medieval-literary-tradition.html.

Moore, Allan F., *Song Means: Analysing and Interpreting Recorded Popular Song*. London: Routledge, 2016.

Morse, Neal with Paul Braoudakis, *Testimony*. Neal Morse, 2011.

Morse, Tim, *Yesstories: Yes in Their Own Words*. New York: St. Martin's, 1996.

Mosbø, Thomas J., *Yes – But What Does It Mean?* Milton: Wyndstar, 1994.

Olsen, Dale A., *World Flutelore: Folktales, Myths, and Other Stories of Magical Flute Power*. Urbana, IL: University of Illinois Press, 2013.

Origen (G. W. Butterworth, trans.), *On First Principles*, in *Readings in World Christian History* (Andrea Sterk and John Coakley, ed.). Maryknoll, NY: Orbis Books, 2013.

Ottaway, Hugh, "Vaughan Williams: Symphony in D and *The Pilgrim's Progress*. A Comparative Note," *The Musical Times*, 94(1328) (1953): 456–458.

Pareles, Jon, "At Lunch with Peter Gabriel; Art, Music, Experience Unbound," *New York Times,* July 13, 1994, C1.

Partridge, Christopher, *UFO Religions*. New York: Taylor & Francis, 2012.

Payne, Philip Barton, "Allegory," in Walter A. Elwell (ed.), *Baker's Evangelical Dictionary of Biblical Theology*. Grand Rapids, MI: Baker Book House, 1996, pp. 14–15.

Peart, Neil, "A Port Boy's Story," *St Catherines Standard,* June 24 & 25, 1994.https://www.stcatharinesstandard.ca/entertainment/music/neil-peart-in-his-own-words-growing-up-in-st-catharines/article_04ae285d-b5aa-53e0-a132-6774cfdd473a.html

Peart, Neil, *The Masked Rider*. Lawrencetown Beach: Pottersfield Press, 1996.

Pelikan, Jaroslav, *Bach among the Theologians*. Minneapolis, MN: Fortress, 1986.

Perry, Shawn, "Ian Anderson & Jethro Tull: Scaling 'The Zealot Gene'." https://vintagerock.com/ian-anderson-jethro-tull-scaling-the-zealot-gene/.

Pettengill, Steve, "Sea of Tranquility Review." https://www.seaoftranquility.org/reviews.php?op=showcontent&id=1553.

Platts, Robin, *Genesis: Behind the Lines 1967–2007*. Edinburgh: Canongate, 2007.

Podulska, Donald M., "Classical Myth in Music: A Selective List," *The Classical World*, 92(3) (January–February 1999): 195–276.

Poloma, Margaret M., "Glossolalia, Liminality and Empowered Kingdom Building: A Social Perspective," in Mark J. Cartledge (ed.), *Speaking in Tongues: Multi-disciplinary Perspectives*. Bletchley: Paternoster, 2006, pp. 147–173.

Popoff, Martin, *Limelight: Rush in the '80s*. Toronto: ECW Press, 2020.

Popoff, Martin, *Queen: Album by Album*. Beverly, MA: Voyageur, 2018.

Prasad, Anil, "Greg Lake: New Perspectives." Innerviews, 2011. https://www.innerviews.org/inner/lake.html.

Prasad, Anil, "Jon Anderson: Harmonic Engagement." Innerviews, 2005. https://www.innerviews.org/inner/jon-anderson.html.

Pritchett, James. *The Music of John Cage*. Cambridge: Cambridge University Press, 1993.

Rabey, Brian, *A Passion Play: The Story of Ian Anderson and Jethro Tull*. London: Soundcheck, 2013.

Reed, Kevin, "Veteran Musician Ian Anderson Comments on Right-Wing Populism with Jethro Tull's The Zealot Gene," *World Socialist Web Site,* February 14, 2022. https://www.wsws.org/en/articles/2022/02/15/gene-f15.html.

Reed, Ryan, "Ian Anderson Wrestles with New Jethro Tull LP's Biblical Themes: Exclusive Interview," *Ultimate Classic Rock*, January 19, 2022. https://ultimateclassicrock.com/jethro-tull-zealot-game-themes/.

Riva, Michele Augusto, Enrica Riva, Mauro Spicci, Mario Strazzabosco, Marcello Giovannini, and Giancarlo Cesana, "'The City of Hepar': Rituals, Gastronomy, and Politics at the Origins of the Modern Names for the Liver," *Journal of Hepatology*, 55(5) (2011): 1132–1136.

Roberts, Chris, "Genesis on Supper's Ready: 'This is Where We Started to Become Significant'," *Prog,* March 22, 2017. https://www.loudersound.com/features/genesis-on-suppers-ready-this-is-where-we-started-to-become-significant.

Romano, Will, *Close to the Edge: How Yes's Masterpiece Defined Prog Rock*. Milwaukee, WI: Backbeat, 2017.

Romano, Will, *Mountains Come Out of the Sky*. Milwaukee, WI: Backbeat Books, 2012.

Romano, Will, *Prog Rock FAQ: All That's Left to Know about Rock's Most Progressive Music*. Milwaukee, WI: Backbeat, 2014.

Rowlands, Jonathan, "John Coltrane's a Love Supreme as Prayed Glossolalia: A Suggestion," *Journal of Pentecostal Theology,* 28(1) (2019): 84–102.

Ruggiero, Bob, "Jethro Tull's Ian Anderson Finds His Inner Zealot," *Houston Press,* December 16, 2021. https://www.houstonpress.com/music/things-to-do/listen-to-the-zealot-gene-by-jethro-tull-and-ian-anderson-12505965.

Rycenga, Jennifer, "Tales from Change within the Sound: Form, Lyrics, and Philosophy in the Music of Yes," in Kevin Holm-Hudson (ed.), *Progressive Rock Reconsidered.* New York: Routledge, 2002, pp. 143–166.

Schwarz, Arturo, "Alchemy, Androgyny and Visual Artists." *Leonardo,* 13(1) (1980): 57–62.

Schwarz, David, *Listening Subjects: Music, Psychoanalysis, Culture.* Durham, NC: Duke University Press, 1997.

Shanes, Eric, *Dalí.* New York: Parkstone International, 2014.

Smith, Sid, "The Making of Chris Squire's Fish Out of Water," *Louder.* https://www.loudersound.com/amp/features/the-making-of-chris-squires-fish-out-of-water.

Sohl, Robert and Audrey Carr, *The Gospel According to Zen: Beyond the Death of God.* New York: New American Library, 1970.

Spicer, Mark, "Large-Scale Strategy and Compositional Design in the Early Music of Genesis," in Walter Everett (ed.), *Expressions in Pop-Rock Music: A Collection of Critical and Analytical Essays.* New York: Garland, 2000, pp. 77–111.

Steele, David N. and Curtis C Thomas, *Romans: An Interpretive Outline.* Philadelphia: Presbyterian & Reformed Publishing Co, 1963.

Stump, Paul, *The Music's All That Matters.* Chelmsford: Harbour, 2010.

Thompson, Dave, *Turn it on Again: Peter Gabriel, Phil Collins & Genesis.* San Francisco, CA: Backbeat, 2005.

Tillich, Paul, "Art and Ultimate Reality," 1959 Dimensions Lecture at MOMA. https://www.moma.org/momaorg/shared/pdfs/docs/press_archives/2449/releases/MOMA_1959_0015.pdf.

Tillich, Paul, *Dynamics of Faith.* New York: Harper & Row, 1957.

Toland, Michael, "Q&A: Michael Moorcock Plays Hawkwind Sci-fi Author Joins Two-Day Tribute to Space Rocker," *Austin Chronicle,* March 28, 2019. https://www.austinchronicle.com/daily/music/2019-03-28/qa-michael-moorcock-plays-hawkwind/.

Tolkien, John Ronald Reuel. *The Fellowship of the Ring: Being the First Part of The Lord of the Rings.* London: George Allen and Unwin, 1961.

Wagner, Jeff, *Mean Deviation: Four Decades of Progressive Heavy Metal.* Brooklyn, NY: Bazillion Points, 2010.

Walker, Derek, "Ian Anderson: Winding Up the Church," 2017 Interview. http://www.tollbooth.org/index.php/past-issues/past-features/2077-ian-anderson-winding-up-the-church.

Walker, Derek, Interview with Neal Morse part 2, Jul 2, 2017 https://walkerwords.wordpress.com/2017/07/02/the-neal-morse-interview-pt-2-deeper-into-the-music/.

Wall, Mick, "Supper's Ready by Genesis: The Story behind the Song," *Classic Rock,* November 19, 2016. https://www.loudersound.com/features/the-story-behind-the-song-genesis-suppers-ready.

Warren, Meredith, *My Flesh Is Meat Indeed: A Nonsacramental Reading of John 6:51-58*. Minneapolis, MN: Fortress, 2015.
Welch, Chris, *Close to the Edge: The Story of Yes*. London: Omnibus, 2000.
Weiel, Natalie, "How Jethro Tull Created Hard Rock's Most Cerebral Album – Aqualung," *Produce Like a Pro,* June 23, 2021. https://producelikeapro.com/blog/jethro-tull-aqualung/.
Weigel, David, *The Show That Never Ends: The Rise and Fall of Prog Rock*. New York: W. W. Norton, 2017.
Wiser, Carl, "Jon Anderson of Yes," *Songfacts*, May 17, 2013. https://www.songfacts.com/blog/interviews/jon-anderson-of-yes.
Young, Michael, "Interview: The Neal Morse Band — Behind the Scenes of 'The Similitude of a Dream,'" *Artist Waves*, February 6, 2017 https://artistwaves.com/interview-the-neal-morse-band-behind-the-scenes-of-the-similitude-of-a-dream/.

Person/Band Index

2nd Chapter of Acts, The, 109, 114n41

Adrenaline Mob, 133
Ajalon, 133
Alcott, Louisa May, 149
Allah, 124
Allan, Marc, 88–89
Altrogge, Mar, 150
Amboy Dukes, 111
Anderson, Ian, 8, 83, 85, 89, 91
Anderson, Jon, 31–50, 55n5, 57n28, 57n35, 57–58n39, 59n60, 60n81, 60n85, 61n89, 158
ApologetiX, 134, 145, 152n13
Aquinas, Thomas, 74
Arcade Fire, 159
Asia, 15, 56n8, 110
Avenged Sevenfold, 133

Babbington, David, 108
Bach, Johann Sebastian, 6, 29n24, 158
Banks, Tony, 13n16, 55n2, 65–66, 73, 80n59, 91n3
Barrett, Syd, 111
Bartók, Bela, 6, 10, 16, 158
Beatles, the, 1, 3, 9, 17, 33, 35–36, 58n53, 95, 99–100, 127n5, 137, 139, 145, 159
Beethoven, Ludwig von, 6, 44
Bent Knee, 111

Billboard, 1, 96–97
Black Sabbath, 90
Blake, Tim, 75
Blake, William, 25, 72
Blue Cheer, 115
Bo Diddley, 13n14
Bradbury, Ray, 29n28
Bruford, Bill, 15, 55n2
Bryant, William Cullen, 104
Buddha, 34, 36, 38–43, 46, 50, 56n23, 124
Bunyan, John, 65, 131, 135–51, 153n28

Cage, John, 13n14, 125
Carroll, Lewis, 65
Chemical Brothers, 12n2
Church, Frederic Edwin, 149
Churchill, Winston, 68
Collins, Phil, 6
Copland, Aaron, 6, 158
Corbett, John, 4, 13n16, 33–34

Dali, Salvador, 78n24, 78n27, 80n50
Däniken, Erich von, 29n27
Dante Aligheri, 149
De Burgh, Chris, 25, 29n27
Deep Purple, 13n16
DeGarmo and Key, 109
Deninzon, Joe, 100, 134
DeYoung, Dennis, 139, 142

171

Dooley, Michael, 150
Doors, The, 95
Downes, Geoff, 15, 33, 52
Dream Theater, 13n11, 60n82, 131, 133, 136, 146, 159
Dunn, Sam, 117
Dvořák, Antonin, 24

Eagles, The, 35, 140
Ehart, Phil, 96–98, 103
Elefante, John, 97–101, 113n13
Elgar, Edward, 6
Emerson, Keith, 6, 13nn15–16, 15, 25, 29n25, 91n3
Emerson Lake and Palmer/Powell (ELP), 3, 6, 10–11, 13n20, 15–27, 29n24, 75, 95, 110, 111, 145, 158, 160n2
Evan, John, 93n19
Ezekiel, 90–91

Fates Warning, 131
Flower Kings, The, 131, 152n4
Flying Colors, 131, 133
Fringe, 111
Fripp, Robert, 16, 27n7, 27n10

Gabriel, Peter, 6, 51, 55n2, 63–66, 69–74, 76n5, 77nn7–8, 78n26, 78n34, 79n37, 79n42, 79n44, 79n47, 80n59, 83, 150, 158–59
Genesis (band), 2, 3, 6–7, 11, 15, 22, 25–27, 31–32, 35, 46, 50, 55n2, 63–81, 83, 90, 110, 111, 131, 137, 145, 150, 159, 161n2, 161n4
Gentle Giant, 2, 90, 95, 100, 159
George, Randy, 90, 132–34, 140, 145
Gershwin, George, 10
Gillette, Eric, 132, 134, 139, 141–42, 145
Ginastera, Alberto, 6, 13n15, 16, 158
Glass Hammer, 159
Glixman, Jeff, 97
Gods, The, 16
Gold, Wally, 97

Grateful Dead, The, 95, 117
Greer, Billy, 97–98
Grohl, Dave, 117

Hackett, Steve, 64
Haken, 134
Harris, Steve, 75
Hawkwind, 29n29
Hawthorne, Nathaniel, 149
Hemingway, Ernest, 149
Hermaphroditus, 73–74
Hesse, Hermann, 34, 36, 38–41, 102, 107
Holm, Randall, 55n1, 58–59n55
Holst, Gustav, 6, 17, 158, 161n2
Hope, Dave, 96, 98, 109–10
Howe, Steve, 15, 33, 38, 54, 55n6, 57n27, 57nn38–39
Howells, Herbert, 6
Humble Pie, 115
Hurnard, Hannah, 149

Iron Maiden, 75

Jeremiah, 90, 135
Jesus, 2, 3, 8, 15, 24–25, 27n8, 42–44, 50–52, 59n58, 68, 72, 74, 80n59, 84–85, 88–89, 97, 107–8, 123–24, 147
Jethro Tull, 3, 8, 11, 24, 75, 83–93, 95
John the Baptist, 2
Jung, Carl, 74

Kansas, 11, 32, 95–114, 131–34, 137, 147
Kauflin, Bob, 150
Kaye, Tony, 13n16
Keaggy, Phil, 114n41, 133
Khoroshev, Igor, 12n2
Kihn, Greg, 118
King, Jonathan, 63, 68
King Crimson, 2, 3, 15–17, 24, 27n7, 29n29, 95, 100, 125
Kirshner, Don, 96, 112n6
Kodály, Zoltan, 10
Kyle, Joseph, 149

Ladd, Jim, 124
Lake, Greg, 15, 25, 27n2, 28n12, 28n14
Landry, Janice, 150
Lazarus, 109, 111
LeDoux, Chris, 150
Led Zeppelin, 3, 35, 115, 139
Lee, Geddy, 115, 117, 119, 121–22, 129n32
Lewis, C. S., 149, 153n31
Lewis, Gereint, 150
Lifeson, Alex, 115, 117, 122
Livgren, Kerry, 11, 32, 95–114, 133
Lloyd Webber, Andrew, 50
Lorde, Audrey, 10

Macan, Edward, 4, 7, 19, 23, 27n8, 28n13, 28n16, 29n24, 29n26, 79n36
MacDonald, George, 153n31
MacFadyn, Scott, 117
Magma, 51, 56n24
Mahler, Gustav, 44
Malmsteen, Yngve, 13n16
Marillion, 2, 12n2, 95, 152n4
May, Brian, 12n4
May, Edward Harrison, 149
Megadeth, 3
Mendelssohn, Felix, 158
Mercury, Freddie (Farrokh Bulsara), 3
Monty Python, 65, 74, 143
Moody Blues, 3, 83, 95, 99
Moraz, Patrick, 13n16
Morse, Neal (including Near Morse Band), 12, 13n11, 51, 90, 111, 131–55
Morse, Steve, 98, 113n12
Morse, Tim, 38, 57n35
Møsbo, Thomas, 34, 39, 44, 55n4, 57n36, 57n38, 58n39, 58n44, 59n63, 60n86
Moses, 84, 87–88, 92n15, 147
Mussorgsky, Modest, 6, 158

Narcissus, 68, 74, 78n24, 78n27, 102, 107
Neal, William, 18–19

New Testament, 65, 75, 79n36, 85, 88, 108, 128n24, 147
Nice, The, 15–17, 95
Norman, Larry, 29n28, 109

Old Testament, 65, 85, 88, 147
Opeth, 131
Origen, 147
Orwell, George, 28n13, 148
Ovid, 70–74, 78n24, 78n31

Palmer, Carl, 15, 18, 23
Parry, Hubert, 6, 64, 72
Paul/Saul of Tarsus, 2, 6–8, 20, 43, 123–24, 128n24
Peart, Neil, 115–19, 121–22, 124–25, 127n15, 128n25, 129n32
Peter (Apostle), 8, 124
Petra, 101, 109
Petrucci, John, 133
Phillips, Anthony, 64
Philo (of Alexandria), 9
Phones, the, 118
Pink Floyd, 2–3, 13n14, 95, 111, 131, 159
Pinnick, Dug, 29n28
Plato, 9, 147
Platt, Ronnie, 99–100
Podulska, Donald, 73
Police, The, 118
Porcupine Tree, 131
Portnoy, Mike, 90, 132–36, 140, 145–46, 152n4, 152nn7–8
Procol Harum, 3, 35, 100, 150
Prodigy, 12n2
Prokofiev, Sergei, 6, 15, 158
Proto-Kaw, 110–11, 114n42
Pythagoras, 70–71, 78n24

Queen, 2–3, 134, 137, 159

Rabin, Trevor, 37, 60n85
Ragsdale, David, 98–100
Rand, Ayn, 116
Ravel, Maurice, 10

Rizvi, Zak, 100
Roberts, Greg, 98–99
Robertson, Pat, 33
Romano, Will, 1, 36, 56n8, 57n39, 61n91, 77n6, 86, 92n11
Rose, Barry, 55n2
Rudess, Jordan, 133
Rush, 11, 26, 60n84, 95, 110, 115–29, 159
Rutherford, Mike, 7, 64, 80n59
Rutsey, John, 115
Rycenga, Jennifer, 40, 47, 56n20, 57n28, 58n44

Salmacis, 74, 159
Sargent Pepper's Lonely Hearts Club Band (album), 1, 17
Sinfield, Peter, 16, 24–25, 27nn7–8
Soft Machine, 125
Sons of Apollo, 133
Squire, Chris, 31–32
Stanford, Charles Villiers, 6
Steinhart, Robbie, 96–99
Stewart, Chris, 63
Sting (Gordon Sumner), 6, 25, 75
Stockhausen, Karlheinz, 13n14
Styx, 14n20, 26, 51, 139, 142, 145
Supertramp, 139, 145
Swon Brothers, 134

Talking Heads, The, 118
Thank You Scientist, 111
Tharpe, Sister Rosetta, 10

Thomas, Ray, 83
Tillich, Paul, 72, 79nn39–40, 92n17
Tiresias, 73–74, 80n51
Tolkien, J.R.R., 3, 148
Tool, 116
Transatlantic, 131–33, 152n4
Twisted Sister, 2

Ultravox, 118

Van Der Graaf Generator, 50
Vangelis, 50
Vaughan Williams, Ralph, 6, 16, 63, 150–51, 158, 160n2, 161n2

Wagner, Richard, 146
Wakeman, Rick, 12n2, 33, 39, 44, 54, 133
Walsh, Steve, 32, 96–104, 112n6, 113n15, 113n18
Welch, Chris, 38
Wetton, John, 15
White Clover, 96–97
Whitman, Walt, 29n28
Who, The, 3, 51, 115, 146
Winery Dogs, 133
Wyatt, Robert, 125

Yardbirds, 115
Yellow Mallow Custard, 145
Yes, 2, 3, 11, 12n2, 13n20, 15, 26, 31–61, 75, 95, 99, 110, 111, 125, 131, 145, 159
Young, Michael, 135

Subject Index

allegory, 65, 132, 144, 146–49, 151, 153n31, 154n43, 155nn56–59, 155n65
angels, 29n28, 56n23, 69, 71, 138, 155n57
Anglicanism, 3–6, 40, 64–65, 77n6, 86–87
Arminianism, 122–23, 128
art rock, 1–2
atheism, 117–19, 124, 126, 158–60
avant-garde music, 5, 33, 45, 47, 125, 158

Baroque, 5–6, 13n19
bass/bassist, 3, 17, 50, 55n2, 96–98, 103–4, 113n18, 115, 120, 127n14, 132–33, 137, 139–41, 152n4, 152nn9–10
bells, 20, 105
Bible, 18, 27, 37, 52, 63–66, 69, 70, 73, 75, 76, 84–85, 93n21, 97, 108, 124, 147
black music, 9, 159
blues/blues rock, 4, 10, 36, 53, 74, 77n8, 83, 86, 109, 137
boogie, 95, 96, 100, 111
bridge (musical term), 38, 121, 141
Buddhism, 39, 42–43, 50, 51, 53, 71, 78n35, 101–2, 107, 124

cadenza, 140
Calvinism, 122–23, 125, 128n22, 129n33
cantata, 109, 111, 116, 145
Catholic, 32, 64, 84, 92n12, 114, 135, 152n16
chant, 5, 36, 38, 44, 87
chimes, 106
choir, 20, 32, 116, 150, 151
chords, 26, 42, 47, 64, 66, 77, 103–6, 120, 121, 138, 141, 154; diminished, 56, 90, 106; major, 106, 120–21; minor, 120–21; seventh, 106
chorus, 20, 41–42, 68, 70, 74, 101–6, 119–21, 124, 128n16, 129n32
Christianity, 2, 8, 10, 33–34, 53–54, 84–86, 88, 90, 95, 101, 107–9, 111, 122, 126, 128n24, 131, 149
church, 3, 17, 20–21, 26, 28, 32, 33, 36, 42, 44, 46, 55n2, 55n6, 55n8, 59n56, 61n90, 64, 65, 77n6, 84, 86–87, 92n8, 108, 109, 111, 114n40
Church of England (COE). *See* Anglicanism
clarinet, 134
classical music, 1, 3–6, 13n16, 13n19, 15, 17, 24, 44, 53, 77n6, 84, 86, 95, 100–103, 109–11, 119, 125, 127n6, 131, 145, 155n65, 157, 158

175

Subject Index

contemporary Christian music (CCM), 45, 101, 109–10, 135, 150
counterpoint, 103, 105, 113n26, 139

determinism, 119, 121–22, 125–26, 129n32
diabolus en musica, 29
drums/drummer, 2, 8, 63, 96, 99, 103, 115, 120, 127n14, 132–34, 141, 152n4

Episcopal church. *See* Anglicanism
evangelical/Evangelical church, 32–33, 45, 95, 97, 101, 108–9, 111, 114nn38–40, 123, 135, 142, 144, 147, 150, 155n52, 158

fanfare(s), 24, 29
flute/flutist, 83, 87, 92n14, 113
folk/folk music, 1, 4, 5, 10, 45, 77, 83, 86, 109, 113, 157–58

grunge, 116–17, 131
guitar/guitarist, 12–13, 17, 46, 58, 64, 66, 87, 96, 98, 100, 103–4, 106, 109, 113n18, 113n26, 114n41, 115, 120, 127, 132–34, 137–40, 152n4

hard rock, 5, 13n16, 92n13, 95, 99, 102, 111–12, 116–18, 131, 137, 140
harmonic progression, 110, 120
harmonics, 120
Hindu/Hinduism, 36, 40, 42, 51, 84, 87, 102, 107–8
hymns and hymnody, 3, 5–6, 23–25, 29n24, 46, 55n2, 59n58, 63–64, 67, 69–70, 72, 75, 76n5, 88–90, 96, 102

idolatry, 40, 85–89, 113n30
intro/introduction (musical form), 68, 103–4, 106, 113n14, 120–21, 140–41, 145
Islam, 40, 86, 124

jazz, 4–10, 15, 53, 137, 157
Jews/Judaism, 6–7, 9–10, 13, 23, 40, 86, 88, 117, 128n24, 135, 147–48

keyboards/keyboardist, 17, 46, 65–66, 93n19, 96, 98, 100, 102, 104, 132–34, 137–41, 152n4

loop (musical term). *See* ostinato
lyric/lyricist, 2–3, 5, 14, 16–21, 23–26, 27n8, 28n12, 28n16, 28n20, 28n22, 29n29, 31–39, 41–42, 44–53, 55n1, 55n4, 56n10, 56nn19–20, 57n28, 57n35, 58n51, 59n58, 65–70, 72–73, 75–76, 78n24, 80n59, 81n65, 83, 85–86, 89–90, 92n15, 95, 98, 100–111, 114–16, 118–19, 121, 123–26, 132, 135–42, 144–46, 150–51, 153n23, 154n34, 161n4

mandolin, 134, 140
math rock, 5
metal (musical term), 13n16, 50, 59n58, 86–87, 90, 99, 109, 113, 116–18, 127n9, 134
meter (musical term), 1, 53, 69, 100, 102, 106, 109, 119–20, 127n14, 141
minimalism, 5
minstrel, 83
Moog, 42
musical theater/musical, 5, 111, 143, 146, 150, 154n35
Muslim. *See* Islam
mystic/mysticism, 27, 29, 32, 34, 36–37, 57n28, 59n63, 77n8, 87, 148

New Age (movement or music), 31, 33, 43–44, 51, 101, 109–10, 134
New Testament, 65, 75, 79n36, 85, 88, 108, 128n24, 147
New Wave, 116, 118

Old Testament, 65, 85, 88, 147
opera, 44–45, 50–51, 143, 145–46, 150–51, 154n35, 155n65

Subject Index

orchestra, 5, 13n16, 99, 116, 131, 134, 150–51
orchestration, 131, 141
organ/organist, 24, 33, 36, 42, 44, 55n2, 56n8, 57n28, 103, 141–42, 153n27
orthodox, 108, 114
ostinato, 103, 120
outro/coda, 104, 106, 121–22, 137, 142–43
overture, 58n52, 136, 139, 141, 143, 145

pantheism, 47–48, 84, 107–8
parable, 18, 147–48, 155n55
Pentecostal, 36, 57n26, 142
percussion, 46, 96
piano/pianist, 10, 46, 91, 103, 105, 126, 140–42
polytheism, 47–48
pre-chorus, 119–21, 124
predestination, 119, 122–24, 127, 128n16
protestant/protestant church, 29, 45, 84, 114n40, 122, 158

psychedelic, 1
punk rock, 53, 60n83, 90, 150

rap, 116, 131
refrain. *See* chorus
reggae, 80, 116
renaissance (music), 5, 66, 83, 110, 131

saxophone/saxophonist, 114n44, 134, 139
symphony/symphonic, 1, 24, 40, 44, 47, 51, 57n28, 58n52, 96, 99, 155n64
syncretism, 10, 95, 101–3, 107, 109–11, 149
synthesizer, 24, 42, 44, 102–7, 140

timbre, 50, 83
time signature. *See* meter
tonic, 66, 106, 120
tritone. *See diabolus in musica*

violin/violinist, 95–96, 98, 100, 103–6, 134

white music, 9, 159

Scripture Index

Hebrew Bible/Old Testament

Genesis	63, 89
1–11	147
1 Sam. 10:5	37
2 Kgs 3:15-16	37
1 Chron. 25:1	37
Proverbs	147
Ezekiel	65–66
33:32	37
33:32-33	91

New Testament

Matthew	
6:9-13	88
25:14-30	18
Luke	
11:2-4	88
Acts	
9:3-9	123
9:13-19	124
11:26	128n24
Romans	20
2 Peter	
2:4	18
Revelation	63, 65–67, 71–72, 79n36, 80n64, 81n65, 158
9:7-10	22–23
19–20	73, 76
19:17	71–72
21	69–70
21:4	27, 28n20

About the Authors

Frank Felice is Associate Professor of composition, theory, and electronic music in the School of Music, Jordan College of Arts at Butler University in Indianapolis, Indiana. His PhD is from the University of Minnesota. He composes music in a variety of genres using electronic and traditional acoustic instruments (not always at the same time), and also plays bass. His profound interest in theology can be seen in his compositions such as "Road to Damascus," "Canticle of Mary," and "Four Antiphons of Hildegard of Bingen."

James F. McGrath is the Clarence L. Goodwin Chair in New Testament Language and Literature at Butler University. His PhD is from the University of Durham in England. He is the author of *The Bible and Music* (2023) and a number of books and articles on topics related to the intersection of religion in general or the Bible in particular with popular culture, including science fiction and music.